FRECKLED

A Memoir of Growing Up Wild in Hawaii

T W NEAL

Cover photo by Kim S. Rogers
Cover design by Emily Irwin
Interior photos by Pop, unless otherwise noted

"The future belongs to those who believe in the beauty of their dreams."
- Eleanor Roosevelt

For Mike, Caleb, and Tawny
Thank you for being the family of my hopes and dreams.

Me, age 2

FOREWORD

Toby Wilson Neal's memoir begins in 1965 and ends in 1983. She writes in the first person, present tense—a child's point of view growing up as a redheaded girl born to hippie surfer parents. From within her narrative it wasn't possible to present a historic account of the overarching cultural and racial tensions in Hawaii at that time. Toby asked me to write a essay that would provide context for her coming-of-age tale, referencing stories from my book *Taylor Camp*, an iconic photographic record of a hippie/surfer community on Kauai's North Shore in the '60s and '70s.

Toby's memoir spans a time of intense transition for Kauai, the oldest and most remote of the major islands of the Hawaiian chain. Back then hippies were all but unknown on Kauai, a "chop suey" community of Hawaiians, Chinese, Portuguese, Japanese, Koreans, and Filipinos.

Television had yet to invade. News in the eight-page *Garden Island* paper was provincial, and the "coconut wireless" was all local politics and gossip. Far away and out of mind, the rest of the world had only begun to affect Hawaii's neighbor islands. Culturally and physically removed from the mainland, unconquered by Hawaii's first monarch, and proud of their heritage as the "Separate Kingdom," Kauai's people practiced a style of localism that not only shut out news and views from the outside but also considered native Hawaiians from other islands as interlopers.

A newcomer to any of Kauai's small, isolated plantation communities and rural villages instantly became the talk of the town. An unfamiliar car or truck was observed with suspicion. A photographer setting up a tripod and telephoto lens at any of Kauai's surf breaks risked a beating as well as having his equipment trashed, as locals fought to keep their island's secrets to themselves.

Local hunters and fishermen divided the island into family territories, usually watersheds in State Forest reserves or plantation-owned uplands, following ancient Hawaiian *ahupua`a* (land divisions) and *konohiki* (fishing rights) on the reefs. Outsiders hunting and fishing these areas would be warned off and then, if the trespass was repeated, met with violence. The same practice ruled the surf breaks.

Hawaii's pineapple and sugar industries were rapidly declining after a fast but short-lived bonanza in the early '60s when they exported technology and consultants to the Third World. After decades of cradle-to-grave paternalism in a unionized sugar and pineapple plantation economy, unemployment forced many of Kauai's people to leave the island in search of jobs far from home.

Kauai's population shrank by almost 50% to about 25,000 in the 1960s—less than a fifth of today's *de facto* count.

Meanwhile, on the mainland, the "leave-it-to-Beaver" illusions of the 1950s were shattered when the Kennedys and Martin Luther King were murdered, and student protesters were shot and killed at Kent State University. Eisenhower's prophetic warning about the threat of the "military industrial complex" was made manifest in the Vietnam War. College campuses across the country erupted while the inner-city ghettos burned. Disillusioned and frightened, many mainland youth searched for somewhere to escape the violence and conflict.

Kauai's low population, abandoned plantation labor camps, and abundant natural food sources, combined with perfect waves, spectacular scenery, and a benign climate made the island seem a safe haven—in spite of its territorial residents.

Taylor Camp began in 1969 on Kauai's North Shore, when Howard Taylor, brother of actress Elizabeth, posted bail for thirteen men, women, and children arrested for vagrancy and sentenced to ninety days hard labor in the local county jail. Taylor had recently learned that the Government planned to condemn his oceanfront property and convert it into a state park, ending his dream of building a family compound on the seven-acre site. In an act of both compassion and revenge, he invited the young mainlanders he'd bailed out to camp on his land.

Rising on the stone terraces of an ancient Hawaiian village at the mouth of Limahuli Stream near the end of the road, Taylor Camp is remembered by many of its former residents as "the best days of our lives." Rejecting the values of their parents, then reinventing them with long hair, marijuana, and a vegetarian, "clothing-optional" lifestyle, the flower-power campers developed a whimsical experiment, ostensibly living a back-to-the-land ethos of fishing and farming, while actually propped up with food stamps, pot-growing, and welfare.

Soon waves of hippies, surfers, and Vietnam vets found their way to Kauai and Taylor Camp—and Toby's surfer parents were among them. When these young *haole* (Hawaiian for non-natives, especially whites) stumbled into the invisible web of rules, customs, and traditions of small-town Kauai society, their wide-eyed joy and wonder was often blindsided by suspicion, hostility, and violence.

The working-class locals quickly developed a love/hate relationship with the surfers and hippies. For many locals, this was their first exposure to *haole* that were poor, ragged, and shiftless. Until then, all *haole* on Kauai had been plantation owners or managers, bankers, doctors, lawyers, publishers, and wealthy businessmen—Hawaii's *kama'aina* elite, the ruling oligarchy (many descended from the early nineteenth-century missionaries) that had dominated Hawaii's society and economy for over one hundred years.

Most locals had not seen *haole* like these before and instantly recognized that the ignorant outsiders, lacking the protection and defense of family and community, were easy prey—perfect to replace them at the bottom of Kauai's social pecking order.

For these young *haole* fleeing the continent, Kauai—even with all its localism and prejudice—was still an answer to a prayer. This wasn't America. It was Polynesia and felt like another world, another time, another place. Many arrived on Kauai with awe and humble respect. They wanted to belong, often joining hula *halau* (schools), studying the language, reading Hawaiian history, and supporting the Hawaiian cultural "Renaissance" that flowered in the 1970s. Some local families recognized this sincerity and welcomed them into the fold—often employing them as laborers on their farms.

These young *haole* might have been dumb, but they did have a crop that made sense to Kauai's hardheaded truck farmers—*pakalolo* (marijuana). While some local farmers with connections to the Honolulu crime syndicate (usually those supplying cocks to the fighting pits of Oahu) had grown *pakalolo* before the hippies arrived, these young *haole* introduced new, more potent and higher-yielding varieties, along with scion propagation that guaranteed seedless hermaphrodites and an almost limitless mainland market. Previously struggling local farmers and ranchers were soon buying new trucks and tractors and making trips to Las Vegas.

Meanwhile, the old-moneyed *kama'aina*—the ruling white upper class—deeply despised the hippies and surfers. The *kama'aina* were under siege politically, economically, and socially. The plantation economy that they'd built and dominated for over a century was collapsing, their cash flow drying up—but they still owned most of the island's land.

Survey flags appeared in the pastures of Princeville Ranch, staking out Kauai's first planned resort community, and signaling the beginning of the real estate boom. In this atmosphere, community and political pressure to close down the camp continued to build. Taylor Camp was finally shut down in 1977, and the tree houses torched by State enforcement officials.

The Kauai of the era covered by Toby's memoir was an anomaly

—a brief period of low population and natural abundance, a breathing space as the engine of the plantation economy wound down, and the real estate bonanza and cultural assault of tourism began to build.

As development boomed, Kauai rapidly changed from a community where a strange vehicle on the road was met with curiosity and suspicion, to a hotbed of resorts, rent-a-cars, and traffic jams. The Na Pali coast, once one of the world's most peaceful and sacred places, has been inundated with back-to-back sightseeing helicopters and tour-boat loudspeakers bombarding the valleys with unholy racket. And many locals can no longer afford to live in the place where they were born.

The photos of Taylor Camp and its people—which I began making in 1971—and their stories, are a tribute to that fleeting in-between moment, a period of our lives on Kauai when we possessed little but youth. Toby's memoir adds a very personal facet, a child's view of a unique time, place, and people.

Me ke aloha,
John Wehrheim

Find John's Taylor Camp film *The Edge of Paradise*, book *Taylor Camp*, and his photography at: www.theedgeofparadisefilm.com

Mom reading to me in the van on Kauai

CHAPTER ONE

SWIMMING

Mom, me, and Pop

Age: 4, Rocky Point, Oahu, 1969

Sand. Big yellow mountains of sand. So much, and a long way, a giant tabby cat napping in the sun. Mom's holding my hand, and I'm naked because we're going swimming when we get to the bottom of the long wooden stairs leading away from our house.

I drop to my knees and dig into the big smooth grains, wriggling my body deep in to feel it all over, sinking in delicious warmth because the sun is hot on my head. When I push my arms into the sand and they come up, my skin is the same color. My freckles look like the beach. This always makes me happy.

The sand feels different as the day changes. Morning, it's gray, cool, and the air is blue. The mynah birds talk, and the ghost crabs are out running on skitter legs over the beach. The coconut tree next to my window makes a sound like clapping when the wind first comes up; it's cheering that we have a new day. And when the day ends, the sand is orange, warm, and soft when we sit on it and watch the sun go down.

I love having no clothes on. I can feel everything better that way. I feel a shivery-good sensation in my legs. I come up out of the sand and walk out of the way by the *naupaka* bush and squat to pee.

"You always do that," Mom says, and I laugh, because what else would I do when I get that feeling?

The ocean is the color of the stones in Mom's silver bracelet as she reaches to take my hand. Her skin is hot and brown and smells like coconut oil, and I want to lick it as we walk down to the water, slow because her belly is so big now with my brother or sister inside —*hapai* it's called.

Mom wades in, and the cold water hits us. I squeal and cling. She laughs some more, sinking down so it covers us, prying me off to hold me by both hands.

"*Opihi*," she says, and she means the little round pointed shells that stick on the rocks. Sometimes we pry them off with a screwdriver and eat them. They taste like rubbery seaweed.

She holds my hands. "Kick! Kick!" she commands.

I kick, the feeling of the water sliding over my skin like the silky blanket I sleep with. I kick and kick and she swirls me through the water, and then puts one hand on my tummy and says, "Now rainbow your hands," and I do, making the paddling rainbow motions she's showed me before, and suddenly her hand is gone and I'm swimming! And I see the yellow beach, our little blue house, the coconut tree beside it, and the windows that watch the ocean.

Then I'm sinking. I gasp for breath, and I paddle harder, but I'm under now, my eyes stinging, but still open to see the waves ahead hitting the white foamy sand and my breath held, tight and burning, until Mom's hand comes and lifts me back up.

I cough and cough. The water stings inside my chest, much more than the pool or the bath. I'm mad that I sank and surprised that I can't swim yet. I was sure I could!

"Again!" I say when I'm done coughing.

"You never give up, my sassy bug. You're going to get this. I know you are." We start over with kicking, and rainbow arms, then she lets me go and I sink . . . but this time I know it's going to work. I hold my breath and keep my eyes open while I kick and rainbow. Underneath I see fish—shiny *aholehole* and green-striped *manini,* and the black rocks on the bottom that make this place called Rocky Point.

I like it under the water. I feel like I can fly, and this time my kicking and rainbow arms bring me back up by myself. I blow out my breath, drops spray off my lips, and I grin big even though my face is barely out of the water.

"You did it!" Mom catches me, and I cling around her giant belly, and the belly pushes back at me. I push back at it, and it's like we're talking. I can't wait to meet who's in there. Mom laughs. "The baby's excited too. You're just going to get better and better at this." She lets me ride on her back as she swims, holding onto the strap of her crocheted top. My legs trail behind, and sometimes touch her, a silky feeling.

Pop's watching from the top of the stairs. He is big and tall, and the sun shines on his blond hair. He has his camera out. He takes pictures a lot, and he's looking to see if there's any surf, because he takes mostly surf pictures. There's no surf today, and I can tell he's grumpy by the way his mouth makes a line—so do his eyebrows. He's usually grumpy when there's no surf or he drank a lot the night before, and I want to cheer him up.

Maybe he will be happy that I swam. I wave to him from the water. "I swam! I swam!"

3

Pop nods, enough so I know he heard me. I should have known that wouldn't cheer him up, but I can't think of anything else.

I drop to roll in the sand again when we get out, because it's warm and feels so good.

Mom hoses us off outside the house, and she chases me with the cold water as I squeak and laugh. We go back out to the beach, and I help her dig a hole in the sand for her belly to go in. She puts her towel over the hole and lies down with a sigh. "Untie my top, will you?"

I pull the cord of her top so there's no tan line on her back; I burrow into the sand beside her and feel it's warm fingers all over my skin.

Pop comes down the stairs. "She really did it this time?" He sits beside us in that way all the surfers do, with his knees up and arms looped around them. His eyes look a little red, how they get after he's been smoking a doobie. *Good.* He's not as grumpy when he's had a joint.

"You know Toby never gives up." I hear the smile in Mom's voice. I lie next to her and rub a piece of her long, chocolate-colored hair between my fingers and suck my thumb, happy.

Nanee, me, Mom, and Gigi

At preschool I heard the ladies talking about ESP. There are two kinds of ESP: the kind where you hear other people's thoughts, and the kind where people can make other people do what they want just with their thoughts.

I always listen to grownups so I can know things— "Elephant ears" Mom calls me. Grandma Gigi, Pop's mom, believes in ESP too. "I can tell when you're thinking about me, so that's when I call," Gigi says. She does usually call when we need something, and I love when her packages come in the mail, even though Pop grumbles that I'm getting spoiled.

I want to have the make-people-do-stuff kind of ESP.

We're at dinner, and the sun has gone down behind the ocean. I can hear the surf outside; it's coming up bigger with a shushing sound.

"Should be good tomorrow," Pop says, sipping his beer. Because my dad's a surfer, we always pay attention to what the surf is doing and the weather conditions. There's "onshore," which means the wind is in my face off the ocean and that's bad for surf—I don't really know why. Then there's "offshore," which is best to make the waves good, and "Konas," which means the wind is light and from the side.

Mom is sitting between Pop and me. Her tummy is super big, almost touching the table, and she's wearing her favorite blue muumuu that she sewed herself. There are some oven-baked fries, special because they are not *goodforyou*, and fish Pop caught, and Mom's salad with bean sprouts. We have white plates with a flower border, a milk bottle filled with daisies, Mom's favorite flower, and everything is pretty and good.

Even after he smoked today, Pop was still grumpy. I can see how he's feeling like a black cloud over his head. Bad things can happen when I make him mad, and I do that a lot because I'm noisy and too bouncy. I'm always trying to get him to like me and see that I'm smart and can do things as good as a boy. Because I was supposed to be a boy and be named James Theodore the Third.

Mom and Pop didn't know what to call me when I was a girl, so they named me Toby after the redheaded boy who runs away to the circus in a movie Mom watched at the hospital. I have no middle name because "when you're old enough, you can choose your own middle name." This worries me. How do I pick the right name? I wish I could just be named James Theodore the Third, even if I am a redheaded girl.

Maybe I can make Pop do something with ESP.

PICK UP THE KETCHUP, I think. *PICK UP THE KETCHUP. PICK UP THE KETCHUP.*

Pop looks up at me. His green eyes have red around them. The overhead light shines on his curling blond hair, going thin at the top. I stare at him, my lips moving, as I think as hard as I can—*PICK UP THE KETCHUP.*

"What are you looking at?" His voice is a low thunder sound. He narrows his eyes. I don't look away or answer. He's going to *PICK UP THE KETCHUP* any second now. I just know it!

"Stop staring at me." Pop gets louder and seems to swell.

I can tell how mad he's getting, but I stare until my eyes hurt because I can feel it almost working—he's going to hear me any minute now. I don't blink. I want to be scary: eyes wide, mouth tight, staring hard as I think *PICK UP THE KETCHUP.* I will make him do what I want!

"I said stop looking at me, disrespectful little brat!" He stands up and his chair flies back and lands on the linoleum with a thud. He's *enormous.*

My mom makes fluttery noises, but it's too late. Roaring something I don't hear, he comes around the table and whips me off the chair by my hair. I crash onto the floor and hold onto my head and use my legs to hold myself up, trying to keep from being dragged—it hurts so bad, as he hauls me down the hall, but I won't cry. I'm stubborn like that. I'm not afraid of pain.

I'm still thinking, *PICK UP THE KETCHUP.* Like it's going to save me. Like he can hear me.

But he doesn't.

He drags me all the way into my little white bedroom, sits on my bed, and throws me over his knees, lifting my cotton dress. He spanks me hard, and it goes on and on.

Tears start against my will. I wriggle and bite my lips and finally scream—a loud shriek because I'm so angry and sad that ESP didn't work; the spanking hurts, and he hates me more than ever now.

The scream's what he's been trying to get out of me, though, because he's done with the spanking. He throws me onto the bed. I bounce, and my head smacks the wall.

I lay there stunned. *I guess I don't have ESP.*

He slams my door so hard it shakes the walls of the little old house.

He rages at Mom outside my bedroom. "Goddamn spooky kid, staring at me like that. I can tell what she's doing; she's trying to get inside my head! Goddamn it, you better straighten her out . . ."

Mom argues with him. I feel bad for her because I hear her crying as he yells about how bratty I am, what a pain in the ass, why did we have a kid in the first place, and now we're having another one.

I put the covers over my head and suck my thumb, rubbing the silky edge of my blankie and thinking about my favorite story. Aladdin can ride a carpet like it was a floating car, and he has a genie in a magic lamp. I wish I could ride a carpet to get away, and if I got three wishes, the first would be that Pop would be nicer.

Mom reads to me every night, and I can't wait to be able to read to myself. Miss K at preschool says I'm almost ready—sometimes I can even read the books Mom has read to me the most because I remember what each word was.

Mom sneaks in with my dinner plate after Pop has gone outside with his evening six-pack. She sits on my bed, and it dips toward her. I come out from my nest of covers and rest my hot, angry face against the mound of the baby under her muumuu, and the baby pushes at me. I put my hand on her belly and push back, and it bumps my hand again.

Mom strokes the hair off my face. "You shouldn't irritate him like that."

I know I shouldn't, but I can't help it. Even when I'm being good I irritate him. He's never been happy with me. She knows this, too.

I'm pretty sure the real problem is that I wasn't James Theodore the Third. "Would Pop like me if I was a boy?"

Mom jumps a little like maybe the baby kicked her. "Oh, no, honey. You two are just oil and water."

I sit up and eat my dinner, my plate on my knees, and I know a secret. *Maybe I don't have ESP, but I can get into his head. And he can spank me all he wants, but I'm not afraid of him.*

It's almost as good as if he loves me.

CHAPTER TWO

A NEW BABY

Rocky Point beach house, Mom, me, and Bonny

Age: 4, Rocky Point, Oahu, March 1969

"Wake up, Toby. It's time." Pop's voice in my dark bedroom. My eyes open. My little room is lit by an angel night-light, and it shines on Pop's face. His eyes are hidden in puffy slits, and his breath smells like beer and corn chips from the party where he was. He's worried, and he thinks it's not a good time for her to do this after they were already out so late.

Maybe I do have ESP after all because I know these things.

"It's time" means it's time for the baby to get out of Mom's tummy. I'm not sure how that's gonna work. Mom's explanation about her "pie" being the place the baby comes out just didn't seem right.

Pop has already gone back down the darkened hall as I get out of bed in my nightie and go get my suitcase. It's small, just my size, and printed with pretty flowers. Gigi sent it to me from the Mainland, and Mom and I packed it a week ago so I'd be ready to go to our neighbor Janet's when the baby comes. I'm excited because I want to see the baby, and now I get to go to Janet's house, too.

I was just at Janet's earlier when Mom and Pop went to the party. She has two cats and a dog, laughs a big laugh, and she takes walks with me along the sandy road behind our houses and never is in too much of a hurry to let me stop and look at something or ask questions. "You're the smartest, most curious kid ever," Janet says, like that's a good thing. I love going to her house.

She, Mom, Pop, and her husband Dave are about the same age, 26. Janet doesn't have children of her own yet, but I get the feeling she wants them because she likes playing with me so much. Dave is a big guy with a loud laugh that matches hers, and he's in the Army and goes to work somewhere every day.

In the warm dark lit by one yellow streetlight, I'm worried as I hug Mom goodbye before she gets in the van to go get the baby out. She smells funny, of beer and *pakalolo* and something damp like wet bread, and her belly is giant and hard when I press my face against her, trying to get my arms around her waist.

"We'll be home before you know it, with a baby for you to cuddle," Mom pants, her voice squeaky.

I'm scared by how she's acting and smelling. I clamp my arms tighter around her.

"We have to go." Pop grabs my hand, peeling me off Mom and tugging me through the dark to Janet's house, right next to ours. He's taking big steps and yanking my arm. I can smell fear on him, and it smells dark and funky, like the cheese I dropped next to the stove that got all moldy.

This isn't fun anymore. I'm biting my lips not to cry because that will just make Pop mad. We knock on Janet's door, and there's a long moment as we stand there in the dark on her porch step. I squeeze Pop's hand with both of mine, hoping he will pick me up or give me a hug or kiss, but he doesn't.

Then the light comes on and Janet's door opens. She has soft blonde hair that sticks up like a halo and makes me think she's part angel. Janet's dog, beside her legs, looks at me with his tongue out like he's happy. Janet reaches down and sweeps me up, away from Pop. I wrap my arms around her neck and put my face in her angel hair and breathe in her smell of sweat and flower perfume.

"She's in labor. Her water broke." Pop's already turned away and disappearing as Janet closes the door and carries me inside.

"Oh, sweetie. You should have just stayed the night with us."

Labor? Water broke? It seems like the baby getting out is a bad thing for Mom. I hold on tight to Janet, still trying not to cry as she carries me to the futon they have instead of a couch. She lies down with me when I won't let go, and we fall asleep that way.

The next morning, we make pancakes. We pick bananas off the stalk on the tree in her yard. They are short, fat, and super sweet, not like the big bright yellow bananas in the store. "Imported to Hawaii from somewhere else, it's so sad," Mom says about those fake bananas.

Janet lets me peel and slice the bananas and put them in the batter, though I have to use the dull knife. The phone nearby has a round dial with holes in it for making a call, and it rings so loud I drop the spoon. Batter splats on the counter, and I look up scared.

Pop always gets mad at loud noises and messes like that, but Janet just says "oops!" and throws a dish towel on it.

Janet answers the ringing phone and turns to me with a big smile and round blue eyes. "You have a sister! Her name is Bonny."

I'm so excited that I clap my hands. I'm going to have a friend to play with all the time, and her name is Bonny! I'm also relieved that Bonny's not a boy they are naming James Theodore the Third. I still want that name for myself.

Very late that day, Pop comes to get me so we can go visit Mom and the baby at the hospital. He's had a nap and a shower and he's happy, which makes me happy, too.

Mom must be okay, then.

We get in the van. "Let's bring her some daisies," Pop says. We stop alongside the road next to the pineapple field to pick Mom's favorite yellow flowers on the way to the hospital in Kahuku. I'm glad I didn't know the hospital is where Mom went to get the baby out, or I would have worried even more.

The hospital is a long, low building made out of concrete blocks painted light green, and they won't let me visit Mom.

"Visiting hours are over," the lady behind the counter says, even though I can tell she feels sorry for us, with our daisies and clean faces. I know I look cute because Janet braided my hair and dressed me in my favorite flowered muumuu that comes to my knees, and I'm wearing the Mary Janes that Grandma Gigi gave me, too.

I can feel my face crumpling up like wet toilet paper. I miss Mom so bad. I need to see her, after how she was acting and smelling weird, and I want to meet my baby sister. I have never cried this whole time. I've been brave. But now I can feel a wave of fright and bad feelings rising up from my toes. It's going to squirt out my eyes and down my chin and all over everybody everywhere because when I feel feelings they are big, strong, noisy, and really annoying to Pop, especially.

He sees it coming and grabs me up, putting my face against his shoulder, and I swallow down my sobs. The daisies are crushed between us and smell strong and piney as he carries me outside. "Shh. I have an idea. You're going to get to see her."

It's getting dark by now. I'm still gulping down my feelings as he puts me down and we sneak around the side of the building. Pop seems to know where he's going, picking his way through long grass under plumeria trees alongside the building, peeking in the louvered windows. He comes to one and lifts me up, so I can see through the slats of glass.

Mom is lying in a bed, sleeping. Her face is puffy and tired-looking, her chocolate-colored hair is all messy, and her giant tummy is gone.

I can't hold back the tears anymore. I cry "Mom!" and the feelings squirt out in a messy flood.

She wakes up and says "Toby!" and it sounds wonderful, like the first time I ever heard her call my name in happiness, her voice so warm it's a touch. I'm so relieved she's okay that I cry harder.

"Thank God there's no one else in this room." Pop's pulling the glass louvers of the window out of their slats and stacking them on the ground. Inside, Mom turns the little plastic things that hold the screen in place and takes it down, and in just a few minutes I'm inside the room, in her arms. Pop climbs in too, with his armful of daisies.

I don't get to see Bonny because she's sleeping in the nursery and I'm not supposed to be here, but getting into bed beside Mom and pressing my face against her sweet-smelling breasts is more than enough.

BONNY COMES HOME TO LIVE WITH US THE NEXT DAY AND POP puts a big sign on the door: *NO VISITORS.*

"They're not going to like that," Mom says, worried. I know who she means by "they." Janet and Dave, the local ladies at my preschool, and all Mom's friends want to come by and bring food and see Bonny.

"We need time alone to get in a rhythm," Pop says. "You want to get some sleep, right?"

It's always this way. Mom likes other people and Pop doesn't. He'd rather it was just us on the whole North Shore of Oahu.

I'm still looking at Bonny, trying to decide if I like having a sister.

She's not what I expected. I thought I'd be able to play with her, but instead she's small and floppy, though Mom says she's the biggest baby ever born at Kahuku Hospital at almost eleven pounds. She's holding Bonny in my favorite spot, on her lap with my sister's head in the crook of her arm, and Bonny's nursing, getting milk from Mom's boobs, which is why they're so big and smell so good.

Mom squirts some milk into my mouth because I want to taste it, and we all laugh because it sprays my face. The milk is warm and sweet like the canned milk with the red label Mom likes to bake into pudding in the oven. She sprays Pop too, and he acts all silly, putting his hands in the air like it's a stickup.

Bonny has white cloth diapers she wears with plastic panties over them, and when she poops it's yellow and smells like papaya. I've already watched how to change her and learned how to swizzle the diaper in the toilet so the poop comes off before putting it in the plastic diaper pail.

We spend several days holed up in the house alone as a family. I have to be quiet all the time and Mom and Bonny sleep a lot. Finally, I go over to Janet's on my own, and we bake cookies. "I don't like having a sister. She's no fun at all," I tell Janet.

"She'll grow up to be your best friend. Having a sister is really special." Janet gives me a hug. "You're lucky to have a sister."

I don't feel lucky. Bonny sleeps in bed with Mom and Pop, where I used to go when I had bad dreams. Pop finally takes the sign down and everybody who sees Bonny says how cute she is, with her green eyes and blonde hair that sticks straight up like a little round chick. All Mom and Pop's friends just want to hold Bonny, and I have to play by myself and not bug her when she's sleeping.

"Why aren't I enough?" I ask Mom one day, as she's picking Bonny up from a nap.

Mom looks at me, and she's surprised. Her eyes are like a stream with green and gold pebbles at the bottom and green around the edge. I have those same eyes; everyone says so, and it makes me happy when they do because Mom is so pretty.

"What four-year-old says something like that?" She shakes her head and puts Bonny up against her shoulder and reaches for me with her other arm. "Come here." I go, and snuggle in my favorite place against her side, the place where Bonny is most days now. "You were so special that we knew we wanted another one," Mom says, after a long time.

I suck my thumb and snuggle closer, holding my blankie with the silky edge, and think about that. I'm pretty sure she just said it to make me feel better.

"She's much mellower than Toby," Pop tells Mom. I can hear the relief in his voice. "Our little Bonny Buddha baby. Thank God."

I feel bad about not being mellow, but I just can't help that I'm interested in everything and like to do stuff all the time.

Gigi and Grandpa Jim, Pop's parents, visit to meet Bonny. They stay at a condo in Waikiki. Grandpa Jim is as tall as Pop and has a big loud voice, and Gigi always smells like chemical flowers, and her hair is a big reddish helmet that the wind can't blow. She jangles with gold and her dresses have a waist. Gigi and Grandpa Jim have lots of money and live in California, and they always bring good presents.

"What kind of place is this to raise a family?" Grandpa booms at Pop. "There are nothing but natives at Toby's school." He follows Pop out of the house, lecturing him.

I frown. I like my school. Miss K, my teacher, thinks I'm smart, and I have lots of friends. Yes, I'm the only kid with red hair and get called "haole girl," but being smart almost makes up for being white.

"This house is so cozy," Gigi says, her hands on her hips as she looks around the tiny front room with its attached kitchen and the windows that look at the sea. "And you have the baby in bed with you?"

I can tell she means the house is too small and that the baby shouldn't be sleeping with Mom and Pop. Gigi and Grandpa Jim bought Mom and Pop a little house in La Jolla when they first got married; I was born there six months later. We moved to Oahu when I was two and I'm pretty sure Gigi and Grandpa still have hurt feelings about that.

Gigi brought me a huge wicker elephant that opens up to hold my clothes when she came this time, and to distract her I give her hugs. "Thank you for the elephant, Gigi." I sniff her perfume loudly. "You smell so nice." Everybody else may like Bonny better now, but Gigi still likes me best. She sits down and pulls me onto her lap. Her charm bracelet is loaded with pearls and diamonds and gold. I love her jewelry and wish she'd take it off and let me play Aladdin's treasure cave with it. "Why do you always smell so good?"

"Chanel No. 5," she says. "A lady always wears perfume."

Mom snorts. "Natural oils are better for people and the environment." Mom's nursing Bonny, sitting on the little futon couch. Gigi doesn't like Mom nursing and thinks Bonny should have a bottle, which I heard her tell Mom when they arrived. "Your figure," she says in her fussy voice, without looking at Mom.

"Breastfeeding is best for the baby," Mom says.

"And she's such a *big* baby," Gigi says, like that's a bad thing.

"Gigi, come see my shells. I have lots." I tug Gigi's hand. Her sparkly rings poke my fingers as I lead her into my room before she and Mom get in an argument. "Let's go look for more on the beach after."

Gigi and I like finding shells on the beach together, and I go with them back to their condo and get to swim in the hotel pool and eat ice cream. Gigi pets my hair and plays with it. My hair is her favorite thing. "Like golden taffy," she always says, and strokes my head like a puppy.

CHAPTER THREE

BEING A HERO

Me and Bonny with Pop's catch of slipper lobsters

Age: 5, North Shore, Oahu, September 1969

Pop goes fishing and diving on the reef in front of the house most days when there's no surf, and he brings his catch in and puts it on the lawn for Bonny and me to play with while he cleans the fish or lobsters.

We especially like the slipper lobsters. They look like brown reef rocks with tiny, shiny beady black eyes on the ends of flat, scoop-shaped heads, and they flip their tails and scoot backward in the water. Sometimes they can even do it in the grass. They click and bubble but don't have poky spines like the blue-green ones with the long antennas.

I always like to touch the fish and know everything I can about them—and everything else too. Mom and Pop believe it's good to ask questions. "Question authority" is something I've heard them talk with their friends about.

"Questions are how you learn." Mom calls me "Little Professor" and says I take after her dad, Grandpa Garth, who is a marine biologist, which means he studies the ocean and fish. "He's coming to work for the University of Hawaii, and you'll get to meet him someday," she says, but she doesn't talk about her parents much—they divorced, married other people and had more kids, aunties who are close to my age. I have lots of aunties and uncles, but I can tell Mom's sad and maybe a little angry about some things that happened, so we don't see them much.

Pop shoots fish with a spear called a "Hawaiian sling" with a long metal pole that goes through a hole in a wooden handle. The spear cocks back using a metal piece and a loop of rubber tubing. Pop made it himself and says he will teach me how to shoot fish when I'm older—but lobsters cannot be shot or trapped. They have to be caught by hand, according to the rules. Pop obeys the rules because he says they are there to help make sure everyone has enough lobsters and fish.

One day, he leaves Bonny and me outside to play with his catch and goes inside. Bonny is bigger now, crawling around at six months old, and she puts everything in her mouth.

"Don't put the fish in your mouth." I flop a large pale *weke* back and forth. Pop told me the *weke* is a goatfish, and it's named that because of the long strings beside its mouth like a mustache. We have a *kala*, which is green and has a horn on its forehead and a wicked blade on its tail, and an *uhu,* which is also called a parrotfish because it is all the colors of a rainbow from purple to red. *Uhu* is my favorite to eat because it has big juicy flakes when it's cooked and not many tiny bones.

Bonny laughs at me flopping the fish back and forth, and a scale the size of a thumbnail falls off the fish where the spear pierced it. It's clear and shiny and reminds me of a moonstone. Bonny grabs the scale off the grass and pops it in her mouth.

"No!" I drop the *weke*. "Spit that out!" Mom has already told me Bonny could choke from all the stuff she's always putting in her mouth, and not to let her do that. I grab her fat cheeks in my hands and squeeze them to make her open her mouth, but it's too late—I see it's too late by the way Bonny's green eyes pop open.

They aren't really green. They're bluish-gray, with yellow spots around the black part in the middle. This somehow makes them look green, and I notice this in spite of my fright.

"Mom! Pop!" I scream.

Bonny arches her back, pulling her face out of my hands. She opens her mouth, but she can't breathe. She tries to cry, her mouth wide, her eyes tearful, but nothing is happening—she can't even make a sound. She throws herself backward onto the ground. Right in front of me she's turning red, and then white.

"Mom! Mom! Bonny's choking!" I scream again, but no one comes from the house. "Help!"

She'll die if that fish scale doesn't come out.

She starts to flop around, just like one of the dying fish, and her eyes roll back. I grab her like I saw Mom do one time, and I throw her hard over my knees and hit her on the back with both my fists. *Wham! Wham!*

"Mom!" I scream. "Help!"

I pick Bonny up and throw her down on my knees again and hit her back as hard as I can. The fish scale flies out of her mouth and out onto the grass, and she starts crying—and that's when Mom comes running out of the back door.

"What are you doing, hitting her?" She scoops Bonny into her arms. "She's just a baby—what are you doing?"

"She was choking, and I got the fish scale out!" I point to the scale in the grass. "See?"

Bonny is scared from the whole thing, and the little crying she was doing turns into full-on screaming. Mom's turning red, her eyes wide, getting ready to whack me, which she only does when she's really mad. I jump up and run away to grab the fish scale. I hold it up. "She was choking, so I turned her over my knees and hit her back like you showed me, and she spit it out! It flew all the way over here."

Pretty soon all three of us are crying, and Pop comes out and I get to tell the story again. I'm proud of saving Bonny. I like the feeling of being a hero.

Pop takes me to get a shave ice as a reward in nearby Haleiwa. Haleiwa is a dirt road over a little bridge, and the shops are small and colorful with fake fronts and creaky wood porches. I'm so excited. Shave ice is really special because it's full of sugar, and sugar is *badforyou*. We walk up to the shave ice truck, and the local guy leans out the window in the side of it. He has a gold tooth in front and a big smile. "What you folks like?"

Pop reads the choices off the board for me to pick one. "Coconut, lilikoi, pineapple, vanilla, mango, lychee, strawberry, and rainbow."

"Rainbow, Uncle! I like rainbow!" The guy laughs because I jump up and down, though I can feel Pop getting irritated.

"We get 'em, honey. Just a minute, cuz time fo' change the ice." I'm too short to see into the truck, straining and jumping toward the window, so Pop picks me up to watch. I hold very still against his stomach and chest so he won't put me down—he gets annoyed when I wiggle.

The guy takes a solid block of ice in a cardboard milk jug, rips the cardboard off, and puts the big, shiny, see-through block in the shaver—a piece of the moon, fallen from the sky, all misty and glowing inside. He winds down on a claw from the top to grip the ice, then cranks a handle on the side. The block spins around and around on a shiny blade, and shave ice flies off into a catcher. Finally, there's enough to pack into a paper cone, and he hoses the ice down with red strawberry, blue vanilla, and yellow pineapple syrup from bottles with a pointy opening on the end. He hands the giant shave ice cone to me. "So *ono*, this one. Enjoy, *ku`uipo*."

"*Ku`uipo*" means sweetheart. I know because Miss K told me so.

Pop sets me down, and I skip over to the nearby picnic table. Pop and the guy talk story about the surf while Pop gets a shave ice, too. I close my eyes to let the tasty colored flakes, just like fruity moonlight, melt on my tongue. I wish this moment could be always.

CHAPTER FOUR

SURFER PARADISE

Fern crowns and beach life with Kala and me

Age: 6, North Shore, Kauai, 1971

Pop is still going to the University of Hawaii for marine biology, which has something to do with the ocean and is what my mom's dad Grandpa Garth is a doctor in. Gigi and Grandpa Jim send money for that because they want him to finish college.

Pop gets more and more grumpy because he says Rocky Point's getting too crowded. He complains that the Oahu locals are getting gnarly with fights on the beach over waves, which is called "beefing"

23

or "scrapping." I've seen it. The men yell and splash water and then tussle like fighting dogs when they get to the sand.

I listen to Mom and Pop talking with their surfer friends, other haoles from the Mainland, and they're worried about drug dealing starting up around Pipeline and Sunset Beach—not pakalolo, which everyone smokes, but other stuff that has a dangerous vibe called horse and LSD and coke. Pop has a shotgun he uses to shoot coconuts off the tree in front of the house, but he doesn't like handguns or believe in them. Pop gets the idea that everyone is carrying weapons, and things are getting dangerous.

When Pop gets an idea he's worried about, he can't let it go. Nothing seems different to me except there are more surfers, more loud parties, more beach scraps, and sometimes I watch Bonny alone at night.

They've been saving Gigi and Jim's money and what Mom makes selling *puka* shell necklaces from shells she picks up on the beach. They've been talking to their Australian surfer friend, Rusty Miller, about going to Australia, a country somewhere far away with good waves and kangaroos. But Rusty moved to Kauai and told them to come there instead because the waves are great on Kauai, and no one has discovered it yet.

To get ready for Kauai, Pop drops out of the University of Hawaii and buys a new van with the money they saved for Australia, a big white Ford Econoline. He builds an inside with wood lining the walls and a built-in bed and padded bench for storage that I will sleep on. There are cupboards, and a food prep area under the big raised bed that you can get to by opening the back doors. Mom makes beautiful red flowered curtains for the windows, and it looks cozy, like everywhere Mom decorates. We get rid of almost everything except some boxes we send to Lihue on Kauai and put in storage for when we get a house. "We'll ship the van over and live in it, and we can figure out where we want to settle on the island," Pop says.

I say goodbye to Janet, and my guinea pig SoShell, the little house with the big windows that watch the ocean, and the big sleepy cat of warm beach.

We drive and camp all over Kauai, from the tops of the mountains in Koke`e to the massive cliffs and sand dunes of Polihale on the west side. When we find Tunnels Beach on the north shore of the island, with its great surf and nearby park with running water and toilets, Mom and Pop declare they've found Rocky Point—only better, because there are hardly any other surfers out at the perfect, peeling break beyond the reef where we fish and dive.

Pop has brought his camera to take photos of the Kauai surfers and sell them like he did on Oahu, but Kauai is a very different island than Oahu. On Oahu, surfers like being in the magazines, but not here. Some of "da local boyz" tell Pop they'll beat him up if he sends anything from Kauai to the magazines.

"I get it. The surf is so great, of course they don't want anybody to know about it, or pretty soon it'll be as crowded as Oahu," Pop tells Mom when he comes back from an early morning talk with other surfers in the parking lot in front of Hanalei Bay, a spot with a nice right-hand break. "But I was counting on being able to make some money for us as a photographer."

There's no work for Mom or Pop on Kauai. No jobs that the locals aren't already doing, and our application for food stamps hasn't come through. Gigi and Grandpa Jim have stopped sending money except for Pop's three hundred a month trust fund. They wouldn't approve of our situation, or that I even know about it, but my parents don't believe in hiding things.

It's been a month since we moved to Kauai, and today we've run out of everything to eat but a little bit of brown rice.

We leave Hanalei and drive the steep, windy two-lane road for miles along the coast to pull up at Tunnels. Pop takes a hidden dirt driveway he found next to a Java plum grove and parks the van at the edge of the beach under the ironwood and *kamani* trees.

These trees are some of the only ones that really like it right by the ocean. Mom says the ironwoods, tall and gray with long, soft, swishing needles, came from Australia. The *kamani*, with their wide, paddle-like leaves, have been here so long people have forgotten where they came from. I've never much cared about either, but I like the *kamanis* better because the ironwoods have little hard cones that really hurt my bare feet. "Haole feet" is what the locals call that soreness. I hate wearing shoes and am trying to get my feet to be tougher.

I grab my red scoop net and run down to the reef in my usual outfit—a cotton swimsuit bottom Mom made for me, no top. I don't see why I should wear one just 'cause I'm a girl. My chest looks the same as a boy.

Pop takes his throw net and heads down the beach to try to catch fish, and Mom stays in the van with Bonny. I walk out onto the low-tide reef, picking my barefoot way across coral worn flat by pounding surf, scanning the clear water. I'm looking for something—anything—to eat. Hopefully one of us will catch something for dinner, or there won't be anything, and I have a hard time sleeping with my tummy growling and chewing on itself.

I bend over a tide pool, peering under the ledge of coral into purple dark. Sometimes, if I'm very lucky, lobsters hide there, and I can spot them by their long, waving antennae. Green striped *manini* and silvery *aholehole* flee as my shadow falls over the sandy bottom, and I get so close to the water that my hair trails on it like floating gold seaweed.

Nothing here. I move on to another tide pool and spot a motion in the water like the whirl a toilet makes going down. A surge happens, then stops. It happens again, with a rhythm to it like something breathing. My heart speeds up at this discovery—but I have no idea what it is.

Walking carefully so as not to accidentally step on a *wana* sea urchin or tubeworms that cut round holes in my feet, I creep around and approach the pool from behind, so my shadow never falls on the water and spooks the fish.

The movement happens again, a surge like a tiny pump hidden in the rocks.

I peer down, feeling the sun on my bare back, my hair floating on the water, and I see an octopus's arm feeling along the sandy bottom. It's as big around as my dad's thumb, pale as the yellow-white sand,

and dappled with brown spots. My mouth waters at the sight. I'm *hungry*. I've never eaten *tako* before, but I know they can be eaten.

I slide a hand into the hole where the creature's hiding and grab whatever's there.

There's a flurry in the water. The part of the octopus's body that I've grabbed is cool and slimy, and there's a tightening sensation as one of the sucker parts wraps around my arm like a whip, pulling me forward, and I stumble into the deep tide pool.

This thing's a lot bigger than I thought! I'm just a little girl and maybe I should not have tried this by myself. I can't let go, though, because the octopus is pulling deeper into its hole under the reef and if I let go, it will get away. I look frantically around for help.

My dad has gone much further down on the reef; I can barely see him in the distance. There's no one anywhere near on the empty arc of beach, with its backdrop of drip-castle mountains robed in shades of green. The big white van under the trees looks deserted; the red flowered curtains are closed. Bonny's only two, and Mom is probably napping with her.

Gonna have to do it myself.

I reach into the water and grab the thing with my other hand, too, and step fully into the tide pool. I brace my feet against the coral bottom, and pull and wrestle and pull and wrestle, tearing off a limb that twitches, writhing in the water, but doesn't bleed. And inch by gradual, panting inch, I drag the creature out of its hole.

Its tentacles writhe up and down my arms and I'm covered with red circles from the suckers when I finally haul my prize out of the hole and up onto the reef. Color flashes over it, and I'm almost hypnotized by the way it turns blue, purple, green, and yellow by turns. Gouts of inky black blood keep squirting out from underneath, and I hope it's not poisonous.

But *tako* can be eaten. The local people make it into a chopped-up blend of salad called *poke*, and they fry it with bread crumbs too. I hold the octopus around the middle, suckering and so heavy, trying to crawl down my belly and legs to get away. I run to shore, trying to keep the tentacles off me, but it's too big and strong. Once the creature's far enough up the beach not to escape, I peel it off and drop it in the sand, running to the van and hollering. "I caught an octopus! I caught an octopus!"

I wake Mom from her nap, and Pop comes back at our yelling. He kills the octopus by stabbing it in the slippery, round head with his fishing knife. The octopus's eye, large and sparkly bronze, looks at me and is beautiful as it dies. I feel a quiver of doubt that I did the right thing, a stab of sadness, but my parents' obvious delight over the future meal fills me with pride.

I did it. All by myself.

Pop flips the creature over and shows me a hidden parrotlike bill right in the middle of all those sucker-covered arms. "Don't let the bill get you," he says. "They have a mean bite."

I had no idea the octopus had a biter like that. My eyes bug out in delayed fright, and the red marks on my arms burn and sting. I'm cold all of a sudden in my bare skin and wet cotton suit; the sun has gone behind the green triangle peak of Makana Mountain, but I can't wrap up in one of the towels.

There's a strict way we do towels. We each have our own, and we can only use it after we've rinsed off in fresh water. The county park's a good half-mile walk down the beach for me to shower, and Mom notices my shivering as I watch Pop clean the guts out of the octopus and chop it up. She washes me off with water from a plastic milk jug that's still a little sun-warm, and I wrap up in "my" towel, crunchy from multiple dryings.

"So, how do we cook this thing?" Mom's made a hole in the sand lined with rocks and got a beach fire going. We have a little stove, too, the green kind you fill with kerosene and pump, but it's too small to handle anything as big as the octopus.

"Not sure. I've always had octopus chopped up in something or deep fried with bread crumbs," Pop says. There is nothing to go with it: no vegetables, butter, not even bread crumbs—just Spike All Purpose Seasoning from the health food store. "Maybe we can grill it."

"Cook it on a stick?" I ask, but they decide the nearby branches of the ironwood trees are too difficult to poke through the tough, rubbery meat.

"Let's boil it." Mom crams all the arms of the octopus into our too-small pot, the pot we use for everything. The tentacles hanging out make us laugh, but she keeps them in with the lid, and sticks the pot on the fire, resting it on a wire grill.

She boils the octopus for a long time.

And she boils it some more, because when she pokes it, it's still hard.

She adds water and boils it again.

Full dark has come. The moon gleams on the black ocean, and the tide comes in, and the fire burns down. Finally, we are just too hungry to hope it will get any better.

Pop hacks the rubbery mass into chunks and we chew it, laughing because it's so tough it bounces your teeth away. It's slimy as well as rubbery, and tastes like smoky salt water. We eat the whole thing. I fall asleep easily that night, tummy full, on my bed that's a storage bench during the day.

CHAPTER FIVE

VAN LIVING

Me reading big books

Age 6: North Shore, Kauai, 1971

Our toys are in storage in Lihue waiting for when we have a house, so for now we don't have much to play with. I miss my familiar bedroom, but I also like the feeling of exploring, of never quite knowing what we'll be doing each day.

Bonny follows me around as much as she can. I'm impatient with how young she is at only two, but I love her fiercely. Janet was right —she's my best friend. But we are so different: I'm salt to her sweet.

My pale freckled skin, daubed with zinc oxide or PABA from the health food store, burns easily.

Hers is the even light brown of a Nilla Wafer cookie.

My hair, bleached by sun and ocean to palest orange, is so fine it drifts on the air.

Bonny's hair is a thick, creamy white-blonde she wears instead of clothing.

I am wiry and strong and always moving.

She is softer and moves thoughtfully.

Bonny sucks her finger and watches me with Pop's green eyes. She's not like I am—needing to touch and understand everything. "Buddha baby," Mom and Pop have always called her.

I come up with ideas for us to do. "How about we build a fort under the ironwood roots?" I love forts. I make them everywhere.

"No." Bonny removes her finger from her mouth with a pop, just long enough to get the word out.

"How about we make horses out of sticks and ride them around?"

"No." This time she shakes her head, too. She doesn't like that I'm much faster at anything involving running.

"We can make Barbie houses in the sand."

Now she nods. We treasure our Barbies, with their silky hair that melts if you get it too close to the fire, and tans that make me think of Sugar Daddy candy. Mom doesn't like how "objectifying" their bodies are, with their ice cream cone breasts, flat butts and long legs with toes already pointed for high heels. The afternoon passes happily as we dig holes and make furniture out of coral, dressing the Barbies in outfits of leaves held together with pieces of vine.

We still haven't found a house, but it doesn't matter because we're okay living in the van by Tunnels Beach. Mom and Pop surf in the morning while I watch Bonny. We aren't allowed out of the van until they return. Pop takes one of his three boards, and Mom surfs on an inflatable mat with green rubber Churchill fins.

When they get back, Mom fixes breakfast on the camp stove, usually oatmeal with dried fruit chopped up in it. Pop goes fishing or throw netting to get fish to trade or eat, or we drop him off at a construction site to pound nails, or at someone's farm to pick papayas or chainsaw trees.

Mom picks up *puka* shells on the beach for the necklaces she sells to people. Bonny and I help find *pukas*. I like crawling along the sand to pick up the round, white discs with holes in them, the spiral ends of cone shells worn apart in the surf. When strung, they look like smooth rolls of Indian wampum we read about in a book, pale as pearls against Mom's deep tan.

When we have to, we drive to Kapa`a, about forty-five minutes away, to use the Laundromat, buy groceries, and go to the library for books. Evenings, we join other *haoles* that gather on the sand in front of a big beach house at Tunnels owned by Howard Taylor, the movie star Elizabeth Taylor's brother. The adults pass bottles and joints and there's guitar playing and singing. We kids fall asleep on towels under the stars when we're too tired to run around in the dark anymore.

We live in the van for a long time—but winter always comes, and winter on the North Shore of Kauai means *rain* and huge surf.

The van gets really small as rain pours down for days and days.

Pop is grumpy from being closed in the van with no work and all of us scrunched in together. His black cloud is back, even with a lot of big surf to ride and doobies to smoke. He's mean and scary, and there's nowhere to get away from it. Everything I do makes him mad and yell, and he finally throws me out of the van one day when I take my Barbie from Bonny and she cries. "Go play outside!"

Bonny gets to stay in because she's little and mellow. I really wish I were mellow.

I get out of the van, opening the door quickly into the rain, and run to hide in my fort under the ironwood roots on Tunnels Beach.

The sand comes and goes on this beach too, and right now it's mostly gone because it's winter, leaving a cave-like place under the tree that's fun to play in on a sunny day—but not today. The sand is wet even under the roots, and I'm too cold to do anything but huddle as far back as I can get, wrapped in my towel with my Barbie, trying to keep dry. The gray beast of the ocean, foaming at the jaws, gobbles away the summer's piled-up sand and blasts me with its chilly salty breath, just like a monster in the book *Where the Wild Things Are.*

Pop comes to get me after a while, angry because he had to get wet to fetch me. We don't have an umbrella, just garbage bag ponchos. "We're going to Kapa`a to the library to get out of the rain."

I step into the water bucket to wash my bare feet before getting in the van. The bucket has a lid and is also the pee bucket at night. Everything in the van has a purpose, usually more than one.

I can't wait to get to the library. At the library, we can be dry indoors, and I can escape into reading. I learned to read early, when I was four, and my mind sees the stories like watching a movie now that I'm six.

I love everything about the library: the tidy stacks of books that take me away on adventures, the sourish smell of them, the carpet I can sit on to read, the water fountain with the rusty button, the flush toilets. Even Mrs. Rapozo, who sniffs when we return our piles of books and checks them for sand between the pages, is one of my favorite people: she stamps the books with a rubber stamper and makes them mine until the date on the little card inside the flap.

But it's a long, wet, grumpy drive to the library today, and sometimes I wish we were like the family in the Sears catalog. Girls with neat, shiny hair wearing pretty dresses sit on white carpets with curly-haired puppies, playing with toys while a mom with a plate of cookies looks on, and a dad holding a baby smiles.

All good things come to us in Hawaii from the magical Sears Roebuck catalog, and I love the catalog even more than one of my picture books—because everything inside can be ordered. I've already worn the ink off the pages of the toy section, wishing and hoping for things like a plastic Barbie mansion and a stable for the Breyer horses I want to collect. The biggest stores on Kauai are Woolworth's and Liberty House, an hour away in Lihue, and they hardly have any toys at all.

I wonder where the Sears Roebuck family lives. Somewhere far from here.

※
༄

MOM AND POP'S SURFER FRIEND, RUSTY MILLER, IS MOVING BACK to Australia and has promised my parents his rental cottage. The place is near Ke`e Beach, known as The End of the Road because the one road that goes around Kauai stops there, at the edge of the steep Na Pali Cliffs.

Rusty is the first person to ever rent the cottage. He found it exploring the jungle after a surf session, tracked down who the owner was, and drove all the way to Lawai on the other side of the island to ask Mr. Allerton, the wealthy island philanthropist who owns the property, if he could rent it if he painted the place and kept it up. In the years he's lived there, it's become something of a legendary spot, with a steady stream of surfers from all over the world stopping in to crash at "Rusty's cabin." Getting the cottage is a big deal because there are so few houses of any kind on the North Shore.

On the day we get the house, we drive to the gap in the trees right after Limahuli Stream, but just before the dirt parking area that marks Taylor Camp, a hippie camp spot. We park the van on the side of the road under dripping guava trees. A path leads down into the jungle, studded with rocks too big for the van to get over. Mom puts our garbage bag ponchos on Bonny and me, and our rubber slippers because of the rocks. We walk down a long muddy trail, through dripping Java plum, mango, rose apple, and kukui nut trees draped in dangling vines like mermaid hair.

Rusty meets us at the empty cottage. He's a wiry man with a head of thick, tufty, sun-bleached surfer hair, bright blue eyes, and a red-and-blond beard. He opens the rickety screen door wide. "Welcome to your new home."

Perfectly square, the house is dark green with white trim and a rust-red tin roof. Inside, the walls are silvery cedarwood planks that Rusty tells us were floated down the coast in the ocean from Hanalei. "Ocean-treated wood becomes resistant to termites. The house was built in the nineteen twenties by a Boy Scout troop for their campouts." Rusty shows us around with his crackling energy. Two tiny bedrooms, a front room, and kitchen make up the layout. There's no plumbing, bathroom, or electricity. Rusty ran a pipe to the stream, though, so there's water to the kitchen sink. We drink it straight from there, so cold it makes my teeth hurt.

Rusty hacked the jungle back with a machete to make the yard, and there's a central patch of sunlight in front of the house. A Hawaiian orange tree grows beside the house, along with papaya and a patch of bananas. Rusty leaves behind a fruit picker made of a bleach bottle tied to a bamboo pole. Right away we pick the sour, juicy oranges, with their yellow, mottled skins—so different from bright Mainland oranges.

My parents are thrilled to get the cottage, and after bidding Rusty a grateful goodbye, we promptly rename it the Forest House.

Lantana, bamboo grasses, and wild roses overflow an area that Mom stakes out for the garden, and she strings up a clothesline for drying our towels and laundry. We wash at the Laundromat in Hanalei, half an hour away, but dry our clothes here in the clearing to save money.

Weeding out the grass and shrubs for her garden, Mom finds the mounds of three graves under antique *lokelani* rosebushes. We leave them alone after just a little weeding and trimming. I like the thought of someone loving this place so much they never wanted to leave it.

We have one of the only gas refrigerators I've ever seen, a small rusty white box whose pilot light blows out a lot. We have a gas stove, too, and shelves where everything is stored. After the van, it seems like so much room. Mom's careful to keep all the food in big glass mayonnaise jars against the rats and cockroaches that come in from the jungle.

Breakfast is oatmeal cooked on the stove with the squishy good-ness of raisins popping on my tongue and local honey drizzled over it. Mom has found a co-op in California, and with the money Pop has from his trust fund, she has big boxes of food shipped each month to Hanalei, the closest town. Lentils, garbanzos, alfalfa, mung beans, dried figs, dates, apricots, oats, and flour so brown it looks speckled, fill the jars on the built-in shelf in the kitchen area, along with honey in a can and peanut butter separating into golden oil and sludgy goodness.

Pop builds me a raised wooden bed frame right next to the screened window in the tiny bedroom I share with Bonny. She sleeps on a foam futon underneath mine, like a bunk bed. The window has trouble closing—damp has warped it, and nighttime rain blows in— but I love that window. From my perch in bed I can watch the leaves at the tops of the Java plum trees fluttering in the wind, and listen to the watery hum of Limahuli Stream, the creek that runs past the house. I read in swishing sunlight that falls in over my books.

There's no electricity, so no radio or records like Mom and Pop used to play on Oahu. Just Pop playing his guitar, and the stream singing its song.

A friendly Hawaiian guy in a brown uniform with his name on the pocket brings our tank of propane to the house on a dolly, bumping it carefully down the boulder-strewn path. Mom gives him a bag of oranges and papayas for "going the extra mile" as she calls it, and she makes him blush and duck his head. She's beautiful, with her big smile, long tanned legs, and ripple of brown hair. People say she looks like the actress Ali McGraw.

Eventually, I explore down the rocky trail leading away from the house all the way to the beach, where there's a shallow, protected swimming hole in the ocean on the inside of the reef. Naked grownups are bathing, washing dishes, and lying in the sun; they're from the village of homemade houses in a grove of *kamani* trees next to us.

When I get back, I ask Mom how come there's a community right next to us made out of plastic, bamboo, and trash-picked wood.

"Howard Taylor, the guy whose house we liked to hang out at over at Tunnels Beach, is a very rich man. He is the brother of Liz Taylor, the star of my favorite movie, *National Velvet*. Taylor felt sorry for the hippies camping in the parks on the North Shore and getting hassled by the locals and locked up for vagrancy. They were even sentenced to hard labor for being homeless! Taylor bailed them out and let them live on his land, and that's why it's called Taylor Camp."

I think this over. "But we aren't a part of Taylor Camp?"

"No. Mr. Allerton owns this land and rents this house to us," Mom says. "We're doing our own thing. We're surfers, not Taylor Campers."

I take this bit of information and tuck it away. If you look at us, it's hard to tell that we're different than the Taylor Camp people, but we live in Rusty's cabin, own a car that works, and my dad has a job. He's now cooking at a restaurant called The Anchorage halfway to Hanalei, and takes the van there most days, or Mom drives him if she needs to use it.

I make some friends at the Camp where there are a few other kids.

Minka's taller than I am, with eyes the color of faded blue jeans, skin like a lion's coat, and blonde hair bleached to the texture of rope by a thousand days in the ocean. Her teeth are overlarge and list about. Minka's happy to have a friend her age to play with, and she takes me to see where she lives in Taylor Camp.

The wind sighs and squeaks in the *kamani* trees that the plastic, bamboo, and plywood houses of the Camp are built of, as I climb a wooden ladder into Minka's tree house.

Their house is one of several actually up in the trees. Minka, her sister Alpin, and their parents are some of the founding members of the Camp. Her mom, Bobo, is a strong woman with a leathery face and long braids who surfs and swims the Na Pali Coast naked and has a surf break named after her. Her dad, Hawk, is a small sturdy man with a straggly beard and is sort of the chief of the Camp.

The people at the Camp don't wear many clothes. There's a lot of sitting around, strumming guitars, working in the garden, rolling joints, and lying on the beach naked. *Pakalolo,* or marijuana it's called, is a constant blue smoke in the air. I'm not sure I like the sweetish smell, the way it tickles the back of my throat and seems to have a texture.

I'm curious about the nakedness of the Taylor Campers. The

men's penises remind me of sea cucumbers in *limu* seaweed nests. Sometimes, when they wear shorts that are too small, their balls leak out like hairy brown potatoes. The women have water-balloon breasts with nipples like raisins, or small ones like cupcakes with a stub of candle on top. Several of the ladies have tiger-stripe marks on their bellies and hips. I ask about them and am told, "they're stretch marks from babies."

I picture babies taking hold of the skin and pulling it in their little hands and wonder how that happened.

Nakedness looks a lot of different ways, but it all kind of smells the same to me—like garlicky sweat, yeast, and sometimes patchouli or sandalwood oil. I get used to it. Minka's mom, Bobo, looks just right naked, like a sea otter with braids.

We mostly wear clothes at our house, and our family doesn't smell because we bathe in the stream and use soap every day. Mom wants me to at least have panties on most of the time, and that's another way I know we aren't like the Taylor Campers, even though the locals think we are.

The first time I see the toilet at Taylor Camp it's because I have to use it. I'd forgotten to use our tidy outhouse at home and have to go poo. Pee is easy, any bush will do—but poo, Mom told me, needs to go somewhere particular so germs don't spread around.

Minka leads me to a raised, completely open wooden structure in the middle of a field with a toilet seat on it about five feet above a hole in the ground. Flies buzz around, and the smell makes my eyes water and my tummy tighten up.

"I can't go here," I tell Minka. I run away into the jungle toward home. I run and run, missing the trail between our house and the Camp, making my way through thick stands of trees and bamboo grass frantically until I find our cottage and the small, dank outhouse in our yard.

It smells like poop here, too, but not in a bad way—kind of sourish, like mushrooms growing, a live smell I don't mind. I lower my butt over the splintery hole in the plywood and sigh with relief to be home. Afterward, I wipe with leaves from the leaf bucket that help keep the poop compost down.

We use a plastic lidded bucket to pee in at night because the outhouse is too far away and it's often raining, which is why it's so green and lush here. Mom dumps the bucket on the banana trees and buries the composted poop for fertilizer. It seems to work because all the trees start growing and making even more fruit after we move in.

I'm going to begin school now that we have a house, a little late in the year because of all our moving. Mom takes me in to register in Hanalei and leaves Pop and Bonny at home. Going anywhere alone with her is a big deal, and I bounce with excitement in the front seat as we drive along the winding, two-lane road with its steep cliffs falling off the side of the island into black rocks and crashing waves.

The school building is a long, low wooden L shape just outside of Hanalei, with a covered porch that wraps around for the rain and red ginger planted all around the edges. The Hawaiian flag, bright with its Union Jack and American stripes, flaps proudly from a tall silver flagpole, and when we arrive some older kids are securing it. I want to help clip that flag on and pull on the ropes until it's at the top and snaps in the breeze.

At the tiny office, Mom has to produce my birth certificate and immunization record, which she fortunately kept up on Oahu.

"You're young to be reading, but it's a good thing since you're skipping kindergarten," the office lady, Miss Inouye, says. Her eyes almost disappear when she smiles, and her face is round and soft, the color of Mom's rising whole wheat bread dough. She reminds me of my preschool teacher and I'm excited, even though I know I'm going to have to take the bus and it's a long way.

"Thought you could learn a little more about our area," Miss Inouye says, and hands Mom a sheet titled *Hanalei School Information* in purple ink.

Out at the van, Mom asks me to read it to her as she drives to Ching Young Store where we have to pick up a few things. I read about the school, and then the town, sounding out when I don't know the words: *"Hanalei Bay is the largest bay on Kauai. The town of Hanalei (population 160) is at the midpoint of the bay and contains Hanalei School, the Wai`oli Hui`ia Church, Ching Young Store and Post Office, the Hanalei Liquor Store, the Rice Mill, the Tahiti Nui Bar, and the Trader mercantile for dry goods. According to Census figures for 1970, there are eleven hundred residents from Ke`e Beach (where the road ends on the Na Pali Coast) to Kilauea fifteen miles to the south.*

Hanalei's wetlands were cultivated by native Hawaiians until the introduction of rice as a staple food crop in the 1830s. Hanalei Pier was constructed to assist in transporting the rice to other locations. Taro has returned to Hanalei and is farmed by several families."

"Why do they grow the taro in water?" I gesture to the field we're passing. Heart-shaped, big green leaves of evenly spaced *kalo* plants rise in pairs from tea-colored liquid, held in by low grassy barriers like quilt squares.

"I think the plants just like it that way." Mom angles the van into the unpaved, muddy parking area next to the Ching Young Store. *Hau* bush and *pili* grass rise up behind it in a wall broken by a potholed mud road leading to some shacks. "*Kalo* can grow in the ground too, but grows bigger and faster in the water. *Kalo* is the Hawaiians' main food crop, and they know how to get the most out of the land."

Flavorless, sticky purple *poi* is the Hawaiians' main food? It's okay with fish and rice, but I like *kalo* best boiled and fried, like a potato chip or hash browns.

"Why don't you get the mail, big first-grader?" Mom smiles, and hands me the keys to open our post office box. Both the little brass key and the van's key are kept on a great big nickel-plated safety pin that my parents clip onto their swimsuits when surfing.

Getting the mail is my favorite thing to do in Hanalei because there are always interesting things that come to our little post office box.

While Mom gets her quilted homemade purse, I skip up the creaky, well-worn porch of the store. The main entrance of Ching Young Store is on the right, and the post office is a half-door on the left, followed by a solid wall of brass-fronted post office boxes in between.

When we first got to Kauai, we had to stand in line with everyone and ask for "general delivery," but now that we have a house and our own post office box, it feels like we really live here. I can reach the fancy brass door of the box myself by standing on my tiptoes in my rubber slippers. A warm draft of air from the street blows up the skirt of the halter-backed dress covered in daisies that Mom sewed for me. Inside the box is a pink package slip. I go to the half-door in the counter and reach my hand up to tap the bell, but Clorinda Murioka, the postmistress, is already waiting in the window because she likes to hang out and talk story with people as they come and go.

"Hi, Aunty Clorinda." Mom wanted me to call her Mrs. Murioka to be respectful, but Clorinda told me to call her "aunty" like all the local kids do. She's all smiling dimples and shiny black hair in a bun, and she takes the pink slip from my hand.

"Toby, what you folks get today? You Wilsons get so many packages!" A few minutes later, she hands the box to me.

If the box is light, it's probably something from my grandma Gigi. If it's a box of food from the co-op, I have to get Mom to help carry it to the van. I check the address. Yep, it's from Gigi. Maybe she sent me something for school. I'd love to have a new knapsack or school supplies.

Mom's gone inside the Ching Young Store and is saying hi to Mrs. Ching, who runs the register from a square station surrounded by glass counters where she can keep an eye on everything. She's short and wears tidy fitted muumuus and half glasses on a chain that she puts on her nose. Mrs. Ching never asks me to call her "aunty," but she likes me, I can tell, because sometimes she'll give me a Bazooka bubblegum from the big jar on the counter if I'm there alone.

I'm always hopeful, but if Mom catches me with the gum, she'll take it away. We don't get to eat sugar like the town kids who run through Ching's store, sticky with shave ice syrup and Tomoe Ame rice candy. Mom says sugar's bad for us. She points out how many of the local kids have silver teeth and tells me it makes me hyperactive.

While they chat about whether or not the Hanalei River will flood this year, I poke around in the dimly lit depths.

Ching Young Store always reminds me of Aladdin's cave of treasures. They have everything: tabis for reef walking, my favorite red scoop nets, spears, knives, fishing tackle, flashlights, matches, paraffin wax Pop uses for his surfboards but you can make candles with—and that's just the non-food aisle.

We can't afford to buy much at Ching's. It's expensive, and we do better with our food stamps if we drive another hour or so into town in Kapa`a or Lihue. Trips into town happen every couple of weeks, with the monthly food stamp pickup at the big white state building in Lihue. We usually get our food right after that at the nearby Big Save: boxes of powdered milk and everything else Mom can't order through the co-op.

Getting food stamps has something to do with not having enough regular money. Pop works whenever he can get a job, plus his job at the Anchorage, but Mom doesn't have a job and the three hundred dollars from Pop's trust fund goes to gas, rent, and the co-op. We really need the food stamps, or we run out of food. Everyone we know gets them, including the local families.

Mom needs matches and kerosene for the lamps, and today she buys me a Tiger's Milk bar, since it's our special day. On the way back home, I lick the carob coating off the peanut butter filling and eat it ever so slowly.

"Go pick us some chard," Mom says when we get back to the Forest House. "And be sure to get off all the caterpillars."

Mom doesn't believe in using pesticides and fertilizers, so Bonny and I pick the snails, slugs, and caterpillars off the veggies every day, and she makes compost to feed the plants from leaves, grass clippings and horse or cow manure. Inside the house, Mom's cooking the kidney beans she left to soak and brown rice. When you combine them, they form "a perfect protein," which means we don't have to eat meat to be healthy.

Mom's veggie plot is growing amazing even though we haven't been here long. I squat in the red dirt of the row and pick a whole pile of the outer leaves of the chard, throwing the caterpillars away into the grass. "Don't kill them. It's bad karma," Mom says.

Karma is when someone dies and, if they were a good person, they come back as a more evolved thing. If not, they go back to start and are born as a slug or maybe a toad. Pop rolls his eyes a bit at the karma of caterpillars, so I'm pretty sure it's okay to squish them. And we kill a lot of fish and reef creatures, but the karma on that is okay, I hope, because we are eating them. Today, we have *uhu* steamed with chard over rice and beans. Sitting on the front porch, eating together, it tastes so good. Especially since Pop's in a good mood, even though he's drinking and that means tomorrow morning will be hard.

Pop goes surfing most mornings when there are waves, but when it's flat, he and I go fishing. The morning after I register for school, Pop puts on an old canvas hat and his surf trunks. I put on my bathing suit bottoms and a little triangle top Mom made, and she daubs my skin with PABA, shaking her head and saying that I'll probably get burned again, but I refuse to wear a hat. It makes it too hard for me to see everything, and my head gets hot.

Pop slings his fishing bag over his shoulder, moving slowly because he's hungover, which means I have to be extra quiet and not annoying. The bag is a dark green satchel that holds gear and the fish we'll get, and it smells like the ocean. He pulls on sock-like reef tabis, Japanese water shoes he bought at Ching's. I don't have tabis because they don't make them in my size.

Pop is the only *haole* guy I've ever seen throw net. He's proud of having been taught how to fish this way by big wave waterman Tiger Espere on Oahu as a thank-you gift for taking pictures of Tiger surfing. Tiger is a big, scary man who dominates the waves on the North Shore and is a badass Hawaiian. If Tiger taught Pop, then it's okay that Pop does it, in spite of being *haole*. Pop just tells the guys who hassle him who he learned from, and that shuts them up.

Pop says that our way of fitting in on Kauai is to not be seen or heard. Henry Paik, a local guy who lives in Hanalei and who is teaching Pop slack-key guitar, tells him that we can live in our little hippie enclave at the end of the road near the Taylor Camp, but we better not go to the places where the locals hang out and take up space or their fish, or "we goin' get plenty humbug."

We've visited Uncle Henry and his wife at their tidy little house in Hanalei, where Mrs. Paik let me play with her collection of painted wood *kokeshi* dolls and we ate a meal of fish, rice, and seaweed. I enjoyed their flush toilet and fancy shell-shaped hand soap.

So far we haven't had any trouble, though we hear of other *haoles* getting hassled and beaten up. A *haole* couple even got shot in their house in Wainiha, and nobody knows who killed them. People from Taylor Camp disappear, and nobody knows what happened, so Pop listens to Henry and does what he says.

The throw net is Pop's prized possession. He bought it for a huge amount of money, ninety dollars, from old Mr. Yoshimura in Kapa'a. Mr. Yoshimura makes the nets by hand with his shuttle and a big spool of see-through fishing line called *suji*. Pop rinses it with stream water after every use because salt ruins it.

Pop slings the heavy throw net over his shoulder easily as he sets off down the trail. I can't even lift it because it weights thirty or forty pounds. Pop looks so tall and strong to me. He can do anything, and he's handsome with his skin the color of caramel and his blond hair like vanilla ice cream. Bonny cries at being left behind, and I feel bad for her, but happy to be old enough to help my dad.

We go down the path beside the stream through tall, white-barked Java plum trees with their little bombs of sour purple fruit, and under the big open shadowy dance of *kamani* trees to get to the ocean. I run with no shoes, my feet like horse hooves by now as I hop from rock to rock. It's too early for the Taylor Camp people to be out, so when we reach the beach, we're alone with the long shiny reef and the wind just beginning to snag the silky water.

Pop takes a moment to drape the circular net ringed in flat three-inch lead weights just so from his shoulder and hip, so that it will open in a perfect circle when he throws it over the fish. There's care in each movement, the beginning of the quiet that is an important part of fishing. He's shown me several times how he arranges the net, explaining the placement of each draped ruffle as it hangs.

When he's teaching me something, it's the best between us. I'm a quick learner, I'm not a whiner, and I'll try anything. I'm still doing the best I can to make him forget I'm a girl.

Pop walks onto the reef as graceful as a bullfighter pictured in National Geographic, and the net is his cape. I follow him, careful not to scare the fish, trying to get what I can with my little scoop net—but my big catch, the octopus, remains a time when I got something good when we really needed it. I've earned my place behind him.

To get a good haul with the net, Pop has to wade at least knee-deep into the surge at the outer edge of the barrier reef. That reef takes the brunt of the ocean's movement and the fish like it there, in bubbly water where food is stirred up for them. The edge drops off into a deep channel with strong currents. Pop doesn't want me getting swept out by a wave, so he makes me stay behind him.

I scoop up tiny *opae* shrimp, their bodies as clear as glass with just the shapes of their guts to define them. I put a couple on the hook of my bamboo pole and jig them up and down in a likely looking pool. I keep one eye on the pool, the other on Pop.

I love the colors of everything: sparkling light on the water, the layered green of Makana Mountain behind us, the dark ironwoods, pale gold beach, turquoise shallows, the deep blue of the ocean beyond. I wish I could paint what I see, but the watercolors I have are too pale, and my pens can't get the right effect.

The sun is getting hotter. I can feel my face heating up with the sunburn I'll have later on because I hate wearing a hat, and Mom didn't get zinc oxide on my nose this morning. Pop has been standing still, only his head moving as he scans the water, holding the carefully draped net just so. Waves crash and boil around him and suck back and forth across his legs. It's amazing that he can hold the heavy net for so long with his arms bent.

Pop bows back in a sudden, fluid way, and throws the net outward in an explosive forward movement. The net flies out of his arms, spinning open in a perfect circle, and drops to disappear into the waves. He leaps after it, grabbing a cord in the center, and hauls back, stumbling and almost falling, making me jerk my pole up with fright—but he gets his footing and leans back, the muscles in his arms and back bunching as he hauls in the catch.

The net's thrashing with fish. Pop scoops the whole flapping thing up in his arms and turns and walks with a long stride back across the reef. I yank up my pole and run after him, forgetting to watch for tube worms and feeling one puncture my foot.

"Ow!" I yell, but don't slow down because I'm too excited. At the beach he tosses the net down on the sand.

A whole school of *manini* is caught in it, green-striped tangs that taste good pan-fried with butter and garlic salt. My mouth waters at the thought. I kneel in the sand and help him untangle the fish, each about the size of Pop's big hand. They have a rough feel to their skin, and lots of poky fins that catch on the net.

"We should just clean them here," he says. "Don't want to stink up your mom's compost heap."

"Okay." I wrinkle my nose. *Manini* are algae eaters, and their diet makes their guts really smelly. He hands me the Swiss Army knife and gets out his fishing knife with the plastic sheath.

He's taught me how to clean fish already. I find a flat piece of bleached white coral and lay the fish, still flapping, on it. I push the point of the knife into the fish's poophole and cut away from myself, anchoring it with my left hand, all the way up to the pectoral fins. The *manini* jerks under my hand, a yucky reminder that it's alive. Being quick is being kind, Pop tells me. Responsible fishermen kill their fish right away to spare them the death of suffocation outside the sea.

Being quick, I hook my finger into the guts and rip them out, tossing them into a tide pool where crabs and other fish will eat them. I breathe through my mouth so I don't smell the guts, and I don't look at my bloody hands. Pop has already cleaned three and is untangling a fourth by the time I've finished one.

Several people from Taylor Camp wander down, looking hopeful. Pop is generous—after all, the fish won't last long in our little fridge with no freezer, and there will be more tomorrow.

A lady from the camp squats beside me naked in her oily tan and *puka* shells, her brown braids trailing the sand. She watches as I try to work fast, cleaning her fish. "You know a lot about this, for a little girl."

"My dad taught me." I'm proud as I hand three fish to her. She walks off down the beach, carrying the fish in her hands, against her bare belly.

Pop is happy about the haul, and he's feeling better now that he's more awake. Maybe his hangover is better. I have to be careful around Pop when he is drinking. I keep count of how many joints, hash pipes, mushrooms, or drinks my parents have. I can look at their eyes to see if it's a good time to ask for something, or if I should just hole up in my room with Bonny and keep the door shut. Sometimes I feel a tight, worried feeling in my tummy about them, but mostly it's good because they are happier when they are drinking or smoking.

We walk back up to the Forest House and into the yard, where the sun has finally reached Mom's garden patch. She's squatting among the plants, weeding in her work muumuu, a shapeless garment dark enough not to show dirt. Bonny's "helping," which means sitting on the ground sucking a finger and digging at the weeds with a spoon.

"We got a lot of fish!" I'm noisy—almost yelling with excitement —but Pop just grins this time. He opens the green satchel to show our treasures, fish lining the inside like stacks of fat green leaves.

Bonny claps her hands and Mom says, "Good job!" and kisses Pop on the mouth. We all take the fish down to wash them in fresh water at the stream.

"Time for you to bathe, too," Mom says. "In fact, I'm done working in the garden. Let's all clean up."

Midday is the ideal time to bathe. The sun has really warmed things up in the yard. But Limahuli Stream, which is rainwater from high in the mountains, is always cold. We take our much-dried and rehung towels with us and walk up the path to a swimming hole just off the road above our house. As usual, there are no cars on the narrow two-lane highway that dead-ends at pretty Ke`e Beach in another half-mile.

I take off my suit, rinse it in the stream, and spread it on a rock to dry. Once in the water, my teeth chatter. Mom gives me a squirt of Dr. Bronner's All-Purpose Soap. The peppermint smell of the soap, with its flip-top plastic bottle, makes every already-cold minute in the chilly stream energetic, not relaxing like a warm soak in the tub at the Rocky Point house.

Limahuli Stream's stones are browny-green with algae, and slippery. I burrow my feet into smooth gravel between the rocks and wash quickly, under the arms and my butt and pie. Mom gives me another squirt to soap up my hair. Pop's naked beside me doing the same, and as usual I keep my eyes off him. Though being naked with the family doesn't feel strange, this is the kind of time when I think of my grandma Gigi and know she wouldn't like how we live. Maga, Mom's mom who was married to my scientist Grandpa Garth, wouldn't care. Maga likes to study other cultures and tell loud stories about natives around the world, and she'd just say we're our own kind of tribe.

Mom and Bonny bathe, too, but Bonny's fussing about being cold. I don't like washing in the stream either at first—it's always too cold—but after I'm soaped up the pool's deep enough to dive forward into. I swim around and crawl over the rocks, pretending to be a mermaid. I cross the swimming hole to sit between two boulders and let a mini-waterfall wash the last of the Dr. Bronner's out of my hair and down the stream.

I love the pressure of the waterfall, the breathless chill, the way it pushes me down like a hand and I have to be strong to resist it. I turn my head and drink, and the water tastes like rain.

Afterward, we wrap in our towels and walk back down the path to our house. We lie in a naked row on our towels in the sun, drying off.

I lift my head and glance over at my family. Pop's on the other side of Mom, an arm flung over his eyes. The sun turns the hairs on his body to gold, the big cage of his ribs sloping down to his flat belly, his root a shrunken mushroom, his legs like fallen trees.

Beside me, Mom's eyes are shut. Her body is dark and long, and she's lost the tan lines from Oahu. Her breasts droop on either side of her chest, empty pouches with leathery tips now that Bonny's done nursing.

Bonny's fallen asleep, tucked against Mom's side. My sister's thick white-blonde hair is bright against Mom's tan. I like the darkness against the light, the velvety baby texture of Bonny's skin against the smooth brown expanse of my mother.

Mom smells delicious, like the coconut oil she puts on her skin. I put my hand against Mom's thigh just to see what it looks like there.

My hand is a small, square miniature of my father's big one. Freckles up my arm look like cinnamon and are the same color as Mom's tan. I'm relieved by this. Sometimes I worry I got into my family by accident because I don't look like Mom except for my eyes, or like Pop except for my hands and feet.

I turn over on my towel and fold my hands under my chin, to watch some ants working very hard to move a seed. They pass it among themselves, and pick it up and set it down, and it takes a long time to get it a short way as they try to help each other.

In my imagination, I shrink down to tiny. I build a cart for the seed, and the ants load it on the cart. Then, I hitch the ants to the front of the cart and sit up high cracking a whip as they pull it to their nest. It still takes a long time to move the seed, even with the cart, but that's okay. We have all day.

CHAPTER SIX

SCHOOL DOES NOT GO WELL

Bathing in Limahuli stream

Age: 6, Hanalei, Kauai, 1971

I'm excited to go to school after visiting the long wooden building with the red tin roof in the middle of Hanalei to register. It's full of hundreds of kids who could be future friends. I'm ready to have friends to play with and excited to learn.

But, after the first few days, I don't like it.

At all.

Getting to Hanalei is an hour-long carsick ride along the narrow curvy road in the big echoing school bus. There are four bridges to cross: two in Wainiha, one at Lumahai, and one outside of Hanalei. The road is super dramatic, with cliffs on one side so close you could touch them with the windows down, and the ocean far below on the other.

The driver goes all the way to the top of our path in the morning to pick Minka and me near Taylor Camp, and we are the first kids on the bus. Then, she picks up the rest—Mahuikis, Chings, Haradas, Makas, Tai Hooks, Wongs, and Chandlers. When we return at the end of the school day, the driver goes all the way to the End of the Road and drops us off first, then drops the others on the way back. The other kids are mad about the extra time they have to spend on the bus getting us to and from our jungle outpost, so they grumble and try to pinch us when we walk past.

Minka and I are the only two *haoles* in our class. Everyone else is shades of brown with black or brown hair, and blonde Minka and redheaded me stand out like two things that don't belong. School is a non-stop day of poking, pinching, tripping, hair-pulling, and name-calling. "Dirty hippie! Stinkin' *haole* crap! Go back to the Mainland!" they hassle us.

Soon I'm happy if the kids just ignore me, and during recess I go to the library if it's open, or try to find a corner to hide in and read. I still wish I had ESP powers and could do things with my mind, maybe zap the mean kids. It was never this bad when I went to public preschool on Oahu. I know I'm different-looking, with freckles and orangey hair, but I've never felt *ugly* before.

I wish for black hair and beautiful brown skin with a longing as sharp as hunger. As it is, I stand out in any crowd like a lit match, and that's not a good thing on Kauai.

To make things worse, I usually forget some item of clothing when dressing in the early-morning dark. Usually it's my rubber slippers, but today, a Monday, I forget my panties.

Mrs. Harada, our teacher, stands at the blackboard in the mornings, using the yardstick as a pointer and reminding us what season it is in some other world. I don't even know what a snowflake is, but I stare at the weather chart and say "blizzard" with everyone else. This morning, I'm separated from Minka. While Mrs. Harada's back is turned, I crawl across Morning Circle in my homemade dress, trying to sit next to my friend and accidentally showing my *okole* to the entire first grade.

Mrs. Harada, gigantic in a purple muumuu with a bun so tight it pulls her forehead wrinkle-free, smacks my bare butt out of nowhere with her yardstick. It feels like being struck by lightning, and I shriek.

"Where are your panties?" Mrs. Harada bellows. "For shame! Go to the principal's office!"

I'm terrified, and my butt smarts in a way that makes being spanked by my dad feel like nothing. I'm not going to the principal's office! I scurry over to my metal desk and hide underneath, grasping onto the metal leg of it. The room bursts into nervous giggling, the other kids whispering and pointing behind their hands.

I've never been yelled at by a grownup except my parents—I'm usually petted and loved by adults. "She's so smart and look at that pretty hair" is what they say.

Mrs. Harada doesn't think I'm smart or pretty. In just two weeks I know she doesn't like hippie kids, and me especially.

"Come out! Right now!" Mrs. Harada smacks the ruler on her hand. This doesn't invite me out. Instead, I wrap my arms and legs around the strut of the desk and hunker down, hiding behind my long hair. *It can't get any worse than this.*

Mrs. Harada pries my arms off, scolding all the while, but I'm pretty strong and reattach, octopus-like. She goes for my legs, and gets both of them, hauling me bodily out from under the desk by the ankles. Once again, my bare behind is visible, but I don't care. *I just forgot my panties. What's the big deal?* I don't say these things, but stubbornness has kicked in. I hang onto the desk with all my strength, biting my lips and wriggling to get away.

The other kids are too scared of Mrs. Harada to laugh, and cluster in a group as far away from our struggle as possible. She wrestles and grunts and scolds, and finally hollers for help from Miss Kinch, a tall skinny lady who looks like Olive Oyl and teaches the next grade on the other side of the room. The two of them pry me out from under the desk, kicking and biting, and I'm physically dragged into Mr. Beck's office. Mrs. Harada sits me on a hard wooden chair in front of him.

Mr. Beck's a large blond man with a kind, weathered face. He knows Pop from surfing, and my dad calls him "Nick" and his wife is "Pam." He lives with his family right in front of a good break at Hanalei Bay called Waikokos. Sometimes we play on the beach with his two sons, Ducky and Hobie, while the adults are out surfing. Ducky's kind of bossy, but Hobie, who's younger, is nice. I like Hobie because he has a lot of freckles and his name rhymes with Toby.

Mr. Beck seemed nice at the beach, but right now he looks annoyed at being interrupted. His big shoulders are hunched in his aloha shirt. His hands are paused on a typewriter that looks too small for his fingers as he peers at me through glasses perched on his nose. He looks like the kind of guy who should be out chopping trees, not typing tiny forms on an old Remington. "What's this?"

Mrs. Harada's tight black bun is coming loose and she's not happy about it, patting the place on her forehead where her hair is unraveling. "This girl has no panties. We'd call the mother if they had a phone, but those *haoles* live out at Taylor Camp." Her voice is mean.

I'm so tired of "dirty hippie," "fucking *haole*," and "stupid *haole* girl, you so ugly."

I look up at Mrs. Harada. "We aren't Taylor Campers. We bathe every day. We have a clean outhouse. My parents mostly smoke weed at night, not all day like the Campers do. My dad has a job, and we live in a real house. *We're surfers*—that's why we're on Kauai. We are NOT at Taylor Camp."

Mrs. Harada turns and glares down at me.

I'm paralyzed. There is nothing scarier than Mrs. Harada's fully loaded eye cannon. She squints mean at Mr. Beck. "You'd better do something about this girl. Toby has an attitude, and it sets a bad example for the other students. So unsanitary. She probably has *ukus*."

"I'll handle this," Mr. Beck says. Hanging behind his desk is a ping-pong paddle whose function I worry about.

Mrs. Harada glides out like there are wheels under her purple muumuu.

Ukus are head lice. I don't have them right now, but I did a few months ago, so I keep quiet. My butt is still stinging. I stare at my knees and pick at a scab. I wish I could jump up, open my wings like Pegasus the winged horse, leap right out the window into the sky, and keep on going.

"We have to talk about what happened. But first you're going to the nurse. She has extra clothes for accidents. Let me show you where it is." Mr. Beck's voice is gentle.

I hop off the chair and follow him out of the office and down the echoey wood porch to the nurse's office. Miss Inouye is both the nurse and the office lady, and she clucks disapprovingly over my many mosquito bites, scabs, and the tube worm cut getting infected on my foot. The two of them check me over from head to foot, and Miss Inouye even looks through my hair for *ukus*, and I'm relieved to be *uku*-free. Eventually, I walk with Mr. Beck back to his office, covered with Betadine and Band-Aids, wearing a pair of too-big panties under my dress.

I sit on the hard chair and stare at the ping-pong paddle. Mr. Beck sees where I'm looking and chuckles. "Don't worry. No paddling today. But where are your panties?"

"I got dressed in the dark and forgot. There's no light in my room because there's no electricity."

"So, you have panties? No one took them off you?"

"No. I just forgot them."

"Well, I'd like for your mom to bring in an extra pair in case this happens again."

I nod vigorously in agreement.

"Why don't you spend the day in my office?" Mr. Beck says. "We'll call it detention. Do you read?"

"Yes, please." I'm thrilled. So far, other than Minka, I haven't made a single friend, and somewhere comfortable and protected to hide with a book sounds like heaven.

I spend the day on the padded bench under Mr. Beck's window, lying on my tummy reading *The Secret Garden,* a favorite. Mr. Beck brings me lunch on a cardboard tray like I'm special.

The school lunches, which I get free because we are on food stamps, are so delicious. A shloop of runny canned peaches in sugar syrup—yum! A mound of spaghetti chopped up and mixed with red sauce and burger—red meat! White flour pasta! My own little carton of milk—so tasty!

And today is especially good because there's a shortbread almond cookie. These special treats are baked in big cookie pans, cut into squares, and marked with a single almond. I save the cookie for last and sit holding it with two hands, gnawing on it with my front teeth. I'm a squirrel with a nut, trying to make the nut last longer.

"You like those?" Mr. Beck looks up at me from his paperwork. "You can have mine." Mr. Beck hands me his cookie.

I love detention.

Mr. Beck has no way to talk to my parents at the end of the school day, so he writes a note, folds it tight, and pins it to my dress. "Don't take this off. Give it to your mom and dad."

I nod.

Bad stuff begins as soon as I leave the safety of his office.

"Stupid *haole* girl, I saw your *punani,*" hisses one of my classmates. *Punani* is the Hawaiian word for what we call "pie" at home, my vagina. "It was gross." Someone lifts up my skirt on the way to the bus and the bloomers, drooping off my butt, get laughed at.

Mr. Beck comes to the door and smacks his hands, a sound like a gunshot that makes everyone jump. "Enough!" he bellows, and points to the paddle on the wall.

Silence falls.

All of us get on the bus with no talking, but I know the local kids are just waiting for a chance to hassle me away from adult eyes. I sit with Minka and fold my knees up against my chest and turn into the corner of the seat, making myself small. Minka can't defend me—she has to worry about herself. But she moves up against my back, a warm presence, and we huddle there together. I imagine a cloak of invisibility draped over us like in one of my fairy tales. In my mind I ride a desert stallion and wield a giant sword with a hooked blade, smiting my enemies.

Mom is pissed off after she reads the note, and especially when she sees the red mark on my butt from Mrs. Harada's ruler. "I'm going in to talk to them. I don't believe in spanking in school." She gets red spots on her cheeks and her eyes flash. Mom is scary when she gets mad, and I'm glad she's not mad at me, even though I was the one to draw attention to our family.

"Don't make waves," Pop says. "We don't want to get them on our case. You never know with the man." A raft of unspoken suspicion of "the man" is behind those words. Pop is always worried about locals and "the man."

I wonder who "the man" is, because Mr. Beck is the nicest person at Hanalei School.

I tell Mom Mr. Beck is the person to talk to. She gets in the van and drives to school, and apparently they get along because he pulls me aside the next day and winks. "I have a bag for you in my office if you ever forget anything," he says. "Tell Mrs. Harada. You can come in and get what you need any time."

I never speak to Mrs. Harada unless I have to, and this message doesn't count as having to. I will try to remember everything I need for school forever after.

The Forest House

CHAPTER SEVEN

PAKALOLO HUNTERS

Reading by lamplight at the Forest House

Age: 6, Haena, Kauai, 1971

We inherit a big German shepherd mix from some Taylor Campers who are moving back to the Mainland. The dog is named Awa, which you say as Ava because it's a Hawaiian word. I'm so happy. I've wanted a dog forever. Awa's so tall that his back comes up to the bottom of my ribs. He is gentle with us but barks fierce to other people who approach our house.

Pop has heard lots of stories of people at Taylor Camp getting hassled and beaten up, so at night Awa is tied up outside to keep an eye on things.

Evenings are very mellow, and mellow is how my parents like it. Pop likes to sit on the porch, smoking his hash pipe and watching the stars come out. Mom cooks, and we eat our simple meal together inside because, once the sun goes behind the mountain, the mosquitoes are terrible even with those green curlicue mosquito punks lit by the door. I hate it when even one mosquito gets in, dive-bombing me in the dark with a high-pitched whine. I've learned to sleep under my quilt completely covered with only my nose sticking out for air.

After dinner, Mom or Pop read to us in their bed from a chapter book. Bon's a snuggler, tight against Mom or Pop's side, sucking her finger. I still suck my thumb, though now that I'm in first grade I only do it at home while listening to stories. I still rub a special bit of the silky-edged blanket I've had since I was a baby, though it's getting really worn-out.

After Bon falls asleep, Mom, Pop, and I read in the front room until bedtime. I have my own tall, molded glass lamp to use, but only under adult supervision because the lamps are so dangerous. I turn the flame up to just before black smoke starts to line the chimney to get the most light. The oil glows like hot honey in the bowl beneath the triangle of flame, and it smells good, too, like pine needles.

Pop is rereading his favorite, Euell Gibbons's *Handbook of a Beachcomber*, Mom is reading a book on macrobiotics, and I'm reading *Big Red, the Story of a Dog*, by Jim Kjelgaard. The author's name is something I puzzle over again and again, wondering about how to say it. I love the story because Big Red is smart and loyal, like Awa.

We're startled out of our reading spell by Awa's ferocious barking, but he's tied up over by the tree and can't reach the porch to protect us. Two young local guys, brown, lean, and angry, come up on the porch and pound on the screen doorframe like they haven't beaten anyone up in a while.

Mom sends me to our bedroom where Bon's already asleep. I get in bed with her on her mattress under my bed but watch and listen.

From my spot, I can see the men's blue-jeaned legs in the light from the lantern shining through the screen door.

They want my dad's *pakalolo.* I don't know why the grownups all love that stuff, though it does seem to mellow you out.

"We don't have any weed for sale," Pop says. He looms in the doorway. He's bigger than they are, and I hope that's enough. One thing I've already learned from all the stories around Camp: when locals are angry, there's never just one waiting to pound your ass.

"Fucking *haole,* we know you get one stash," one of them says. "And we're not buying. You give 'em to us."

Word about Taylor Camp's *pakalolo* growing, which is one of the ways they get money, has gotten out to the community. "Get lost," my dad says. "Go try the Camp."

They argue awhile through the screen door, and finally the guys swear and stumble their way off the porch, heading up the long trail back to the road. Pop turns and picks up the club he keeps behind the door—a guava branch as thick as a man's wrist.

Pop looks like a Viking with the club in his hand, his green eyes fierce in the lamplight, bigger and meaner than those mokes. "Lock the door and keep the girls in the back room. I'm going to make sure they don't come back," he says to Mom. He steps out into the dark.

Mom hurries over to "lock" the door—a simple hook and eye latch on a screen door that couldn't really stop anyone. Outside, Pop lets Awa, who's been barking the whole time, off the tie-out rope.

Awa streaks up the trail after the men, a ghost-hound nightmare disappearing into the looming black jungle. We can hear snarling and barking as he chases the men up the trail. Pop follows at a run, his flashlight bouncing, and is soon swallowed by the dark. Bonny whimpers in her sleep, and I snuggle close to her and pull the blanket up over our heads.

After a long time, Pop and Awa return. He says the young men ran back to a car parked up on the road and joined three other men who'd broken into and vandalized our van. Awa ran them off, scaring them into driving away. Pop was just backup for our dog.

"The Camp's getting to have a bad reputation in the community."

Pop is sweaty and amped up, mad about the van's broken windows. "If we didn't have Awa, they could have beaten us up and stolen our *pakalolo*."

He and Mom discuss what's happening between the locals, who hate the influx of hippies into the community, and the hippies who just want to be left alone to enjoy the paradise that is Kauai. It's not a good mix—in fact, very little mixing actually goes on. We all stay separate in our own places on the island.

"From now on, we lay low. No hanging out where the locals go," he says. I thought we were already doing that. "We'll just keep such a low profile they'll forget we're here. That's what Henry says we should do."

I always try to lay low at school, too, but it's lonely and there aren't many places to hide. They spot me because of my red hair, and in class I can't help raising my hand if I know the answer, in spite of kids hissing, "No ack, *haole* girl" from behind me.

"No ack" means *don't stand out*. Don't get above yourself. "The nail that sticks up gets pounded down," says Mrs. Harada.

I try not to '*ack*,' but I love learning stuff and knowing the answers.

Not seen and not heard does seem to be the way to go, but those guys came all the way out to our hideout way in the jungle! Pop says he wishes he never sold his shotgun, and he worries about having his camera stolen. He still takes pictures, but no longer tries to sell them. It's crushed something in him to give that up, but everyone's afraid to publish any photos of Kauai. People might find out what a paradise it is here, and the locals don't want that.

I'm not sure why everybody keeps saying this is paradise. I still like Oahu better.

CHAPTER EIGHT

JUNGLE CHRISTMAS

Forest House reading with Mom, me, Bonny, and Awa

Age: 7, Haena, Kauai, 1972

Christmas approaches, and we decorate the classroom with cut out snowmen and Santas made of construction paper with cotton balls glued on. We're learning the *Twelve Days of Christmas*, memorizing the traditional song. I've never seen a partridge, or a pear tree, or a turtledove, or a French hen, or a lord a-leaping, but I like to imagine what they might be.

Even Minka and I like the *"Hawaiian Style" Twelve Days of Christmas* better, and Mrs. Harada accompanies us singing both songs on her ukulele as we practice for our Christmas program. I'm learning to speak pidgin like the locals, and this song is fun because we aren't usually allowed to speak pidgin in class.

Numbah Twelve day of Christmas, my tutu give to me

Twelve television, eleven missionary, ten can of beer, nine pound of poi, eight ukulele, seven shrimp a-swimmin', six hula lesson, five steenkin' peeg, foah flowah lei, t'ree dried squid, two coconut, An' one mynah bird in one papaya tree!*

And then, really huge packages arrive at the post office from Gigi and Grandpa Jim just in time for Christmas. The boxes are so big they have to be kept outside on the porch. I can hardly stand it; I'm so excited to see what's inside them.

We decorate our house by covering the little Norfolk pine Pop dug up and put in a pot with strings of popcorn, but the ants are so bad we have to take the popcorn down. So, we make strings of Job's tears and *hale koa* seeds instead. The *hale koa* seeds grow in flat brown pods on scrubby, tough little trees along the roadside, and we just pull over to pick the pods.

A fiber on the side of the pod, like the zipper on a sleeping bag, pulls down to open the pod and reveal, inside, a neat row of shiny brown kernels the size and shape of sunflower seeds. On our way back from our town runs we stop and pick the purplish-gray, finger-tip-sized Job's tears from where they grow among the sharp-edged clumps of bright green grass, usually beside one of the irrigation ditches used to water the sugar cane fields which cover most of Kauai.

We sit in the lamplight in the evenings and punch through the *hale koa* seeds' tough shells with a needle. I like the way three brown *koa* seeds look with one silvery Job's tear, and make that my pattern as Mom, Bonny, and I each work on a different strand.

Another day we make decorations to hang on the tree from an idea Mom has—a *puka* shell with flat toothpicks coming out like rays, and another *puka* shell glued on top of the toothpicks to make a star.

I get frustrated with making the stars. The glue is too runny, and the toothpicks fall out before they can set, making me grumpy and ready to throw things.

"Slow down. Be patient. Do one side, balance the toothpicks, and when the glue has set a bit, put the other *puka* shell on." Mom leans in to show me, and I inhale her smell: sweet darkness of hash, her favorite thing to smoke, coconut oil, and sweat. Her smell is a beloved tender nose-prickling that always makes me want to press in close. Pop smells different: heavier, darker, and always the tang of the ocean.

Bonny, age three, has a sweet milky smell even though she doesn't nurse anymore. She makes her own ornaments by filling one side of a clam with glue and dropping little shells in. Her way looks easier, and I decide to make a Baby Jesus with a clam shell, a variation on what she's doing.

Mom spends hours walking the beach and picking up shells while I'm at school and Bonny's at Mommy School, a babysitting co-op she set up with some other moms at Taylor Camp. This means there are a lot of shells to choose from in the cookie tray where Mom has rinsed them and left them out in the sun a few days to make sure all the hermit crabs and algae have died.

I find a pale, freckled clam shell and make the Baby Jesus out of the round, blank "door" of a turban shell and a black-spotted cone for his body "wrapped in swaddling clothes." Baby Jesus comes out so great that I decide to make the whole Jesus family. Mother Mary is a cone shell balanced on "feet" of a broken fragment of cowrie, her head a nice round pink *puka* shell with a veil of another carefully selected cone shell fragment, this one so worn by surf and sea it's a gentle violet. Papa Joseph is much the same construction but with brighter colors.

"Toby, these are wonderful. You're making a crèche set!" Mom always calls it a crèche set instead of a Nativity because she went to school in Switzerland. My grandpa, Dr. Garth Murphy, was a famous marine biologist and the world expert on sardines for a long time, so Mom grew up on Oahu where he worked for the University of Hawaii. My grandparents knew the rich and famous scientist Linus Pauling and his family as friends, and when she was fourteen, Mom went and lived with the Pauling family in Switzerland and was their au pair. That's why she crosses her sevens with a little line, too.

Mom and Pop call themselves "spiritual," not religious. They believe Jesus was a great teacher, along with Buddha and Yogananda, a guru from India whose teachings they like. We also don't do Santa in our family. "Begin with a lie and then add commercialism" is Pop's opinion on Santa. I am careful not to tell any other kids he's fake, though. Other kids get to believe in him if their families want.

Pop's learning guitar, plunking on his chords in the background next to his own glass lamp. The quiet concentration of the shell project and the sound of his music fill me with happiness, swelling inside me until my skin is tight, a balloon blown up just right.

Even though there's no Santa, Mom and Pop like the stocking idea, and when Christmas comes at last, we hang the fabric stockings Mom sewed at the Rocky Point house from nails on the wall. Bon's and mine are both a bright, crazy Hawaiian print with little bells sewn around the top. The bells are already beginning to rust from the damp of the jungle. On Christmas morning, the stockings contain most of our presents, bulgy with treats like carob balls and licorice candy sticks from Ambrose's, a box of maple sugar leaves, a store-bought orange so bright it hurts—all the way from Florida. A glorious pen and watercolor set are wedged in with a new flashlight in mine.

I chew my fingernails, waiting to open those big boxes on the porch as we go through a strict present-opening process with agonizing slowness: each person opens a gift by age, and no matter how small, we all witness and exclaim before we can go on to another one.

Finally, Bonny and I can open the gifts outside from Gigi and Grandpa Jim. Pop uses his Swiss Army knife to slit the wrapping and reveal the box inside of the one with my name on it. I clasp my hands and hop up and down with excitement. "It's from Sears!"

When Pop strips the box away, a hot pink bike is revealed. A woven plastic basket with pink plastic flowers attaches to handlebars decorated with glittery plastic streamers, and a swooping, glitter-embedded rubber banana seat invites me to hop on.

"I love it!" I shriek, loudly, and glance over at Pop. His face tells me it's okay to be loud because it's Christmas, and he is already cutting into the second box to reveal a smaller bike in an aqua color with training wheels, for Bonny. We both hold hands and hop up and down, yelling with happiness. I don't know how to ride a two-wheeler, but I can hardly wait to try.

Mom's mouth is pinched, and her eyes are sad as she picks up the flower-decorated front basket of my bike. She usually doesn't like the presents Gigi sends us, so I feel bad that I like them so much.

"Lots of plastic," she murmurs. She doesn't like plastic, never has. Says it rapes the earth.

I don't understand what that means.

What I know about plastic is that it doesn't rust when everything else metal rusts in the jungle, and it doesn't swell and get squeaky and split like wood things do here. Black mold can grow on plastic, though, and I know that mold will grow on my plastic flowers unless the bike is covered up—but the flowers will last. They will probably last longer than the rest of the bike.

Mom's sadness is oozing out today, and I hug her, and whisper in her ear. "My pen set is the best present of all. Thank you."

She's begun to be sad a lot lately, and sometimes hours go by where she stares at the tops of the trees and doesn't say anything. I want to cheer her up, so I give her a kiss. I really do like the pen set;

it's only a little bit of a lie. She puts her arms around me and squeezes me hard.

Pop mutters over the little bags of screws and the tiny-printed assembly instructions, but it's only an hour or so later that I've got that hot pink bike positioned at the top of the sloping, boulder-strewn, bush-choked path as it leads past the house and toward the beach.

Mom and Bonny stand behind us, and Bonny can already sit up straight on her bike with the training wheels, though it's a little big for her. My bike actually had some too, but I wouldn't let Pop put them on—I'm ready to roll, the faster the better. Pop holds me upright with the little handle on the back of the banana seat as I get on and put my feet on the pedals.

"I'll hold you up and run alongside," he says. I wonder how he can with all the bushes beside the rocky trail, but I don't care. My heart is pounding and I'm itching to *GO*.

"Push me," I command. He does.

I wobble and weave down the trail, picking up speed with Pop running behind. Mom and Bonny yell encouragement. It's like I'm flying, and it's amazing!

Suddenly I realize I'm going really fast and have no idea how to slow down.

Pop trips over some vegetation and lets go. I'm roaring down the slanting, bumpy dirt path, trying to dodge the rocks and shrieking with delighted terror. I'm heading into the stand of Java plum trees at the end of our clearing when I lose balance and crash into a lantana bush.

I'm winded and scratched as I try to crawl out of the prickly bush. My bike lies in the path, tires spinning, already getting smeared with red Kauai dirt. Pop runs over and picks me up to see if I'm okay. My knees have hit something and are scraped, lantana thorns tangle my hair, but I'm panting with excitement. "Let's do it again!"

And so, we do. Again and again, until I'm careening down that forest trail all the way to the ocean and making the Taylor Camp kids jealous.

"Barbie doll," one of the hippie moms calls me, but I don't care because I know everyone's just jealous of my beautiful hot pink bike. I teach Minka to ride my bike too, and we take turns crashing into trees and rocks.

It's a very good Christmas.

CHAPTER NINE

DON'T GO WITH STRANGERS

In the van, still sucking my thumb

Age: 7, Tunnels Beach, Kauai, 1972

Mom discovered at the meeting with Mr. Beck to give him my extra clothing and discuss "how I'm adjusting" that I only legally have to be in school three days a week.

So that's all the days I go because I hate the hassling and the bus ride so much. "You're smart, Toby. If you stay home, you'll have to make up for those two days a week on your own," Mom says.

"No problem," I tell her. I can already read books in the sixth-grade reading section easily, and while I don't like math as much, I have no problem keeping up with the boring worksheets Miss Harada gives us.

One non-school day, we drive into town while Pop's at work and do our usual: go to Ambrose's health food store, Big Save for kerosene for the lamps, and then stop by Kapa`a Library for books.

On the way back to the Forest House, Bonny's fussy and tired so Mom pulls up at Tunnels Beach. It's still our favorite beach, great for fishing, surfing when the waves are good, and finding *puka* shells.

Mom and Bon take a nap on the bed in the van while I put on the bottoms of my swimsuit, pick up my red scoop net, and go out to the reef where I once caught an octopus.

The wind's beginning to settle in late afternoon, and the tide is fairly low with hardly any surf—good conditions for reef picking. "Surfers and fishermen study the ocean like Mainland people study the weather on land," Pop says.

The great golden length of beach is empty; the towering peak of Makana Mountain that the tourists call Bali Hai looks near enough to touch. The sea outside the skirt of reef is aqua and Prussian blue, two of my favorite watercolor hues. I like matching the fancy color names on tubes of paint, to the shades of real things I see.

I hunt over the reef with my net, walking light on the balls of my feet, careful of tube worms. On the reef and while fishing, I can be quiet and move slow, which is hard for me other times. I keep my shadow behind me and my eyes scanning for movement.

I spot something—that surge and pump in the water that means an octopus is hiding in this hole. I circle around, my heart speeding up as I try to get a look at it under a big rock in the middle of a tide pool. The rock's big, the tide pool's deep. I'm going to have to climb in and grab for it blind—only I can tell by the surge that this octopus's at least as big as the other one. Now that I know about the snapping bill in the middle, I don't want to just grab and hope for the best like last time.

I glance up, scan around, and spot a local boy walking on the beach carrying a fishing pole. His stringer of fish, surf trunks, and tabis tell me he knows fishing and the reef. I trot to the sand, practically hopping with excitement, waving my net to get his attention. "Hey! I found a *tako* under that rock over there. Can you help me get it?"

He's brown and tall as he looks down at me, his dark eyes a secret glitter under a mass of thick black hair sorting itself into curls and hanks. His lean body isn't fully grown yet; he's still a teenager but looks capable. "Show me, *haole* girl."

I lead the way to the big rock and he squats and investigates. "Yeah. One big *tako*. We need my spear. I live right across the street; let's go get it."

"Okay." I follow him back to the beach. I'm curious to see his house—I know a few of the kids that live up there from the bus, but not to speak to since they usually call me *haole crap* or *fucking haole* or, on a good day, *dirty hippie.* I don't remember ever seeing this boy, though. He's too old for our school. He called me *haole*, but not in a bad way. Just like describing something, and I'm fine with that. I am a *haole*, after all.

I glance over at the van, which is a long way off. It's too far to run to tell Mom where I'm going. We'll be back before she ever needs to know I went anywhere.

We walk up the beach into young ironwood trees. Ipomoea vines, with their purple morning glory flowers, trip me, and the boy takes my hand and helps me up, the fishing pole in his other hand. "Just a little further."

He's being so nice, even holding my hand. I probably go to school with his little brothers and sisters who hate me. He leads me to where a path heads into the vacant lot separating the beach from the road. The houses are just on the other side of the road, in clusters and clumps like hens with chicks, several of them as small as our Forest House. They're separated by grass, and parked boats, and lots of pickup trucks.

"I want to show you something." The boy tugs me off the path into the ironwoods.

A prickle of alarm—his hand has gone clammy, and I smell something sharp coming from his skin. I try to get my hand away, but he doesn't let go. He pulls me forward and stops at an open spot surrounded by ironwoods. "I want to show you something," he says again.

"What?" Curious. I've always been too curious.

"Kneel."

"No. I don't want to."

He pushes me on the top of the head, forcing me down, and I kneel.

I'm really worried now, and glance around for help or how to get away, but I can't see anything or anybody but the green of the ironwood saplings and the strange glitter of the boy's eyes as he opens his surf trunks. "Have you seen one of these?"

"Yeah. All the time." His root is a slightly different color than Pop's or the other men at Taylor Camp, but it's nothing unusual.

He frowns. He doesn't like what I said. Does he think he's showing me something special? His eyes are hard and shiny as kukui nuts on one of those tourist leis. "Have you seen it do this?"

I look. His root is getting bigger and bigger as I stare at it, and my eyes widen. "No."

"Kiss it." His voice is gravelly. He grabs a handful of my hair and pulls me closer.

His hand in my hair hurts, and I don't like the smell of him. "No, I don't want to."

"Kiss it, or I'll get my spear and come after you—and your family. While you're sleeping, fucking *haole* crap."

He hates me. I hear it in his voice, and now I'm really scared. I look up and his eyes are squinty and mean.

I kiss his root. It smells funny, but it's not too gross.

But that's not enough.

He makes me put it in my mouth and tells me if I bite him he'll hit me. His hands are twisted up in my hair to control me. I keep my eyes closed, shutting out the way things look. Trying to shut out the strange musky smell and the sounds too, trying to shut out how I feel, how what's in my mouth is choking me. But I can't shut out thoughts of him hurting us, and he's holding my hair too tight, and I can't breathe. I start to cry, snorting and snuffling with his root in my mouth, because I'm scared of him spearing us at night, in our beds.

I choke and spit when he's done with whatever he's doing.

His root is gone. He pets my head and seems to feel bad. "I'm sorry," he says. "I'm sorry. Stop crying."

I'm still kneeling, and I finally open my eyes. Everything is fuzzy from crying. He squats down so that he's close to my face, and he kisses me, which seems really strange since he hates me so much. He pets my hair some more, like I'm a cat, smoothing it down my bare back.

"It's okay. It's okay, I'm sorry," he says. *It's not okay.* But I can tell he's trying to make me feel better somehow, and I let him hold me close.

This whole thing is weird, and kind of gross, but nothing too scary. Not like the terrible thing he said about spearing us, or when those guys came to our house looking for *pakalolo.* I start to cry again, remembering that, but make myself stop so I don't make him mad.

The boy straightens up and fastens his trunks. His voice comes out hard again. "If you tell anybody that we did this, I'll spear you and your *haole* crap family."

I bite my lips to keep from sobbing out loud. Tears run down my face as I imagine the spear stabbing my parents and Bonny.

He holds his hand out to me. "Let's go catch that octopus now."

"I don't want to." My voice comes out all shaky. "I don't want you to spear us."

"I won't. As long as you don't tell." I wonder what I'm not

supposed to tell—what he did with his root? I'm not scared of that, I'm scared of his threats, of how mean I can see he really is.

"Come on, let's go get the spear. Only for the *tako*, I promise." His voice is soft, and he reaches to take my hand. I almost let him because he's being nice again, and I want him to be nice.

But what if he takes me to his house and spears me there? What if he lets his brothers and sisters beat me up? I've seen his eyes, and I know he hates me.

I jump to my feet and do what I should have done when he first started leading me into the trees—I run, straight into the thick iron-woods toward the ocean.

I burst out of the trees, scratched and burning from the branches, and run straight to the van. My face feels numb and hot at the same time. My diaphragm spasms because it feels like I can't get enough air. I pull open the van's door and jump in, and scramble around locking all the doors and rolling up the windows.

"What are you doing?" Mom wakes up on the back bed, her hair fuzzy and face crumpled. Bonny's still asleep, a soft blonde mound.

"He's going to come spear us." I crawl into the back and cling to her, tight as a baby monkey. "He's going to spear us." I burrow my wet, hot face into her boobs.

"What?" Mom goes rigid, her arms tight around me, her voice getting loud. "Who said this to you?"

I tell her a local boy made me do weird things with his root in the bushes and he threatened us with his spear.

She gets really quiet and rubs my back until the sobbing and hiccupping finally stop. And then she tells me not to go anywhere alone with strangers.

Not go with strangers? I don't remember ever hearing that before. Until today, the world, other than school, has been full of interesting and kind people, adults especially. She checks me over for any marks. There are none. "You're going to be okay," she says, soft but fierce. "We have to talk to Pop and decide what to do."

We drive the van to pick Pop up from work, and I eye the clustered houses across the street as we drive past them, wondering which one the boy lives in, wondering what his name is, wondering if he went back for his spear and got the *tako* on the reef by himself. He probably did.

I'm sad that we didn't just catch it together. I wish so hard that we had just caught it together. It could have happened that way.

Mom tells Pop when she picks him up that a local boy made me do weird things. They make me tell the story again. I'm so worried that he'll spear us in our beds at night that I cry again. Pop says no, that won't happen. We have Awa, and Pop will protect us with his club.

They discuss what to do, but since I don't know what house the boy lives in or what his name is, they decide they can't do anything since the boy is a local. We can't draw attention to ourselves with the locals, and the police are "all cousins, in each other's pockets."

"If it was one of the Taylor Camp kids it would be different," Pop tells Mom in the front seat as we drive back to the Forest House. "We'd be able to do something."

I'm disappointed.

I thought Pop and I would take Awa and Pop's big guava branch, and Pop would go to each house in that cluster where the boy said he lived, and he'd demand to see the boy who'd threatened his family with a spear—and the boy would come out and I'd point to him and say, "That guy! He threatened us!" And his parents would give him lickens, and he would know he couldn't hurt people and get away with it—even if we're *haoles*.

CHAPTER TEN

THE TREES ARE TALKING

Me, Minka, and Awa's puppies

Age: 7, Forest House, Kauai, 1972

Our stuff from Oahu was eventually brought down to the Forest House in a series of trips from Lihue with the van—but the house is so small that Mom gives a lot of it away to the Taylor Campers, or by leaving it on the steps of the Hanalei Trader, a store where an informal "free store" has begun on the porch.

Mom even gives away their silver wedding candlesticks, her jewelry box, and the string of pearls from her high school graduation. "Stuff just weighs you down. Practicing detachment," she says with that far-off stare she gets, like she's not really there. That's been happening more and more, and it worries me.

My toys, so beloved and missed at first, seem babyish now. I give most of them away after Bonny picks what she wants. My favorite things are my art materials and books, though I read so fast we are always having to get new ones from the library. I don't keep any of my own books—they mold too quickly in the jungle.

We've been at the Forest House about a year, and I've found a way to deal with school—besides only going three days a week, I hide in the classroom with a book during recess. At lunch, I sit with Minka and give away the good parts of my lunch whenever other kids ask for them. I'm good at hopscotch, though, and if Minka and I get to the squares first, sometimes we can play a game with a bit of broken chain to mark our spots until the local girls spot us and chase us off.

I play with Minka at home, but her reputation is even worse than mine. When we're together we get called "fucking *haole* bitches" and "dirty, stinky hippies," but when I'm alone it's just "*haole* crap," which is slightly better. Eventually, I'm tired of hiding with my books, and I like playing hopscotch and four square, so I begin to try to join games. Sometimes I get to play with the kids that aren't popular; a chubby Filipino girl named Glenda even lets me sit with her at lunch when I give her my desserts.

I can run fast during PE and some of the boys like me, like Samson Chandler who's Hawaiian and lives in Wainiha and rides my bus. He sticks up for me and tells his friends I can play, and because he says to let me, I get to play four square with them because I'm fast and play hard. I feel bad about leaving Minka behind, but if I don't, I'll never make any other friends.

Now that I'm in second grade I have Miss Kinch. She's a little nicer than Mrs. Harada. She even calls on me when I have my hand up because I usually know the answer and do my homework, especially anything to do with reading. I've been tested and I'm average at math, but I can read at a high school level. Things are getting a little better until Kira Yoshimura, the prettiest girl in my class, decides she really hates me.

Kira is usually Miss Kinch's pet (Miss Harada's too) but, for some reason, one day Miss Kinch calls me up to the board to write the spelling words for everyone to study. Kira usually does it, and when I turn around from doing my best handwriting on the chalkboard with the spelling words, her narrow, hate-filled eyes give me a shiver.

She's tiny and cute, like the Japanese kokeshi doll Mom got me at a garage sale, with shiny perfect hair and clothes, but she's mean as a centipede and just as sneaky. The small, pretty blue centipedes are the most venomous, and that's what Kira's like.

"No *ack*," Kira hisses. She sits behind me and pulls my hair or pinches the back of my arm whenever I raise my hand. "Go back to the Mainland, *haole* crap," she whispers whenever I have to pass her.

I think about telling on her as I sit down at my battered desk to rearrange my colored pencils. Rearranging my colored pencils always makes me feel better. I put them in rainbow order and sharpen each one carefully with my little plastic sharpener, and then I slide them back into their cardboard box just so. Folding the lid of the box shut and tucking it in my desk, I decide not to tell. Telling on the kids who hassle me only makes it worse. Later, they add "snitch," "tattle-tale," and "liar" to the list of things they call me, and Kira's someone everyone listens to. Even the adults.

Haole Crap, Kira's nickname for me, catches on and sticks. I try to stay out of her way, but she hunts me down at recess with her posse of girls, and wherever I've found to hide, they torment me with pinching and name-calling.

A black female Shepherd named BlackCoat appears at our house from Taylor Camp one day and joins Awa in doggy marriage. They have puppies, and I get to have a puppy for my very own, which makes me even happier than my bike. I name him Argos after Ulysses's faithful dog.

As soon as Argos is weaned, I begin to spend more and more

time away from the house, playing with him out in the forest because things are getting weird at home. Pop is gone a lot working or surfing, and Mom is sad and spaced-out, usually napping while Bonny is at Mommy School with the other Taylor Camp kids being babysat.

At last Hanalei School is out for the summer, and Argos and I build a fort halfway between our house and Taylor Camp for Minka and me to play in. I build the fort up against a Java plum tree with sticks tied together and cover it with big, fan-shaped palm leaves to keep the rain off. I use a nice little rock inside for a table. I like to draw out there or play Barbies when Minka joins me. I bring my drawing stuff back and forth each time because it rains almost every day, and my fort isn't waterproof.

The drawing paper is expensive, good-quality art paper on a big spiral pad that my fairy godmother Catherine Elber sent in the mail. She's a friend of Mom and Pop's that met me when I was a baby in California. Ever since, she's called herself our fairy godmother because she loves fairies and Bonny and me. I'm always drawing or illustrating a story, using colored pencils or pens, and my nice Grumbacher watercolor paints from Aunty Jan.

Eventually the other puppies are given away, and only Awa, BlackCoat, and Argos remain. The fleas are terrible and bother us more than the mosquitoes, but Mom doesn't believe in using a bunch of chemicals to get rid of them.

One day, coming back from Hanalei, we spot two women hitchhiking on the road. They're carrying a surfboard and a surf mat, which is what Mom uses for surfing, so Pop pulls over to give them a ride. They climb in the van, telling us they hear there's good surf near Taylor Camp, and they plan to stay at the Camp for a month.

The surfing sisters from California are named Patty and Debbie, and they have huge smiles, big laughs, and waist-length, ripply blonde hair. Mom and Pop like them and offer to let them stay with us instead, in the shack where my dad shapes his surfboards. They are delighted to accept, even though the shack is just a flimsy hut made of bamboo and plastic.

Patty is a great artist, and Bonny and I spend happy hours with her drawing together. Her art is fun pen-and-ink, and I learn a lot from her. Every day the girls go surfing at nearby breaks with Mom and Pop. Because they are barely in their twenties, they still like to play games, so Bonny and I play board games and Red Light Green Light and Simon Says with them. They come into the house and join us for evening reading time since they don't have a lamp at their shack. With Patty and Debbie there, it's like having two fun big sisters for a whole month.

But after they leave, Mom begins to act strange and sad again. Sometimes she does more than meditate, which she's always done— now she just sits and stares into space. She plays with us less, and when she does, it's like she's not really there. She doesn't keep the house clean like before. Sometimes she wanders around the clearing, crying and talking to herself. She gets mad a lot, screaming when Bon and I bicker or forget something.

I always check her pupils when I get home, which I've been doing since the Oahu house to keep on top of things. Lately her pupils are always big, which means she's been smoking *pakalolo* or eating mushrooms.

"I can hear the trees talking," she says one day. "Can't you hear them talking?"

I listen hard, and don't want to disappoint her, so I say, "I think so." But all I hear is the wind in the leaves, and the creak of branches, and the loud chirps of the cardinals who come to eat the papaya seeds on the compost pile.

One morning I go down by the stream and Mom's there, naked, her long hair hanging around her in silky brown ribbons. She's digging a spoonful of bright red dirt out of the riverbank with a spoon. "I have an iron deficiency." She eats the dirt, scooping up water to wash it down. After she swallows it she says, "There's a lot of iron in this soil. It's *goodforyou*. Want some?"

"No thanks." I don't want her to make me eat the dirt, so I tug on the rope I have around Argos's neck, hurrying into the jungle. I think guiltily of the junk food school lunches I love and how upset

83

she'd be if she realized how *badforyou* they are. The lunches are the only thing I miss about school during the summer.

Argos happily follows wherever I want to go, clambering over the rocks behind me. He's going to be a big dog because his paws are big, but his body is still roly-poly and fuzzy. He's golden tan with black markings on his face, back and tail, like his father, Awa. He is the perfect best friend, even sleeping in my bed with me.

I'm reading the Pippi Longstocking series now. Pippi makes me feel better about my red hair. I wish I could live in my own house with all my pets like she does. I also love the Anne of Green Gables stories because Anne has red hair and is a reader, too.

During our evening reading time, Mom's doing worksheets in a big blue binder. "You're doing school too?" I ask, pointing to the literature she's reading.

"It's spiritual stuff. I'm learning ancient wisdom and things like telepathy," she says. I read the title. OCCULT AND ALTERNATIVE STUDIES it says. "Telepathy's like ESP."

"I can't do ESP. I tried." I still like the idea of ESP.

"Well, sometimes I can hear thoughts, the thoughts of the spirits of those who were here before us."

I don't know what to say. Mom worries me, so I open my book, so I can disappear into the story.

Pop pretends not to hear this discussion. He's repairing a tear in his throw net, using a bamboo shuttle and a roll of fishing line. He shakes his head and walks away from her when she says weird stuff, but they don't fight. They like things quiet and peaceful.

But Pop's gone during the day at his job, so he doesn't know how Mom gets lately, and I'm afraid he'll get mad if I try to explain how weird she's acting. I'm worried and try to cheer her up and distract her out of her moods, but she either ignores me or yells. "Can't you entertain yourself for even a minute, for God's sake?"

That's not fair. I'm super good at entertaining myself. Janet used to say I could have fun in a paper bag, and it's true. I'm good at making things and inventing stories, and I'm never bored—but I miss the Mom who laughed and hugged and read to us a lot. This withdrawn, sad Mom with her faraway stare, who mutters and wanders and eats dirt, makes me feel lonely and scared.

Bonny's always easygoing, and she entertains herself or we play together when I'm at the cottage. She's still too little to go with Argos and me into the jungle though, because she can't climb around like I can, and she gets really puffy and itchy from mosquito bites, which don't even make a bump on me anymore.

Mom acting strange makes me go to Taylor Camp more to hang out with Minka. We make tree houses for our Barbies at her place, constructed out of cardboard boxes that food from the co-op came in. I like it at her house, with its smells of *pakalolo*, cooked food, and incense. Minka tells me to watch out for a certain guy.

"He might try to get you to come with him somewhere." Minka's eyes are light blue, like a really sunny day when you can't see into the sky. "He likes to touch you and make you touch him back. It's gross."

I'm always watching for men with that glitter in their eyes. "Don't go with strangers," I say. "Run like hell."

"Even if they're not a stranger, run like hell," Minka says, and we laugh.

One day when I go over, Hawk, Minka's father says he needs us to help him. I've never been to the big room roofed in clear fiberglass where they dry the *pakalolo* the Camp grows. There's a picnic table in the middle, and clusters and clumps of the *pakalolo* hang upside down from rafters above it. The smell inside is thick, sweet, earthy.

Hawk sits me down next to Minka and shows me how to properly roll a joint.

I smooth out a thin, delicate Zig-Zag paper, and lay a row of bud, which is fuzzy seeds mixed with a little leaf, at one end of the paper. He shows me how to pack it tight by pressing down with my fingertips, and roll the joint carefully, keeping it from getting lumpy or loose, pressing it as I go.

"Just like rolling up a sleeping bag," Hawk says. "Real tight and cozy." He winks. He has Minka's light blue eyes and a little scraggly beard like lichen. He's nice and laughs a lot.

There's an odd taste as I lick the edge of the crinkly paper to seal it and twist the ends. Now I know how to make joints as well as pack a bowl, which Pop taught me, so I could fix his for him in the evenings.

School starts again, the usual torture, and one day I come hurrying down the long path afterward, eager to see Argos and go to my fort to recover.

Usually Awa, BlackCoat, and Argos bark to say hi when I come home, running out from under the house in a whole family. But today when I get to the house, there's no Argos with his whipping tail and licking, no happy greeting barks from BlackCoat. Only Awa comes out from under the house, silent and alone. His head and tail are down, and his eyes are sad. I pet him to cheer him up.

Mom's sitting on the steps of the front porch. Bonny's in her lap, sucking her finger and playing with Mom's hair, her head against Mom's chest. Mom's staring into space, but her face is pale with red blotches that I can see even with her tan.

"Where's BlackCoat and Argos?" I ask, a bad feeling starting in my chest. It shortens my breath into little pants of terror. *Something has happened.*

"Argos has another home," she says. "We gave him away."

"What?" My voice rises into hysteria. "BlackCoat too?"

I can see why we got rid of the other puppies. I know it was a lot of dogs to feed and a ton of poop to clean up. Fleas hop onto my legs and bite me even now.

"BlackCoat went back to the Camp," Mom says. She's smoking a joint, the hand not holding Bonny lifting it to her mouth.

I run to where the dogs sleep in a family under the house and dive into the smelly dirt to look for my puppy. There's nothing there but an empty handful of silence when once it was full of beloved dogs.

I scream and scream as I come out. I hit the side of the house and grab the dogs' water bowl and throw it. I yell all the bad words I've learned at school. "Stupid crazy bitch cunt whore dirty hippie!" I scream. "Argos was my puppy! MINE! Not yours to give away!"

Bonny puts her fingers in her ears and plasters herself against Mom. I know she's afraid of me, and I wish Mom were too. I stand right in front of Mom, screaming in her face. I want it to be so loud she has to listen, but she looks through me and beyond me at something I can't see.

"Don't talk to me like that," she says, and takes another drag on the joint. "Too many dogs."

I'm sick with grief and want to throw up.

My parents can just get rid of anything: a pearl necklace, a beloved puppy. They don't care about me. They don't care what I need. What hurts me, haunts me, scares me, tortures me.

"I hate you! I hate you!" I scream and run out into the forest.

I'm crying, and it's not nice little girl crying. Powerful, terrible feelings take me over and explode out of my body, feelings I've always been scared to let out because they're so strong. The crying is huge and snotty and loud. I hit everything around me, grabbing a tree and banging my head on it, kicking bushes that lash back at me. The pain feels good, soothing the bone-deep grief and fiery burning rage as all the things that are wrong with my world erupt all at once.

I'll live alone out here, build another fort farther away from the house—a bigger one, where I never have to see Mom and Pop again.

Blinded by tears, stumbling, I look for a spot, somewhere by the stream. But I can't imagine living out in the forest without the safety and comfort of our dogs.

Argos was my friend.

He loved me and made me feel safe and special no matter what, and he was *mine*. Mine! My beloved puppy, who cared about me just as much.

I scream over and over again until my voice is hoarse, banging my head on a kukui nut tree in a glade next to Limahuli Stream, and finally hug it tight, the harsh bark rough against my hot, bruised face.

Spangles of light surround me, as if the trees cry drops of sunlight with me, falling like gold coins over the bamboo grass. I slide down to rest, curled up in the roots.

Gradually, I feel the forest all around me absorbing my pain, soothing me.

There are tiny songs and sounds just out of range in the shushing of the wind in the leaves—Mom says she can hear the trees talking. Maybe the sounds are the *Menehune,* the Hawaiian little people, and fairies, imaginary companions from my books. They feel sad with me because they knew how much I loved my puppy, how happy I was playing out here with him, how his loyal love soothed all my hurts.

I get hungry and forage for stuff to eat: fern tips, guavas, Java plums, flyblown fallen mangoes. By nightfall my stomach is sour from too much fruit. The mosquitoes have sucked off about a pint of blood when I finally return to the house in the dark. Diarrhea cramps my stomach, and I cry some more in the outhouse because the dogs don't come out to walk with me back to the cottage. Only Awa's lying on the porch, his big square head resting on his paws. His expressive brown eyes, marked like eyeliner, are sorrowful.

He misses BlackCoat and Argos, too.

I go into the lamplit front room. Mom's in bed, Bonny's in bed, and Pop meets me. I know better than to call him bad names, and I'm all cried out and too sick to say anything. His face looks sad but scary and determined, too. He doesn't comment on my tear-streaked face or scratched, bruised body. He doesn't ask where I was—he knows, and he doesn't care. He knew I'd have to come back eventually.

"We're moving," he says. "This place isn't good for your mom."

CHAPTER ELEVEN

THE BEST FACILITY

Toby, Mom, and Bonny

Age: 8, La Jolla, California, 1973

My grandparents' Mediterranean style stucco house across from La Jolla Beach and Tennis Club in California is floored in marble and has white carpet and cream-colored furniture made out of steel tubing. We're staying in two guest rooms while Mom gets treatment for her "nervous breakdown" at a place my grandma Gigi calls The Best Facility.

Mom goes to therapy at The Best Facility hospital every day, takes her medicine, and sleeps the rest of the time, which was the agreement she made so that she didn't have to actually live there in the hospital. When I ask Mom about what she does at therapy, she says, "It's Freudian."

I have no idea what that is, but it sounds like Friesian, which is a really beautiful kind of black horse with long tasseled legs, one of my favorite breeds from *The Big Book of Horses*.

I like to imagine Mom goes into the big square building with its tiny windows and, once inside, walks into a stall to groom and then ride her own special Friesian stallion. But I'm pretty sure that's not what therapy is or Mom would look happier when she came home. Instead, Mom's eyes are glassy, and all her movements are slow, like she's stuck in a jar of honey.

No one tells me what's going on, so I sneak to listen in to Gigi and Grandpa Jim talking about the situation. If Mom doesn't take her medicine and go to therapy every day, they will "put her away." And I know that's not good. "Thank God we got them out of that nigger shack," she tells Grandpa Jim.

What's a nigger? It sounds bad. Maybe it's a bad word like haole crap. I've never heard that word before, and it makes me feel yucky that Gigi hates our beloved Forest House.

Maybe it's the fleas. They really were nasty, but I feel guilty even thinking that because I miss our dogs so much—Pop gave our hero Awa away to a farmer in Kilauea, and now it's like we were never there in that special place with the lokelani roses in the shadow of Makana Mountain.

Gigi made a big fuss at the state of me and my sister's hair and clothes when we first got off the plane from Kauai, not to mention Mom's toad-in-the-headlights stare. I wonder if Gigi knows that I ran around naked and bathed in a stream until recently. I don't tell her that because she'd get upset. She raises her voice and yells "Jim!"

for my Grandpa when she gets upset, and I'm a little scared of Grandpa. Everybody is.

Pop, who had to pack up all our stuff after asking his parents for help and pushing Mom and Bonny and me onto a plane, arrives a few weeks after us. He barely talks, and is gone all day supposedly looking for work, but when he returns in the evening his eyes are brighter, and he smells like booze. He tries to avoid Gigi and Grandpa but sometimes they catch him sneaking in.

Grandpa Jim's a big man who smells of lime aftershave and always wears clean chinos and soft golf sweaters with little animal logos stitched on the chest. He made millions by owning a factory that makes rubber road cones, and by being one of the first to have his products produced in Japan after World War II. Now, in 1973, he's doing great. Because he started his business during the Depression, a very bad time according to my grandparents, he can't understand why Pop is "still floundering" and hasn't "settled down" to a career.

"You need to get off your duff, son," he booms. "There's no free lunch. Get that hippie wife of yours cleaned up and get a real job."

I hide out with Bonny in our guest room with a book, listening in so I can be ready for whatever happens, and frowning because I'm confused. Actually, there *was* free lunch, and we qualified for it.

I don't understand how everything is fancy here, and obviously Pop's parents have money, but how poor we were back on Kauai. If I had a choice, I'd pick being rich and having a job over eating nothing but windfall mangoes and rice and beans when the food stamps run out at the end of the month.

Gigi has bright blue eyes and auburn hair teased up and sprayed into a helmet. She wears rows of pearls and fitted Lilly Pulitzer dresses. She smells like the big poufy powder puff she has on her "vanity," a little table with a marble top where she sits on a satin stool and does her makeup.

I come into her big bedroom and watch her with that curiosity that has already gotten me in trouble—but she likes me visiting. She pats me with the artificial-smelling pouf that I know Mom would hate and brushes my hair with a silver brush. She pets my hair, running its strands through her fingers.

"Like taffy," she says, her voice as affectionate as it ever gets. She's been saying this about my hair since I can remember. Maybe I'm not ugly after all, though I'm feeling pretty strange in the clothes she bought me—matching flowered tops with stretchy, scratchy polyester pants, and shoes.

Shoes. All the time, we have to wear shoes. Tennis shoes for tennis lessons, ballet shoes for ballet lessons, and saddle shoes and Mary Janes for school. I am immediately enrolled in all of the above since my grandmother is thrilled to take over my daily schedule.

My hair is neatly cut with a row of bangs in front and a ruler-straight line at my shoulder blades. I'm put in third grade now that I'm eight at La Jolla Elementary school, blocks away from the house. For the first time in my life, I look like all the other kids—but I'm not. I'm different, and I think they can smell the remnants of Dr. Bronner's and garlic oozing out of my pores.

Though I'm wearing clothes that help me blend, I walk to school, which no one does.

I sit cross-legged on my little plastic chair instead of with my legs down.

I take my shoes off at the doorway of the classroom like we did in Hawaii—wearing shoes inside is rude.

"Put your shoes back on, honey," my teacher says. "We wear shoes all day here." Her voice implies I'm from somewhere nasty. Yes, people wear their shoes all day here—ugly, pinchy ones worn with thin little socks with itchy lace on them.

No one is brown here.

Everyone remembers their underwear every day, as well as their shoes.

Jif peanut butter, clear purple jelly, and white bread are considered actual foods.

There are no plumerias, no rubber slippers, no pidgin English with its lilting singsong, no almond cookies, and the ocean is very cold. I don't hear "*haole* crap" anymore—but I don't feel welcome, either.

By the time I'm attending there, I've missed so much school that all I can do well is *read*. I struggle with math and every other subject, but I'm a fast learner, try hard, and I can read at college level, so I catch up quickly.

After my work is done in class, I draw on all my papers. Renderings of princesses, warriors, and horses decorate everything.

"So artistic!" my teacher says, with a tone that says artistic isn't actually good. "Why don't you put all your drawings in one place, on their own paper?" She draws sad faces on the worksheets I doodle on, but drawing makes me feel better.

When I'm drawing, I'm in a story—and it's always somewhere imaginary, glorious, interesting, with quests, dragons, horses, gold, and warrior princesses.

We aren't like other families. We weren't like the local families on Kauai, and we aren't like the families in La Jolla, California.

I'm trying to understand it, but I still don't.

One day my dad calls school and says that he's going to pick me up instead of me walking home as usual. I stand on the sidewalk, waiting with the other kids whose parents are right on time in their Mercedes and BMWs.

I'm wearing one of my homemade hippie sundresses with a halter top, in the middle of a California winter. I dressed myself in it that morning because I looked out the window and thought the sunshine just beginning to touch the trees meant it was warm, like sunshine in Hawaii—and my mom made this dress for me back when she cared. I made my own lunch and walked to school this morning, realizing I'd made a mistake in my outfit as soon as I reached the end of the driveway, but out of time to go change or grab a sweater.

And I've been shivering all day.

Pop pulls up in front of my well-dressed classmates in our old white van, which we shipped over since we're here longer than we thought we'd be. The van's battered and rusty now, and the bright curtains are faded and patched with mold.

Pop's grown a beard that encircles his head and shoulders like a golden throw rug, and he's wearing a flannel shirt, jeans, and Birkenstocks. The other parents with their shiny cars stare at us as he grabs me in a big, *pakalolo*-smelling funk of a hug with the jollity that weed and a six-pack bring out in him.

"Let's spring you from this joint," he says. "Go down to Windansea for a picnic."

I pull back, mortified, aware that my bare legs in their Mary Janes are adrift and visible. Other La Jolla dads didn't come rolling in reeking of pot, swinging their third-grade daughters up, exposing their panties, and driving off in rusty vans with a daisy whirligig on the front.

I slide down to the ground and peg him with the stare he calls Getting into His Head.

"Why don't you have a job? Why can't you be like the other dads and wear a suit? Why don't we have a regular car?" I look up into Pop's bearded face, my hands on my hips. I'm asking these questions because I really want to know, because Mom and Pop raised me to Question Authority. That used to be something they believed in.

But as Pop's face changes, going hard and red, I know I made another mistake. These aren't questions Pop wants to answer from Grandpa Jim, or from anybody—*least of all me*. His sassy, redheaded daughter who wasn't a boy and can't keep her mouth shut.

"Get in the van." Pop's green eyes go narrow. I should be scared of him. I really should. "Way in the back. I don't want to look at you."

If only this was one of the days we all walked as a family on the beach at La Jolla. Those are our happiest days since we moved here. We start at the Beach and Tennis Club, and we walk all the way to Scripps Pier. Mom and Pop buy a coffee at the stand there, and Bon and I get hot chocolate, and we walk all the way back.

I love that long silver beach with its squeaky sand, sparkling with mica. I do ballet, practicing the steps I'm learning at my lessons, by jetéing over mounds of washed-up kelp, keeping an eye out for sand dollars.

If the tide's low, I hunt over the cold, clear tide pools at the end of the beach, finding turban shells and hermit crabs and even an abalone one time. I like to feed bits of kelp to the anemones to watch them close up. I shouldn't have asked those questions.

I climb in the side door of the van, and slide it shut with a whoosh and a hard bang—it no longer closes easily. Crawling all the way back onto the bed, which smells musty and lonely, I lie down and look out the back window. I just said what I was wondering, which they used to tell me to do.

Pop drives to my grandparents' house, and instead of taking me to Windansea for a picnic, he stops the van in the turnaround in front of the house without speaking. After I get out with my little backpack, he drives away.

The double front doors unlock with a key that hides under a fake rock next to the bougainvillea hedge. I tiptoe inside the house where I can't get anything dirty and all the furniture's white, and the first thing I do is take off my shoes.

I peek into my parents' room. Mom is asleep with the bottle of her special medicine called Thorazine on the nightstand.

Mom's gotten thin. Her tan has gone yellow, and her hair is tangled on the pillow. Looking at her makes that familiar, uncomfortable feeling of angry/sad roil in my belly, the feeling I have around her so often now. Bonny is at her preschool, Grandpa Jim is at work, and Gigi's at her club, so I have no one to talk to.

My Uncle Steve is going to college, and he lives in the guesthouse behind the big one where we are staying. Uncle Steve's an artist, and he lets me visit him at the studio that's also his apartment. Downcast, I go to his place, breathing in the delicious smell of linseed oil and paint as I open the glass slider to his place.

Today he's at his desk working on something, but he lets me dab about with a watercolor set. Steve's a tall man like Pop and Grandpa Jim, but thinner built than my father and only twenty-two. He has the same green eyes, but his are set at a slant on broad cheekbones, catlike. I love Uncle Steve with an uncomplicated love, not like the mixed feelings my parents stir up in me because he's so patient and tells me that I'm an artist, too.

Eventually, I hear my grandmother come home.

"Yoo-hoo!" She sings her usual returning cry. "I'm home!"

I scramble up from painting with the watercolors. "Can I come back later, Uncle Steve?"

"Sure, anytime." Uncle Steve babysits Bonny and me sometimes. Once he let me stay up way too late and watch *One Million Years B.C.* with Raquel Welch. Raquel's fur bikini has me eyeing my grandmother's mink stole—in fact, I sneaked into her closet and played with it one time, but I haven't dared drape it around myself like Raquel yet.

Bon's enrolled in an all-day preschool, so I hardly see her until nighttime. Pop will probably bring her home when he returns from Windansea. Once again, I feel a stab of sad/angry. What did I do that was so bad? I just asked him what I really wanted to know.

Back in the main house, I hug my grandmother around her girdled waist, catching her as she's moving by. "Hi, Gigi."

She smells of chemical flowers from the cut glass bottle of Chanel No. 5 on her vanity. The first time I came in unexpectedly and saw the things she wears under those bright flowered dresses, my eyes bugged out. Her bra was pointy, and the girdle with its Super-Flexx Diamond Tummy Control Panel looked really uncomfortable.

"Foundation garments," she says. "Ladies wear them under their clothes."

I remember the woman from Taylor Camp squatting beside me as I cleaned fish on the beach, wearing nothing but her braids. I saw her pie as I cleaned the fish, because she wasn't even wearing panties. I guess she wasn't a lady, and if foundation garments make you a lady, then my mom isn't either.

"You have paint on your hands!" Gigi exclaims. "Go wash!"

"It's just watercolor," I say, going to the kitchen sink.

"Use the guest bath." She gestures. "Ladies use private facilities to wash their hands, not the kitchen sink."

I go into the little guest bath with its cut crystal fixtures, white carpet-covered toilet, and gold-plated sink. I wash the watercolor off, but I don't want to unwrap one of the pile of fancy soaps and use it up, and I don't want to wipe my hands on the fluffy monogrammed towel and mess it up either.

I end up flapping my hands to dry them and wipe the rest of the damp on the front of my dress as I come out. Gigi sees this with her x-ray vision—she always seems to catch me when I try to shortcut something.

"There's a perfectly good towel right there." She's rubbing the big colored stone rings she wears like her fingers hurt. They're so big, they must.

"I'm sorry, Gigi, I didn't want to mess up the towel."

She puts her hands on my shoulders, small and bony as bird claws, but heavy because of her rings. Stacked on her wrist are gold chains, bangles, and a charm bracelet I long to inspect. In fact, I wish she would take off all of her jewelry and let me play Aladdin's Cave with it.

"Look at me."

I gaze up at her. Gigi's breath smells like Tums, and her eyes are very blue. One has a tiny square of black in the blue part. "This is your home now. You can dry your hands on the towels; use anything you need. We have a maid who comes and cleans. Just don't—rub paint or mud into the furniture."

"Okay." I don't know what a maid is. Does she mean Conchita, the nice lady who comes every week and made me pancakes one day? Conchita takes all the sheets off our bed and washes them. I help her, and she likes that.

Gigi straightens up and touches my hair, her favorite thing about me. "Don't forget. You have ballet tomorrow."

I love my ballet lessons over at the Beach and Tennis Club. I'm old to be just starting, behind at the lessons like I was at La Jolla El, but I try really hard to make up for that. I wear a black, slightly scratchy leotard with pink tights, and soft ballet shoes that make me feel graceful. I always slide and skip, pointing my toes, when I wear them.

Bonny takes the lessons with me. She's just turned four, and still has a little plumpness around her middle and cheeks that remind me of Argos. In her pale pink tutu with her long silver-blonde hair hanging down her back, she looks really pretty. While people say, "Toby's cute with her freckles and red hair," they say, "What a beauty!" about Bonny.

"Good thing I'm smart," I tell myself when I hear that. I've only been at La Jolla Elementary a few months, and I'm caught up already. But being smart doesn't seem as good as being pretty, especially since Bonny's smart, too.

The next day in ballet class, one hand on the barre, practicing my plié, I keep an eye on my green-eyed, blonde-haired sister jumping across the room in her interpretation of a *jeté*. Mom's walked us to the lesson, and she's watching from a chair. She claps her hands, her mouth open in a big smile I haven't seen in ages as she watches Bonny's bouncing.

I like physical challenges. Mastering the plié and footwork, holding my hands and body just so, definitely count as challenges. We older girls run through the room in a line, *jeté*-ing, and I feel like I can fly. I really give it my all, hoping Mom will smile watching me, too.

"You're picking it up fast," my teacher says, and nods approvingly, but looking over, I can't tell if Mom was happy or not—she's got that glassy look again.

Our grandparents' house is right across the street from the Club, and after the lesson we walk past the pond and tennis courts, across the mini golf course and between the tall date palms. I run to do a cartwheel and more *jetés* as we walk home, unable to go slow, and I skip and spin all the way to the front door.

Mom hardly seems to notice anything I'm doing. She's slow and clumsy from the medicine, shuffling along at Bonny's walking speed, looking down at my sister. I feel invisible, and it hurts—and that makes me want Bonny to hurt too. Sometimes I pinch Bonny when no one can see and pretend a bug bit her when she cries.

I'm also learning tennis at the Club. Bonny doesn't like tennis.

She runs away from the ball and complains of being hot—but put me in front of one of those machines spitting a yellow sphere at me every thirty seconds, and I'll go all day. I even like the little white pleated skirt with built-in panties and the collared polo shirt I wear for lessons. My cousin Jennifer, Uncle Chris's daughter, is already a very good player who wins contests and everything. I want to do that, too.

I miss my fort in the forest, and the window with the sunlight where I read, but the things I liked best about that place are gone— my puppy. Mom's happiness.

We visit Nanee, my great-grandmother, on Sundays. Mom takes less medicine on Sunday so she can drive and hold a conversation. Nanee lives in a big tall building that has a man in the elevator who pushes the button for you, and she's short and round and smells like baby powder. She gives great hugs and smiles the whole time we visit.

Nanee has none of the fast-moving sharpness of Gigi, even though she's Gigi's mother. She wears tons of sparkly rhinestone jewelry, and if I get up close and ogle it, she takes off whatever I want to see and lets me wear it and play with it while I'm there.

"Such a magpie," she says, smiling. "You love sparkly things, don't you, Toby?" She says it like it's a good thing.

Mom loves Nanee, too, and when we're there, we all relax. Nanee lets Bonny and me roll around on the silky carpet and furniture because it's so soft, and she just laughs at our antics. "You girls are just like kittens!" She doesn't seem to care if we're ladies or not.

When Nanee puts a box of Turkish Delight down on the coffee table, I glance at Mom to see if it's okay. Turkish Delight is a fruity, chewy candy covered with powdered sugar, and Nanee always gives us a few pieces. Mom's staring in our general direction, but her eyes don't seem to be registering anything, so I take three pieces of Turkish Delight and chomp them down, my cheeks bulging, as Bonny and I play Go Fish with Nanee.

Mom has that little smile on her mouth that says, "I'm here, and it's okay."

That little smile doesn't reassure me. I wonder if she's getting better. Nobody tells me anything, and I'm not sure that this shuffling, vacant, sleepy Mom is better than the emotional, angry, acting-strange Mom.

One day when I'm alone with Pop, I ask him what's wrong with Mom. He's sitting on the fancy white couch in the living room, putting new guitar strings on his Martin. He hardly ever plays it here in La Jolla, so I like to watch and listen when he does because it reminds me of home in the evenings in the Forest House.

"They tell me she had a psychotic break and paranoid schizophrenia, which is a fancy name for crazy. But I think it's just that she took too much acid and peyote while doing that occult study course. She tried to kill herself three times while we were out there, you know."

I didn't know.

Even with my curiosity, even with how much I love Mom and try to observe and stay on top of things, I missed some big stuff that was going on.

"Why?" I ask. My lips feel numb, imagining having only Pop and Bonny as our family and living here with Gigi and Grandpa forever. "Why would she want to kill herself?"

"The tree spirits were talking to her, and they told her to. I had to get her out of that place because the *mana* was so strong."

Mana. The Hawaiian word for spiritual power. It's true—there was a lot of *mana* at the Forest House. I'm thankful I didn't know Mom was trying to die while we were there; I would never have stopped worrying.

Pop tightens his new set of guitar strings. He turns the knob on the head of the guitar, plucking the string with the thumbnail he keeps extra-long for guitar, and it makes a *pweeeeew* sound. He blows a black plastic tuning whistle and adjusts again.

These two sounds have never really made sense to me because they don't match, but somehow they do. I've never been able to figure out how he knows when they do. When he tried to teach me, the strings hurt my fingers too much. It was the one time I just didn't want to make him happy enough to persist through that pain.

"Sue lay in the road naked and waited for a car to hit her," he goes on, talking to the guitar as much as me. "The cops got called one time, and another time the driver just told her to get out of the road and go home."

He doesn't tell me about the third time, and I don't ask.

I picture my mother's long tanned body spread-eagled in the narrow, winding, lightless road as she stares up into the stars overhead, talking to the spirits, waiting for death as a car comes around the turn.

The squealing of the brakes.

The fear, the yelling, the confusion.

That all of this went on without me knowing is huge. I should have been around the cottage more, keeping an eye on things. Guilt stabs me in the guts, and I fold up small, holding the couch's fancy gold satin cushion, letting Pop's soothing plunking comfort me as I lie down and suck my thumb.

A few nights later, I overhear my parents talking in their room. "I hate this place." Mom's crying. "It's killing our family. Our spirit. Who we are. We have to go home to Kauai."

I can hear my dad's rumbling whisper but can't make out his words. I stare at the ceiling, sprayed with white swirly plaster stuff that has glittery gold bits in it. Bonny and I have twin beds separated by pale carpet. I glance over at my sister. She's asleep, her finger still in her mouth, and I get out of bed and climb in with her. She moves over without waking up.

I do that many nights, and Bonny doesn't seem to mind. She's always there with me, my best and only friend, even though I'm jealous of her sometimes.

Home. Kauai. Most days here in La Jolla, Kauai seems as fake as Neverland in my Peter Pan book. But sometimes, when the window's cracked so I hear the morning wind in the date palms that surround the Beach and Tennis Club below us, or there's a big swell breaking on the La Jolla Shores Beach and I can hear the surf, I'm back at the little cottage on the beach at Rocky Point. Sometimes when the trees outside cast shadows over my book as I read in my grandmother's guest room, I'm back in my little bed next to the window at the Forest House, and there's nothing before me but a long day of playing barefoot in the friendly jungle.

I close my eyes and imagine it. In my mind I can be there without mosquitoes, bullies, weird guys with glittery eyes, or a beloved puppy suddenly gone.

CHAPTER TWELVE

LADY LESSONS

Mom and me

Age: 8, La Jolla, California, 1973

I'm getting used to La Jolla, and I'm even starting to like it. I've ridden in my new friends' Jaguars and Mercedes, swum in their pools, petted their poodles. I come back from one playdate super excited. "Sarah has an elevator in her house!"

Mom makes a squinchy face. She's definitely feeling better because she says, "How ridiculous."

Gigi and Grandpa Jim take us all for a family dinner at the La Jolla Country Club once a week. I like this because of the tasty food and that I get a Shirley Temple. Other than that, it's boring and one long "lady lesson."

The evening always begins with a cocktail in the formal seating area at home. Bonny and I wear matching long party dresses with white, ruffled yokes and flowered, flowing material that Gigi bought us. Hers is blue, mine is red, and we both have on Mary Janes with itchy white lace socks.

Pop drinks an amber drink with ice that Grandpa gives him. He usually has two before we get out the door, and I can see his mood improve by his second or third. Mom drinks white wine and wears a shirtwaist with a belt and that little smile. Grandpa makes Bonny and me ginger ale with a lime slice at the wet bar and forbids us to spill. We sit on the stiff white couch, and Gigi coaches us on making conversation: "Begin with a compliment when you greet someone. Notice the weather. Talk about anything but religion or politics."

We need to take two cars to get us all to the club. Gigi and Grandpa don't want us driving the van, since "it's not suitable," so we separate into their cars: Mom and Bonny drive with Grandpa in his big black Cadillac, and Pop and I drive with Gigi in her cream-colored Thunderbird.

In the back seat where they can't see me, I lie down and wriggle around, enjoying the softness and breathing in the smell of the leather, which makes me think of saddles and riding the Black Stallion across a starlit desert as the car glides up the steep drive to the Club.

We pull in under the portico and Pop, who's driving, hands the valet the keys. Pop's big bushy beard gets a glance, but he's packed into one of Grandpa's suits, so he passes muster. I've already been told that "ladies must wear dresses or dressy slacks, and men wear a coat and tie at the Country Club."

"Thanks, Henry," Gigi says, as the valet comes around and opens her door. He lifts her out by the hand like she's a queen. I open my door and hop out, slamming it. Henry smiles—he didn't have time to get my door. He's shiny black from head to toe, and his teeth look like pearls.

"You like to do things yourself," he says. I nod, staring open-mouthed at his beauty. His skin looks like purple-black satin and his hair seems like it would feel good to touch. I haven't seen many black people—we didn't have any on Kauai.

"Ladies wait for the door to be opened," Gigi hisses in my ear, grabbing my hand too tightly and tugging me away from staring at Henry. Bonny and Mom are already standing with Grandpa, waiting for us in the fancy lobby with its gigantic vases of flowers and the crystal chandelier dripping stars and rainbows of light over the patterned carpet.

We gather under Grandpa's formal portrait, painted to commemorate his stint as President of the Board for the Club. Set in a big, curlicued gold frame, his rugged face looks off into the distance like Christopher Columbus considering new worlds to conquer.

Tonight, Gigi's wearing her red Chanel suit with the gold buttons and her real diamonds. She begins her oft-repeated spiel, gesturing with her sparkly hands. "After your Grandpa sold his rubber factory, he made investments in stocks and real estate. Now he gives his time to managing those and guiding worthy organizations like the La Jolla Country Club."

"Honey, they've heard it," Grandpa says. "Let's eat." Holding Bonny's hand, he ushers Gigi ahead of him toward the dining room. He likes Bonny better than me, but Gigi likes me better, so it works out. Gigi takes my hand and we walk into the restaurant. Grandpa and Bonny follow. Mom and Pop bring up the rear, leaning into each other as if they'll tip over otherwise.

The hostess leads us to a round table for six by the window. The Club's dining room looks out over the ocean and the rest of La Jolla, twinkling with lights as the sun goes down. The way the window curves, it seems to me that the whole town and the ocean beyond is held inside a fishbowl along with the setting sun, and I want to plaster my face against the glass just to look and look.

We sit where Gigi tells us to, always an important decision that she spends time considering aloud. This time, I'm between my grandparents, Bonny is next to Grandpa, and Mom and Pop are across from us behind an expanse of draped white tablecloth.

Facing me are rows of utensils, a couple of glasses, and a fancy gold plate that's not to be eaten from, decorated with a napkin folded into a swan. I remember my "lady lesson" from the last time we were here and take my napkin, shake it out, and drape it over my lap.

Gigi pats my arm approvingly.

A waiter comes to take our drink orders. Bonny and I tell him, "Shirley Temple, please," when it's our turn.

After that, we can hold the massive leather-bound menus. Gigi points a coral-colored nail at the Children's Choices section. "Something from there will be more than enough."

I order the Hamburger and Pommes Frites. Bonny gets Mac and Cheese. My dad and Grandpa Jim have Ribeye and a Baked Potato. Mom has the Vegetarian Selection. Gigi has Veal Piccata. After we order, she leans down to whisper in my ear. "Ladies never eat much in front of other people. And they always watch their weight."

Watch their weight? What does that even mean?

The bread comes in a steaming basket that makes my mouth water. Gigi's eye is on me as I lift the white napkin covering hot sourdough rolls and use the tongs on the table to lift a roll onto my plate. Remembering my lesson from last week, I tear off a fragment and butter it lightly, pop it into my mouth and chew with my mouth closed and elbows off the table. She nods, and then frowns as she spots Bonny cutting her roll in half and buttering the whole thing.

"No, no," she says. "Just little bits. Like this." She demonstrates.

I glance across the table. My mom's eyes are narrowed. She's not appreciating Gigi's instruction of us, and just like noticing that she picked the Vegetarian Selection, I can tell she's feeling better. She's finished her chardonnay and orders another with a raised finger and a tap on her glass.

I've eaten my roll, but I know better than to reach for another even though I'm still hungry. Conversation about golf, fishing, and the stock market go on over my head as my burger arrives at last. I pick it up in both hands and open my mouth wide. I get a tap on the wrist from Gigi. "Wait until the senior lady takes her first bite."

I shut my mouth and put the burger down, looking around. No one is eating yet.

Gigi takes her first bite of Veal Piccata, and, still conversing about golf, Pop and Grandpa Jim do the same. Mom's got that little smile on as she pokes at her Vegetarian Selection, something green with pasta.

"Use your knife and fork," Gigi instructs.

On a burger? I frown. That can't be right. I stab my burger with my fork and saw at it—too vigorously, knocking my Shirley Temple so that it wobbles.

"Slow down. Smaller pieces." Gigi demonstrates how to cut a piece off of my burger and take a bite. "A lady cuts everything with knife and fork."

I manage to get through about part of my burger that way, when she lays a cool, soft birdy-hand on my wrist once more. "Only eat half of your food. Maybe three-fourths. Otherwise, you'll get fat. You're picking up some weight already." She pinches my cheek, and it's true. I've noticed my cheeks are fuller.

I've spent so much time being hungry that it's hard to imagine worrying about being fat, but I guess I need to be concerned about that, too.

I hear a funny sound from across the table, and it's my mom, breathing hard through her nose and giving Gigi stink eye, her lips tight. She stands up suddenly. "Come, girls. We're going to the ladies' room."

Pop and Grandpa Jim hustle to stand up too, and wait for Mom to get out from behind her seat and Bon and me to get up. She takes our hands and we walk rather fast, for ladies, to the restroom.

Inside the fancy bathroom, Mom squats down and pulls us close, her arms around each of our shoulders. I breathe in her beloved Mom-smell—sandalwood oil and skin. Nothing artificial.

"Don't listen to Gigi. Eat all you want; however, you want.

Okay?" She strokes our hair and pulls us in against her. The three of us hug for a long moment. I am so happy she's feeling better.

Returning to the table, my appetite is gone. It's too much work to cut my burger, and the stress of Mom against Gigi makes me a little queasy as I pick at my fries. The half-full plate carried away earns me a "good girl" murmur from Gigi, and then I feel disloyal to Mom. I entertain myself for the rest of the meal by chasing the cherry in my Shirley Temple, trying to suck it onto the end of my straw and keep it there without getting in trouble—I'm pretty sure ladies don't play with their straws that way.

Later, after bedtime, I'm hungry. I sneak into my parents' room and tell Mom, who's lying on her side of the bed reading Yogananda's *Autobiography of a Yogi*. She tiptoes with me into the big cold kitchen and gets me a lemon yogurt, and one for herself. We perch at the glass dining room table and eat them with Gigi's silver teaspoons.

"Ladies might not eat much at dinner, but later they go into the kitchen for snacks," Mom whispers, and I lean against her warmth. *Mom's back!*

CHAPTER THIRTEEN
COCONUT ISLAND

Me in a tree

Age: 8, Kaneohe Bay, Oahu, 1973

We're in La Jolla nine months altogether before we move back to Hawaii. By then, I don't want to leave, because all I can think of is how miserable school was in Hanalei. I'm liking school now, despite having to wear shoes. Mom says I don't have to go to Hanalei School this time; she's going to homeschool me. I have worries about that, but I don't say anything.

Gigi and Grandpa don't agree with us going back to Kauai, and there are lots of loud arguments and Gigi blinks a lot and hides red eyes. They've even bought us a cute little house on a street nearby, to get the family to "settle down." But Mom and Pop are determined. Kauai matters more to them than anything I've seen them care about, except surfing—and Kauai and surfing are tied together.

I'm especially sad to leave sweet Nanee and my buddy Uncle Steve when we say goodbye, but I'm glad to leave the guest room of a house where I never stopped worrying about messing something up. We all want our own house again, so Pop goes to Kauai ahead of us to find a job and that house.

Mom, Bonny, and I fly over to Oahu for that month to visit Mom's dad, marine biologist Grandpa Garth. He has paid for our tickets so that Mom can also bring Judy, Lauren, and Bettina, his daughters from a second marriage, and babysit them while they visit too. They are not allowed to visit him alone, and Mom is there "to make sure they're safe."

I've never spent any time with Grandpa Garth that I can remember—whatever happened between Mom's parents happened before I was born, and she's not close to him.

Mom's nervous and snappy as she herds all five of us girls onto the plane from California to Oahu. "He's the first person ever to earn a Ph.D. from Scripps Institute of Oceanography in La Jolla," Mom tells us as we get settled in our seats. "Your grandpa got his doctorate the year you were born, Toby. He's the world expert on sardines. Their population is dwindling, and he's been influencing fishing policy by using data to show that overfishing is leading to the problem."

I have five aunts total from both my Grandma Stella and Grandpa Garth's second marriages, but this is the first time I get to meet and spend any time with Judy, Lauren, and Bettina. Judy's a year older than me, with brown eyes and long brown hair, serious and quiet. Lauren, the middle daughter, is a year younger than me, has Grandpa Garth's dark eyes and black hair. Bettina is almost three and has lighter hair.

It's so weird to have aunts that are young enough that they seem like cousins or something.

Grandpa greets us at the Honolulu airport with a rented passenger van. A black-browed, handsome man with hair turning silver at the sides of his head, he has a booming voice that makes the younger girls jump. "The gang's all here! What a family—my grand-daughters and daughters are the same age!"

"Except for me," Mom says acidly, settling herself beside him in the front passenger seat as we arrange ourselves on bench seats in rows in the back.

"Except for Sue, of course," he says, equally acid.

Grandpa Garth's science career is why Mom grew up in Hawaii, moved to La Jolla, and traveled so much in Europe when she was young. Their family knew all sorts of famous and interesting people because of his work. Maga and Grandpa Garth divorced when Mom was seventeen because of his drinking and hitting, and because Maga had met Egidio, a handsome policeman in Rome, while there for one of Grandpa's fish conferences.

Mom is the oldest of four kids, and it was a bit scandalous at the time when her parents divorced and then both of them remarried. Mom had to leave college to come back home and take care of her brothers, Garth and Eric, and her little sister, Jan. She did that until she was nineteen and Grandpa got remarried to Judy, Lauren, and Bettina's mom—but their marriage eventually ended too.

Grandpa's over hearty when we arrive at his house, a big two-story on pier posts with a yard that ends at the huge expanse of calm

Kaneohe Bay. "You've got the run of this whole place. Just don't get in my way!" His laugh sounds like distant thunder.

Grandpa Garth works for the University of Hawaii as a professor during the day, and it's apparently a stressful job because he closes himself away in his study drinking in the evenings, even on the first night we arrive. Mom tells us all to be quiet and leave him alone, and we don't need to be told twice.

The brackish ocean's right there, lapping at the edge of the yard of Grandpa's house, and a long pier in front points toward a tiny atoll across a deep blue channel. I'm thrilled to throw off my mainland clothes and shoes and run down to the edge of the water with a big red scoop net I find under the house. Unlike Kauai and Rocky Point where we lived before, Kaneohe Bay is shallow, wide, and very calm, with a silty-mud bottom—ideal for fishing and catching stuff.

Judy and I become friends the first day as I show her how to catch *opae* with the net, and thread them, still flipping their tails, onto a hook on a couple of spare bamboo poles. We jig for *papio* off of the pier. I get the feeling Judy's not used to this kind of thing, but she doesn't complain, which I like. Lauren and Bettina stay in with Bonny and Mom, baking and playing in the house.

Grandpa Garth notices us fishing and comes down in khaki cargo shorts and a faded green University of Hawaii *Rainbows* tee. He puts on a faded canvas fishing hat that looks like it's been around the world, and his deep brown eyes sparkle with intelligence from beneath the brim. "Want to put out some crab traps?"

"Sure!" I'm super excited and grab Judy's hand, giving her a tug toward the flat-bottomed skiff with a little trolling motor tied to the pier. Grandpa Garth piles wire cages into it as we sit together on a bench in front. Each trap has a scrap iron weight at the bottom, and a bleach bottle tied to it so it can be found again.

Once loaded, he poles us across the still, shallow water of the inner bay with its gray bottom and long, squishy sea cucumbers. Mom and the other girls wave to us from the shore. Mom has a little worried frown on her forehead, but Grandpa's in a good mood, and I can tell it's going to be fine.

He maneuvers the boat into deeper water and shows us how to set the crab traps, baited with pieces of bacon he brought down from the house. We drop them around the Bay in a pattern, marked by the floating bleach bottles, to check on the next day.

"Now that you know how, you can take over baiting and bringing in the traps," he tells us. I'm thrilled about this and can't wait to see what we catch the next day. "Samoan crabs, mostly," he says, when I ask him what to expect. "Slipper lobsters, sometimes."

My mouth waters. Samoan crabs, with their pointy-edged shells and blue-lined claws, can grow to be huge. They like mud and mangroves, which Kaneohe has in plenty. The slippers, horseshoe-shaped brown lobsters with beady black eyes, are bottom dwellers that dig into silt or sand.

"I'll show you my lab," Grandpa says, once the traps are set. His lab is why he's living in this house right across the channel from the University of Hawaii's facility on Coconut Island, he tells us, and points to the atoll I noticed on the first day. Coconut Island is a hockey puck peppered with palms only a few hundred more yards out to sea, across a deep turquoise channel.

"The island is a natural atoll with its own very healthy barrier reef." Grandpa's deep voice booms from his barrel chest, and I can easily see him teaching college—he has a voice you want to listen to, and a face that's hard to look away from. "In the thirties, the heir to the Fleischmann yeast fortune bought it, made artificial ponds and other changes to it, and built his house there. The University of Hawaii owns half of it now, and the wealthy Pauley family owns the other half. Coconut Island's an ideal location for research because it's right in the middle of reef habitat and near open water too, so we can study marine animals in varied natural environments. We have a lot of studies going and also teach students out there."

I am so excited to go to Coconut Island to see his lab that I bounce on the seat where the life preservers are. He doesn't make us wear the jackets, which means he knows we can swim and handle ourselves. Well, I can, at least. Judy looks back at the shore, her eyes squinty and her face pale, but doesn't say anything.

Grandpa Garth pulls on the rope attached to the small outboard and fires it up. The skiff moves along well, sliding across the deep-water channel on the other side of the mud flats and all the way to the atoll.

We tie the boat at the dock on Coconut Island. I'm almost hopping with excitement but restraining myself from talking too much as Grandpa takes us into the marine biology building. The steady heartbeat of bubblers fills a dim and fishy-smelling barnlike place, where rows and rows and rows of glass tanks crusted with the drying salt of splashed ocean water line walls and aisles of shelving. No kids ever get to come here, I can tell. I'm lucky to see this.

Grandpa tells us all sorts of things about the tanks' contents, but I only really notice the huge cylinder tank in the center of the room, filled with sardines circling and circling in a shape like a tornado. They're individually small, but make a shape like one big thing, silver and fluid as mercury. They remind me of a beehive—busy, organized, and not interested in us at all. I press my face against the curved Plexiglas. I could watch them all day.

"These are my babies." Grandpa Garth sets a big square hand on the tank, gazing into the whirl of sardines. The reflection of their passing lights his face, and I can feel how much he loves those fish— maybe more than the people in his life, which makes perfect sense to me as I take in their beauty.

We continue on past offices and classrooms, then walk out of the building to look at ponds and docks around the island's edge as he tells us about the invasion of mangroves into Kaneohe Bay. He picks up a green, pointed mangrove seed floating beside the dock. About the size and shape of a pen, the seed's slightly rounder on one end. He shakes the water off it and gets our attention with his intense dark eyes, holding it up by the bulb.

"These mangrove pods floated to Hawaii, and they're taking over the ancient fish ponds and choking out the native Hawaiian birds' habitat. If you see any of these seeds, pick them up and throw them away, but not anywhere that they can grow—all the way into the trash. Pull up any baby trees you find when you're playing around in the mud."

We promise to fight the Mangrove Invasion every day.

On the way back, I catch a nice, hand-sized *papio* with my bamboo pole from the skiff, and when we check the traps, I pull out a Samoan crab caught without a fuss or getting pinched. At the house, Grandpa tells Mom, "This girl is a natural!"

I get to cook my fish by myself at the stove. I feel really good that Grandpa noticed how good I am at fishing, and I can tell Mom likes that too.

Mom's trying really hard to be nice to Grandpa and my aunts and keep everything fun and interesting for all of us girls. She makes meals for everyone and cleans the house. I'm still a little worried about her, but she seems pretty much back to how she was before the crazy started.

During the day, Judy and I roam the bay in the skiff, setting the crab traps and pulling in buckets of Samoan crab and slipper lobster, which we eat nightly. The younger girls play at home in the yard and under the house.

Mom gets the idea to surprise Grandpa by having us make a "natural history museum" on the shady side of the house next to the hedge. This project is something all of us girls can do, so each day we scavenge for interesting things. We add treasures daily: a sunbleached cat's skull, eggshells and bird nests, road-flattened toads, lobster molts, coral and shells. Judy and I look the names of things up in Latin, and write them in our best handwriting on little paper tabs. We plan to impress Grandpa Garth with a grand tour when we have it finished.

A few days after we start the museum, Grandpa tells us we're having a barbecue down by the dock. "Caught something big," he says, his eyes glittering. "Come see." The gaggle of us follows him down the slanting lawn to the barbecue area near the dock.

A dead five-foot gray reef shark lies on the grass, its glassy, opaline eye staring up at us. Dark patches on its rough skin make it look like pictures I've seen of salmon exhausted from spawning.

"Shark steaks!" Grandpa says in his over hearty voice. "Something new for you girls, I'm sure." He brandishes a huge buck knife, and squats beside the carcass. "Judy and Toby, hold the fins and tail so I can gut it."

I hold the dorsal fin reluctantly, breathing through my mouth because it stinks in a dark and funky way, worse than most fish I've gutted. Judy's face is white, and her lips are folded together, but she holds the tail by her thumb and forefinger, because I know she's even more terrified of her dad than holding the shark.

Grandpa Garth stabs the knife, grunting with the effort of getting through the tough skin, into the poophole of the shark. Muscles bulging, he saws and strains as he slits it. Guts bulge out, springing free as if pressurized, and a wave of rotting meat smell rises. Judy lets go of the tail and runs for the house, her sisters in her wake. Bonny comes and holds the tail in Judy's place.

"You two girls aren't afraid of a little blood, right?" Grandpa pulls the ropes and bags of guts out. The smell is nauseating, a solid thing I have to find a way to breathe through. Bonny squinches her face, but we both hang onto the shark's wriggling carcass to steady it.

I've gutted enough fish with my dad, even game fish like *aku* and *papio,* to know that this shark wasn't well. "Grandpa, it doesn't smell right," I say. "Do you think it might have been sick? Should we eat it?"

My grandfather glares at me, hands covered with blood, neck red with anger, giant knife in hand. "I'm a marine ichthyologist. Do you think I'd feed my family bad fish?"

We eat the barbecued shark steaks because he says we have to. Mom protests, but he won't let her fix anything else. The slabs of shark are greasy and rancid, and reek of the rot that was in the fish's gut. Bonny and I both eat what's put in front of us and get to have ice cream after. The other girls cry and don't finish theirs, but get the ice cream too, in the end.

We all feel the lash of Grandpa Garth's disappointment.

He must have been right that the fish was okay because we don't get sick. But after that, we stop making the natural history museum.

Another evening, near the end of our stay, Mom slices carrots for dinner, and gives some to the five of us to snack on. We're hungry and ready for dinner, but Lauren complains that Mom hasn't peeled the carrots.

"I never peel the carrots. All the nutritional value's in the carrot skin." She's said this before. In fact, I don't remember ever eating a peeled carrot.

Lauren fusses that she doesn't like them that way; that's not how they have them at home. Mom ignores her, continuing with her meal prep. Lauren disappears and returns a few minutes later, towing Grandpa Garth out of his den.

Red veins stand out in his neck, and he seems to have grown huge, like the Hulk. His face is almost purple. "SUE. Peel the fucking carrots," he snarls.

Lauren pales with terror at what she's unleashed and lets go of his hand.

Mom, stirring something at the stove with three-year-old Bettina on her hip, doesn't look up. "I don't feed food without nutrition to children."

"You don't know what you're talking about." I can tell Grandpa wants to swear more. A lot more. His voice is like a cannon firing fierce, loud words. "You never have."

Lauren runs to the room she's sharing with her sisters. I slide down from my chair, giving Judy's hand a tug, pulling her with me. We make for the back door. Four-year-old Bonny's still sitting at the table, looking bewildered at the raised voices, a thunderstorm breaking around her. She sees us leaving and follows at a trot.

"I'm preparing meals that are healthy for the kids." Mom raises her voice behind us. "If you don't like it, you can do it yourself."

"Goddamn it," bellows Grandpa Garth. "There's no science in that statement about the carrots. You've never had any sense."

By then, Judy, Bonny, and I are under the house in the fort we've been making down there. Scrap carpet on the ground, dusty old sail material, and discarded household castoffs have all found new life in our grubby playhouse.

Judy covers her face with her hands as tears slide down, her long hair hanging around her like a blanket. Bonny and I snuggle against her, one on each side. I think of Lauren in the girls' room, alone, and hope she's okay.

"He can't find us down here," I say, and hope it's true.

"I don't like it when he yells." Fear and sadness are in Judy's words. Grandpa hit Maga a lot, and that's why they divorced. Probably he hit my aunts' mom, too. Is Mom going crazy again, standing up to Grandpa like that?

More yelling goes on above us. I'm glad we never showed him our natural history museum. He's mean and scary and doesn't deserve it!

I hear the giant crash of something being thrown. Bettina shrieks in fright like a teapot left on too long. Waiting for the sound of glass breaking or people getting hit, I chew my nails and taste the quicksilver of blood. Mom's going to get hurt and have to go back to The Best Facility . . .

Finally, Grandpa's footsteps echo heavily overhead as he thumps back to his private domain and slams the door. Silence falls.

"Let's go see if they're okay." We hurry up into the house.

There's a big iron pan on the floor, leaning against the wall. Mom's putting sliced, steamed, unpeeled carrots in a bowl, setting them beside a casserole on the table like nothing happened. Bettina is still on her hip, red-faced and crying.

"Wash your hands, girls," she says. "Where's Lauren?"

"I'll get her." Judy disappears down the hall as Bonny climbs back up into her seat.

Mom soothes Bettina and puts her in a booster seat, and I go hug her, then Mom. When I put my arms around Mom, I smell the sharp sweat of her battle with the Hulk soaking her muumuu. Delicate trembling zaps through her body like she's plugged into an electric socket.

"I love you," I tell her, but what I mean is, "you're brave."

I wonder if she has the same secret power I have—to Get into His Head and come out unbroken.

CHAPTER FOURTEEN

BACK TO KAUAI

Me with a kitten

Age: 8, Wainiha Store House, Kauai, September 1973

We circle in to land on Kauai ten months after we left it to take Mom to the Best Facility. Deep cobalt sea, crinkled like metallic wrapping paper, wraps around green velvet mountains and makes me realize I was more homesick than I let myself be. Getting off the plane at Lihue Airport, my fine hair lifts off my shoulders in celebration because the air is so moist and soft. I gaze up at the clean blue sky filled with cotton candy clouds, and the nearby mountains almost melt my eyes with their intense color.

The long, low airport building, open and windy, resembles a big metal shed more than anything. We hurry down the moveable stairs off the Aloha Airlines plane with its familiar orange hibiscus and run to hug Pop, waiting for us in the shade under the wide tin roof. He's wearing a big grin on his face and a tee shirt and corduroy shorts with rubber slippers. We're wearing the slippers we bought in Kaneohe, and as we run across the blacktop, I love that none of us are in regular shoes.

"We're home." Mom leans into Pop like she'll never let go, her face pressed into his shoulder. Kauai *does* feel like home, and I realize how much I didn't let myself remember. Now Gigi's house, with its white carpets and "lady lessons," seems like the imaginary place.

A man drives a golf cart trailer into the shed, and we get our bags directly off it. Pop leads us out to an old car in the parking lot, a dark green, wide-assed, square-cornered Rambler American sedan, only a little rusty.

"The car came with the place we rented." Pop's voice is happy and excited; this is a good thing, because we left our faithful white van on the Mainland. "Wait till you see the house I found for us." He opens the trunk to put our suitcases in, and it's as big as a swimming pool.

"There's enough room back here to put you girls in with the suitcases if you start bickering," Mom laughs.

I bounce in the bench seat in back, and the springs squeak. "I love this car!" Bon and I bounce and squeak, bounce and squeak, all the way through Lihue on the two-lane highway that leads through the island's capital. Pop is so happy to see us that he never makes us stop.

We bounce through Kapa`a, then Kilauea, then Hanalei, and even further. Pop tells us about where we're going to live. "We're going to be in Wainiha Valley. The river running through it goes all the way to the heart of Kauai, Mount Waialeale—the wettest spot on earth in measured rainfall."

I didn't know these facts, but I know Wainiha.

I've driven through the steep, rugged, heavily jungled valley hundreds of times on the bus, or on our way to Tunnels Beach and the End of the Road, crossing the twin metal bridges of the thick river that runs like a vein down the middle of the valley, splits, and rejoins itself again near the ocean. A wind-battered beach marks the river's sandbar, and black rock cliffs line its edges. Like Hanalei, the Wainiha River floods most years in winter. The only things that really thrive in the valley are taro, mosquitoes, and toads—but it's summer now, and beautiful.

Our new rental is the tiny defunct general store, right on the only road leading through the valley, a building that has been closed for years. Rusty old red gas pumps lean toward each other beside a boarded-up door leading into the termite-ridden, empty storefront. Behind that unused area is an attached cottage where we're going to live.

Bonny and I haul our suitcases up rickety wooden stairs into a bright, wooden-floored bedroom with a window that looks at the back yard. A pair of beds Pop made from scrap lumber fills the L of one corner of the room. We push our suitcases under our beds to hold our clothes, and we're home.

Mom meets with Mr. Beck at Hanalei School. She shows him a high-quality homeschool program "used internationally by diplomats, celebrities, and missionaries overseas" called Calvert School that she proposes to teach Bonny and me with. He signs off, approving it, and I don't have to go back to Hanalei School—at least for the remainder of the year.

Mom buys the Calvert School with Pop's trust fund money.

Everything needed, including creamy paper marked with wide blue lines in light-blue tablets and all-wood, silky pencils, arrives in a box. The lessons cover biology to Latin and are challenging and interesting. Each day Mom reads her Teacher Manual and explains the assignment, and I do my work at the kitchen table with the sun falling through the window. Bonny sits beside me, working on her preschool version.

Instead of getting a job this time, Pop starts his own business as a fix-it man. A steady stream of broken toasters, radios, waffle irons, vacuums, and lawn mowers appear on the stoop of the old Wainiha Store, and he opens a little shop in Hanalei town. He's as happy as I've ever seen him with work, challenged by new puzzles to figure out how to fix—but he still needs quiet in the mornings because he starts drinking in the afternoon and wakes up hungover.

One day, not long after we get back to Kauai, we go to a party, which doesn't happen often because Pop still doesn't like crowds and other people. It's at a private home in Anini Beach, with a lawn that rolls down to the beach. The adults get started drinking and smoking *pakalolo* right away as Jimi Hendrix whales on his guitar on the record player. Bonny and I put on our bathing suits and head down to the beach with the other kids.

I know several kids my age there, including Kenny Bryan, whose father, Vinnie, is a surfer friend of Pop's. We splash through a waist-deep sand channel to an outside reef. Unusual long rippling strands of seaweed grow there, and we pretend to be merpeople, draping the seaweed all over ourselves and giggling as we swim around with pretend wigs on.

Bonny comes out to the reef to join me. The water, more than waist-deep on me, is at her shoulders. Her eyes are bright green with excitement to be out here with the big kids.

"Go back!" I yell at her, pointing to the shore. She can't swim very well at her age, and the water's too deep for her. "You're too little to be out here." Mom never said anything to me, but I know I'm supposed to watch her in situations like this.

Bonny's face crumples with disappointment, and I turn my back on her. She's usually my best buddy, but I have other eight-year-olds to play with today.

Diving in and out of the water dressed in seaweed, I eventually check to see if Bonny's on the beach where she's supposed to be, playing with the other little kids with their buckets and pails.

She's not there.

I feel like I've been socked in the stomach. My heart seems to stop beating.

I look up the long slope of lawn leading to the house. But she wouldn't have had time to get all the way up there.

I turn all around, looking for her.

Way out in the ocean, looking just like one of those white bleach-bottle crab trap markers, is Bonny's bobbing blonde head. She must have been swept out to sea through the sandy channel on her way back.

"Bonny! Bonny!" The water drops into deep right off the reef's edge, and I fall into it heading toward her. I can't get her myself—I'm too slow and weak, and she's too far out. Frantic, my whole body vibrating with terror, I splash in to shore, screaming. "Help! Help my sister! She's swept out to sea!"

I can't find our parents. I accost the first able-bodied adult I see, Kenny's dad Vinnie, who's sitting on a towel drinking beer with some other people.

"Vinnie! You have to help! Bonny's swept out to sea!" I pull on his arm. "You have to save her!"

His face is kind but disbelieving. "Calm down. Tell me what's happening."

I point, hopping up and down in my panic. "There she is! That's her head, floating way out there! She came to play with the older kids, and I sent her back to shore and she . . . she didn't make it. The rip must have taken her out." Tears start and my throat closes. "Please help her, please!"

"All I see is a bleach bottle. It's a crab trap marker."

"No! No, it's her. She's got really blonde hair!" I'm still looking around for our parents, but they must be inside the house.

Vinnie makes a joke and sets his beer down—he's not taking me seriously. I spot a big old surfboard under the house. "It's my fault. I'll get her myself."

I run and grab the board by the nose and start dragging it across the lawn. Snot and tears obscure my vision as I plow toward the beach, but I'm running, stumbling, and I feel like I have superhuman strength as I drag the big board toward the water.

Suddenly the board's plucked out of my hands.

Vinnie looks down at me. "Because you're so sure, I'll paddle out and check on that crab trap."

And then he moves fast, running with the board down to the water, launching with a splash, and paddling like an arrow toward Bonny, who's drifted so far out she's barely visible. I run up to a rise on the lawn, and turn to watch. He reaches her and grabs her by the back of the swimsuit, hauling her up onto the board. I'm laughing and crying and clapping my hands.

I run up to the house and finally find my mom with a bunch of other moms. *Pakalolo* smoke is thick in the air. "Mom, I've been looking everywhere for you! Bonny drowned!"

Dead silence.

Then Mom surges to her feet and runs past me toward the beach. The other moms grab me, exclaiming and asking what happened. I realize that I should have said, *"almost* drowned."

I run after Mom, yelling. "She almost drowned!" I scream. "Almost! Vinnie's getting her!"

Vinnie's already on his way back, paddling the board with Bonny draped over the front. Her head is down so we can't even see if she's alive. Mom runs right into the water in her pretty muumuu, and scoops her up.

Bonny's hunched over, barfing, throwing up salt water as they reach the beach. Mom's crying, and I'm crying, and even Vinnie's crying. Vinnie gets his beach towel and wraps it around Bonny when she's done throwing up.

I'm sick with guilt that I didn't make sure she got to shore safely, that I was mean and yelled at her. I hug myself with my arms, shiv-ering in my wet swimsuit and biting my bleeding nails.

Mom's eyes light on me, and seem to catch fire like hot coals. "You! You were supposed to watch her!" she screams. "And you told me she *drowned*!" She reaches down, grabs a big piece of driftwood, and whacks me. I yelp and scramble away as she chases me, huge with rage like Grandpa Garth on a bender.

Vinnie grabs her arm and takes the stick away forcefully, throwing it on the ground.

"She saved Bonny's life!" He yells at her. "I almost didn't go out, but Toby was getting this huge old board by herself to go save her!"

Mom stops, gulping air, anger seeping out of her like air out of a balloon. "Oh," she says, suddenly aware of the whole party emptying out from the house and everyone coming down to watch our drama on the beach.

"You shouldn't have said she drowned," Mom hisses at me. She wraps Bonny tightly in the towel. She carries her up to the house, calling for Pop.

Vinnie squats down to me; he's a tall man with kind brown eyes. "You were very brave. I almost didn't go out. *You* saved her."

"I should have been watching her properly!" I burst into tears. Vinnie hugs me, and my friend Kenny pats my back.

I don't know what would happen to us if Bonny had died. My imagination shies away from that horrible thought as guilt eats at my stomach. Vinnie can say I saved her all he wants, but I know how things are in our family—I was responsible, and I didn't take care of her.

CHAPTER FIFTEEN

COURAGE LESSONS

Me river fishing

Age: 9, Wainiha, Kauai, 1974

When homeschool lessons are over, Bonny and I play outside, roaming around the river, and up to our neighbors' houses off the dirt road behind our house. I make friends with horses staked out along the riverbank feeding on the thick buffalo grass. A gentle brown mare, tied up beside the lazy green river, is my favorite. Feeding her bits of her favorite kinds of grass, breathing in her smell, and leaning my forehead on her neck, I can imagine she's my own.

Now that we live further away from Taylor Camp, we're better accepted, and we play with the Kaipakas across the street, and the Richardson boys down the dirt road.

Darren Richardson is a famous surfer from the North Shore of Oahu who's moved to Wainiha with his family for the same reasons Mom and Pop have—the great, uncrowded surf on Kauai. He's a tall handsome man with a big crest of blond hair and lots of tan muscles. All of the surfers respect him because he's won contests at Pipeline and has pictures in Surfer Magazine. Darren and his wife, Betsy, have been friends with our parents since the Oahu days. Now that we live in Wainiha, our parents like to hang out with beer and joints in the evenings on the Richardsons' porch a few houses down, talking about the surf, while we kids run around outside.

Knight, Betsy's son from her first marriage, is a year older and big for his age, with blond hair and a ton of energy. His little brother, Royal is Bon's age, and they play in the house and on the porch while Knight and I go further afield. Knight loves risks, and I'm always a little scared of what he comes up with for us to do. I try not to let it show, but he seems to know and dares me constantly.

One day he takes me into the jungle behind their house. "Let's play tiger hunt."

Turns out, "tiger hunt" involves digging a big dent in the ground, lining it with sticks we sharpen with Knight's pocketknife, and covering the trap with branches and leaves. When it's finally done, we stand back to observe our treacherous handiwork. Anyone coming along here wouldn't see it, and could break a leg or pierce a foot. I frown with worry. "I'm not sure this is a good idea. Someone could get hurt."

"Yeah, the tiger. And you're the tiger." Knight adjusts the leaves to his satisfaction.

"No way."

"Someone has to be the tiger. I'll go behind this tree and when you get trapped in the hole, I'll kill you quickly." He brandishes the pocketknife.

I look at him, then down at the trap. "That doesn't sound like fun."

"I'm not really going to kill you. Are you chicken, or just a girl?" he sneers.

I hate being called chicken, or "a girl," and he knows this.

Pretty soon I'm in the tiger trap, having positioned myself to fall in between the sticks as best I can, but it's muddy and hazardous, and that's even before Knight leaps down from where he was hiding in a nearby tree, yelling. I play my part, growling and swiping at him with a paw. He leaps on me, squashing me into the mud at the bottom of the hole. He puts his pocketknife to my throat, pretending to slit it with a dramatic gesture. I don't flinch when he puts the blade against my throat, but it's scary enough for me to instantly play dead, making him drag my lifeless tiger corpse out of the pit.

"That wasn't so bad, right?" Knight's panting a little because I made him haul my dead weight, keeping my eyes shut and going totally limp. I didn't want to chance him cutting me, and I'm just glad that he's not pretending to skin me, too. I stand up, rubbing at the mud on my arms and legs and scratches from the sharpened stakes.

"Don't tell the parents." He squints blue-green eyes.

"I'm not a baby." I squint right back.

"Okay then. Now let's do a snare trap. I'm going to hang a loop of rope off a branch and you can walk into it. I'll catch you with it, and haul you up into the tree."

Knight's nicer to me as time goes on because I pass his repeated tests of bravery and friend-worthiness, and I'm even excited when he says one day, "I've got something cool to show you. We have to hurry or we'll miss it."

Knight leads me, Bonny, and Royal into the jungle behind the Ham Youngs' house. "Where are we going?" I whisper. The younger kids are behind me, and I'm getting really worried because I'm responsible for them. The Ham Youngs are serious locals. We'll get lickins for sure if we get caught sneaking around on their land.

"They're getting ready for a luau. Seriously, this is cool." Knight pushes me through some dense bushes toward a fenced area.

I hear a lot of hollering. A strange grunting and squeaking. Then, a terrible, high-pitched screaming—*a woman is being attacked!* Some awful crime is being done, and I'm about to see it. My heart is drumming so hard that I'm dizzy as Knight drags me forward by the arm.

Still screened behind some bushes, I peek into the large wooden pen we've arrived at.

Two brawny local men and a teenage boy, all stripped to the waist, are chasing a huge black and white spotted pig around the pen. It's as big as a sofa, and they've roped it by one foot. The pig's objecting, loudly, punctuated by the yelling and swearing of the men. Only one hind leg is captured by the lasso, but that seems to be enough to slow it down because it finally stops, and one of the men runs up and whacks the pig on the head with a leather mallet. The blow makes a hollow thump like dropping a melon, but doesn't do anything but make the pig scream even louder.

The little kids are crowded against me, their eyes as big as tennis balls. We're going to get in so much trouble if anyone catches us! I try to pull back, turn away, but Knight has his hand on the back of my neck.

"Watch!" he hisses in my ear, squeezing my neck hard. "I thought you weren't chicken."

I watch.

They whack the pig repeatedly, cursing, but it keeps darting and squalling, knocking the men aside with its big head, slamming them into the sides of the pen. Suddenly, one of the men darts forward, and a blade in his hand slashes deep into the pig's neck.

Blood fountains and sprays over the men's half-naked bodies. It smells like licking a penny.

The pig's screaming goes on and on, until finally it begins to drown in gurgles and wet sobs.

I remember how it felt to have a knife against my throat. Now I know what it looks like when something dies that way.

The great beast folds its tiny hooves and finally keels over.

I want to look away but can't. I want to retch but can't. I glance down at my sister and put my arm over her. Bonny's eyes are huge, and her face is greenish.

"Cool, isn't it?" Knight says. We don't say anything.

The men work the lasso around the pig's other hoof, tighten the loop, and toss the rope over a crossbar over the pen. The three of them, hauling on the rope, pull the pig so that it's hanging from its hind feet, swaying and massive. The man with the knife puts a white paint bucket underneath its head, then stabs it deeper in the neck. More blood gushes out, filling the bucket.

My eyes feel burned, as if I've stared too long at the sun—I haven't blinked since the whole horror show started.

After the blood bucket is filled, the knife man stabs the pig in the belly, and like when I gut a fish, saws from its hindquarters to under its front legs. The intestines spring out like pressurized stuffing, along with reek of blood and shit.

I've had enough and turn away, pulling Bonny with me—and this time Knight lets me go. The little kids break loose and run past us up to the house.

"Are they going to tell?" Mom and Pop wouldn't like it that I let Bonny see something like that.

"Royal knows better than to tell, and your sister better not," Knight says matter-of-factly, cracking his knuckles.

"She won't." *I hope.* But I bet we have to sleep together tonight from the nightmare.

"You can see my fort," Knight says graciously, since I haven't barfed and didn't run away until the very end. "I built it myself."

"Okay." I've never had an idea Knight would even consider, and this sounds relatively fun and harmless out of the selection of activities he's offered so far.

"This way." He leads me down the dirt road, and over to a good-sized guava tree. Pieces of wood, listing to and fro, are nailed to its trunk. Knight climbs, and I follow. Up, and up, and up.

Finally, sitting side by side on a one-by-four board nailed to branches at the top of the tree, we look out across Wainiha and the river mouth and the big sandbar, all the way to the ocean.

"I can check the surf from here." Knight already surfs with Darren out at Hanalei Bay and, even though he's just a ten-year-old, people already talk about how good he is. We stare out at the ocean. I hold the board I'm sitting on so hard my fingers hurt because it's swaying in the wind and there's nothing else to hang onto.

"Blown out," I say, referring to the surf conditions.

"It's only glassy in the mornings." He's condescending.

"I know that." I don't surf yet, but I do everything else in the water, and I resent his attitude. "This is a pretty boring fort. There's nothing to do up here."

He narrows eyes the color of sea ice at me. "I've got something else for us to do."

Uh-oh. Now I've pissed him off.

I follow Knight as he shinnies back down and lopes back to the house. I wait outside while he goes in and gets something. My heart speeds up when I see it's a gun.

"It's just a BB gun." Knight smiles and cocks it, leaning it on his shoulder like an old-time cowboy, then swinging it down to point at me. "You scared?"

"No," I lie. I can imagine him shooting me with it, can actually feel the sting of the BB pellets. "But I'm kind of tired. I think I'll see what the parents are doing." I can hear their voices, their laughter, even smell a little *pakalolo* on the air coming from the front porch.

Knight clamps a hand around my arm. "C'mon. You'll like this."

I seriously doubt it.

This time we go down the rutted, potholed dirt road toward our house. Because it's wet Wainiha, the potholes are mud puddles right now. Knight jumps into them with both bare feet and splashes me. I do it back, and he laughs. We splash and laugh that way until we get to a vacant lot, and it's the closest thing to fun I've ever had with him.

At the vacant lot, Knight swishes through the damp grass ahead of me to where a low barrier of sawhorses surrounds a very deep pit, at least fifteen feet straight down into raw red dirt, filled with water at the bottom.

I pull back, afraid of being pushed into the hole in some parody of Tiger Hunt. I'd never get out. I try to act casual as I peer from a distance. "What's this hole?"

"It's a cesspool for when they build the house on this property." Knight rests his BB gun on one of the sawhorses. "See the toads?" He points down into the pit. "This is target practice. One point if you hit the toad, two for a leg, and three if you get one in the eye."

I look over the sawhorse.

Hundreds of toads splash and croak in the water at the bottom of the pit.

I love toads and often play with them, putting them in little corrals made of sticks and pretending they're fairy broncos, or trying to race them with Bonny. The silly creatures come out and sit in the road after rains, so the streets are often covered with big brown squashed toads with their guts coming out of their mouths from the cars running over them.

Their eyes remind me of the octopus I caught—sparkly bronze and intelligent.

Knight takes aim and shoots into the pit. "Two points!" he crows. "Your turn." He pushes the gun into my hands.

I take it reluctantly. "I don't know how."

He takes the BB gun back, cocks it for me, hands it to me. "Point and shoot. Nothing to it. Like shooting toads in a barrel." He laughs.

"I don't want to."

Knight's eyes get narrow and his mouth thins out. He seems to get bigger right in front of me. "You scared?"

"No. I like toads, is all."

"Toby. Toady! Toby, Toady!" he chants. "I think that's a great name for you. I bet the kids at school will think so, too." He attends Hanalei School, and even though I'm homeschooling right now, this is a small island and the last thing I need is "Toady" catching on with the local kids.

I step up to the sawhorse, and rack up twenty points with the BB gun before he finally lets me go home.

Walking back to our house alone, I hate him for making me shoot the toads: poor helpless things, twitching and hopping and unable to escape.

And I hate me, for letting him push me around as if I couldn't escape, either.

CHAPTER SIXTEEN

THE BIG FLOOD

Pop's famous homemade canoe

Age: 9, Wainiha, Kauai, 1974

Winter's come with its stormy surf and heavy rain, and Pop's in one of his dark moods, and Mom's begun forgetting things and staring into space. Pupil checks show that she's smoking a lot of hash, and Pop is drinking daily.

With the rain outside, there's nowhere to get away to, and it's hard to stay quiet all the time. One day when I'm singing in the morning while jump roping in the lean-to garage, Pop comes roaring out of the house, red-faced and furious. "I told you to shut up and be quiet!" He paddles me with Mom's hairbrush, drags me into the house, and throws me onto my bed. I stifle the crying with a pillow and hear them fighting outside the door. *Will Mom have to go to the Best Facility again?*

Bonny comes in from wherever she'd disappeared to while Pop was spanking me and climbs into bed with me. We snuggle, trying to tune out the yelling, and I read her a book.

I wake up to the roar of rain on the old tin roof and stare out the window. It's raining so hard it seems like we're underwater, and the gray light of morning barely penetrates. Streams of water fly off the channels of the tin with such force it seems like we're in our own personal waterfall.

Mom's muttering swear words and running around putting down pots to catch the drips. The rain goes on and on, even worse than usual, and the power goes out. Bon gets clingy, sucking her finger and hanging on Mom, but I just wonder if it's going to get too dark to read. As long as I can read, I can get through anything. I put on my usual shorts and T-shirt, and Mom makes eggs at the gas stove with Bonny hanging onto her leg.

Pop turns on the battery-operated Weather Radio, holding it against his ear to hear above the roar of water outside. "Sounds like it's gonna flood."

I hear a familiar yell outside. Knight runs by our window, excitement in his voice cutting through the roar of the rain: "No school today! Hanalei School closed for flooding!"

Darren must have had his Weather Radio on, too. Hanalei School closes at least once a year when the river overflows its banks and no one can cross the bridge—so the flooding must also be happening in Hanalei.

"Let's go see if the river's coming up," Pop says as we hurriedly finish eating. We put on our see-through plastic ponchos and the rubber boots that are critical to life in Wainiha. I can't find mine so I put Mom's windbreaker on over my shorts and tee shirt.

When the rain backs off a bit, we walk to the front of the house —the part that's the abandoned store. The flood is already fifty feet away, mowing a liquid path across the road and swirling around the supports of the houses across from us. I've never heard of a flood coming this close to the store before, in all the stories of Wainiha's flooding. My heart speeds up and sweat breaks out inside Mom's big parka, warming me up in my skimpy clothes.

My friend the brown mare is tied in the vacant lot next to the river where it's already flooded! I jog down the road, my heels rubbing in my damp boots, and get ahead of Pop in his big green slicker. It's hard to see through the rain, but I can hear the mare, neighing and frightened, and when I spot her, the water's above her knees.

"Oh no!" I grab Pop's arm. I'm afraid to walk deeper into the floodwater than midway up my knee-high boots—I can see the full force of the river just beyond the mare, roiling past in angry choco- late swirls studded with logs. "We have to move her!"

"She's not our horse." Pop doesn't want to get into the locals' business, and the horse belongs to one of the local families. *"Don't remind them we're here"* has become our motto. So far it's worked—we haven't had the kind of trouble we hear still goes on elsewhere.

The mare neighs again. The water's still coming up, and she's going to be swept away and drown, I'm just sure of it. "We have to move her. The locals will understand we did it to save her." I push forward into the water. Water swirls up, filling my boots, cold and gritty. Every step is like trying to move with a cement block on my feet.

"Shit," Pop says, but he follows me.

We get to the horse and I shush her, petting her nose. I hold her neck rope, past my knees in the flood, as Pop unties the stakeout rope from the guava tree she's tied to. Once he has it undone, with me on one side and Pop on the other, we walk her toward dry ground. Mom and Bonny are standing on the dry area of the road, cheering us on.

The brown water has completely filled and overflowed my knee-high boots, making walking in the water slow and clumsy—but the mare, frightened of what's happening, breaks into a trot.

"Whoa!" I tug on the rope around her neck, but it isn't enough to slow her down. I trip and fall into the water, and it's enough to frighten the mare into a full gallop. Pop yells as the rope burns through his hands.

I get up out of the water, spitting and soaked from head to toe, as the mare gets out of the flood and gallops down the road, the rope flapping in against her flanks and scaring her even more.

"Hope letting that horse go doesn't get us in trouble," Pop says. "We aren't catching her now."

The rain slants down in cold, drilling pellets. I push my wet hair out of my face, shivering. My mouth tastes like salty dirt as I slosh toward dry ground, turning my head to watch trees and branches tumble by in a slow-motion dance as they move downriver. The twin metal bridges further back are still above the water, but hum with a high-frequency sound of strain.

The flood's broken the sandbar, and the river gushes into the ocean but swirls back because of waves churned up by the storm. Looking out to sea, the whole bay is a brown, churned-up expanse like foamy hot chocolate.

A woman comes splashing from the deeper end of the road, bedraggled and panicky. "Help us! We're stuck in our house!"

The phones and electricity are out, and no rescue vehicles can get through the flooded areas between us and Hanalei, anyway. Other residents have begun joining us from the drier end of town, and the adults put their heads together and come up with a plan. Someone brings a rope, and the biggest men go to the front and wade in to lead us to the house. Knight is right in there behind the men, clearly thrilled to be helping, and gestures to me to come. I grab onto the rope, not about to be left behind, and become part of a human chain heading back to the woman's house.

As we approach, the floodwaters rise to my waist, sucking and cold. I'm barefoot, having taken off the useless boots, clinging to the rope with both hands. The current is strong, pulling me sideways, as we finally reach the woman's driveway.

The whole bottom floor of her house is flooded, but it's a two-story, and two small children and the woman's elderly mother are clustered at the top of the exterior stairs. Beside the house, their VW Bug bobs in the current, tied by its bumper to a sturdy guava tree.

We walk the family all the way back to shallower water, passing them from person to person along the rope, and helping them to the dry part of the road.

By then I'm shaking with cold and have poked my foot on something. Pop spots me in the rescue effort and yells at me from his place on the rope. "Go home, Toby, before you get swept out!"

I slog back to the house reluctantly.

Fortunately, the water's stopped rising just short of the red gas pumps in front, and the pilot light hasn't blown out on the water heater so I get to clean up in a hot shower. The house is steamy inside because Mom is fixing food, a huge pot of rice and bean stew, for the rescued people and neighbors who collect on the porch of the old store.

Pop goes on to help with rescues all along the valley for the rest of the day. Cut off from any services by the flooding in Hanalei, it's up to us to help each other. The usual barriers are suspended—there's no rich or poor, local or *haole*. Just people helping each other survive and get through a crisis.

As the water begins to go down, Pop and two other men comb the banks, looking for two babies who were swept out of their mothers' arms as the women tried to escape a house further up in the valley.

He gets home as the sun is going down.

The rain has finally stopped. Foul mud and every kind of disturbed thing that the water plowing through the jungle has torn loose, has been deposited on the sandbar in giant mounds of rotting debris. At least ten cars are mixed in—most people didn't think to tie their vehicles to trees, like that VW Bug. The air is dank and misty, full of so much water it's like breathing rain, and reeks of mold and decay.

Pop and the men found one of the babies, eighteen months old, miles down the stream. She was still alive, stiff and nearly unresponsive with shock, and caught in a cat's claw vine studded with inch-long thorns.

"The baby was blue with cold." Pop is heroic, fully alive like the night when he and Awa chased away the local guys at the Forest House. His eyes are bright green, unclouded by alcohol or the dark moods he gets, even though he's shivering and wrapped in a towel next to the gas stove, whose door Mom has opened as a heat source. "She was barely breathing. A miracle she was alive. I helped untangle her from the thorns. One of the men put her under his shirt against his skin to warm her up, and we got her back to her mother. She's going to be okay."

The other baby, naked and drowned, was found on the beach the next day.

I dream about the drowned baby. I see its pale limbs among the wet driftwood on the shore, its face bluish and eyes open and glassy. Other times I dream about the baby hanging in the thorns above the water, alive but trapped and dying.

Bonny tells me she dreams about the babies, too, and we get in bed together when either of us has a nightmare.

After the flood and our part in the rescues, everyone greets us by name and waves when they drive by. People are saying it's the worst flood in Wainiha in fifty years, and by living through it and helping others, we've earned a place in that rugged valley.

CHAPTER SEVENTEEN

RIVER CAMPING

Tent in Wainiha with Bonny, Mom, and me

Age 9, Wainiha River vacant lot, 1973

The flood's gone down, but now Mom and Pop are arguing about money. Bonny and I go out in the yard to play with our kittens, and Mom gets picked up by a friend to drive into town to "get some space." Pop goes into the garage area to work on one of his fix-it projects.

Bonny and I are still playing in the back yard when Mom is dropped off in front of the store about an hour later.

"Help." She staggers toward us down the little path beside the house.

I run to grab her because she's hunched over and bleeding. She smells of booze and *pakalolo*, and there are hundreds of tiny glass cuts in her face and an oozing bump on her forehead.

"I'm okay," she says to our exclamations. "I was in a little accident, but I got a ride home. I'm okay."

"Mom was in a car wreck!" I bellow, fear making my voice too loud as she leans on me. Pop comes running out and helps her into the cottage.

He half-carries her into the bathroom and sits her on the toilet where the light from a bulb and the window are good. He's murmuring and talking to her, dabbing at her face with a towel. "What happened?"

"My friend was drinking. She ran the car into the cement abutment at the Hanalei bridge." Mom's eyes are shut and her face is pale except for the bleeding marks on it. I can see glass gleaming in the cuts. "I didn't have my belt on."

"Why didn't you get help in town?" He's trying to dab at the blood, his big hands shaking and clumsy.

"No insurance. And I told you, she was drinking. I didn't want to be around when the cops came. A guy gave me a ride home."

Bonny and I mill around anxiously in the doorway. "Should we call someone?" I ask. We don't have a phone, but we can go across the street to the Kaipakas' and borrow theirs. Never far from any of our minds is how much an ambulance will cost, and that we don't have health insurance.

"I think I can get this glass out." Pop pulls open the drawer in the sink, digs around. Mom lists sideways and rests her mashed, bloody head against the wall, shutting her eyes.

"Where are the tweezers, kids?" Pop demands.

We were playing with them outside, under the back steps, doing one of our pretend games. I think it was my idea to take the tweezers from the Medical Kit, a zippered bag that's strictly off-limits. Bonny and I glance at each other, horrified.

"WHERE ARE THE TWEEZERS?" Pop's turning red and scary.

Bonny and I turn and run outside. On our hands and knees in the dirt, we crawl around under the house, looking for the tweezers. Looking and looking, as Pop yells and rants overhead. Finally, we find them, and Bonny runs back in—she gets along better with Pop. I'm terrified of what's going to happen that we took something from the Medical Kit and didn't return it—one of the family rules that must never be broken, and now I understand why.

Pop is at it for what seems like hours, picking slivers and shards out of Mom's face. She yelps and cries and Pop growls and snarls as Bonny and I take turns hovering in the doorway. Finally, he puts her to bed, covered with Band-Aids. We're all so traumatized that Pop forgets to punish us for taking the tweezers.

But Mom still doesn't feel well. She isn't getting better, and lies around a lot feeling queasy. Eventually she goes to Dr. Goodman in Kilauea, who takes cash and trade—and she returns bright-faced with excitement. "I'm pregnant!"

Bonny and I are super excited and dance around the kitchen. "I know it's a boy this time," Mom says. They're not naming him James Theodore the Third. It's part of their rebellion against Grandpa Jim and Gigi, and I'm happy about that. I'm still trying to be the quiet, brave, rugged James Theodore the Third that Pop wants.

After some weeks and a lot of discussion, Mom and Pop decide to name the baby Francis, after Saint Francis of Assisi, who they feel a spiritual connection to.

"Francis. That's going to drive my parents nuts," Pop says with a grin.

BAD NEWS COMES TO US JUST AS THE RAINS ARE TAPERING OFF. THE Olonolong family wants to rent the Wainiha Store, restore it, and open it for business again. Our landlord gives us notice.

Mom and Pop can't find another house. There are no rentals on the North Shore that we can afford. We set up tents to live in across the street from the store, in a vacant lot behind Mom's friend Ricky's house.

Ricky lets us run a hose from her house to our campsite. Bonny brings her kitten, Macadamia Nut. We both had kittens until recently. Mine was an orange-striped one named Tommy. A neighbor's dog, loose off his rope, ran into our yard and snatched Tommy right out of my lap. He whipped the kitten back and forth and broke his neck before I could even stand up. Macadamia Nut, Bonny's kitten, had the presence of mind to climb on top of Bonny's head out of reach of the dog, and our screams brought the neighbor before the dog knocked Bonny over to kill Macadamia Nut, too.

The two of us get one tent that we share with Macadamia Nut, and Mom and Pop are in another. Pop builds a clear plastic roof that connects our two tents and protects our cooking area, which is a board nailed to a couple of Java plum trees to hold the Coleman stove. Pop sets up a sneaky trail, winding between the trees, so that no one will see us come or go from our illegal campsite.

The plan is that we park our car on the shoulder of a nearby road, and wait until no cars are coming. Then we run across the street and enter the jungle when no one can spot us. On the way out, we hide behind a big tree and then dart across the street when the coast is clear. If someone drives by, we try to look like we're just out for a casual walk.

Doing this whole plan while transporting our stuff from the store cottage to our jungle camp is not easy, and Pop decides it's not enough. We need to dye all of our clothes green so we're camouflaged. "We can't draw attention to ourselves. We have to lay low."

I sincerely hope we find another house to live in before school starts in another two months because Mom's already told us she doesn't feel healthy enough, being pregnant, to do homeschooling. I reluctantly surrender my stuff to the dye bucket, and stand in my panties with Bonny as Mom pushes all of our clothes down under the dark green dye water with a stick.

Mom giggles as she stirs the clothes with the stick, stuffing them down as they try to bubble up. "I feel like a witch, stirring my brew. This is ridiculous."

Pop gets mad at her laughing. He swells—it's like he expands with heat inside that turns him red, and he's really very big already. The colors of his eyes break into the parts that are blue and yellow as he opens them wide. He breathes deeply through his nose, his big surfer arms flexed. "Sue," he growls, and he sounds just like scary Grandpa Garth when he says her name like that.

Mom stops giggling and focuses on keeping all the clothes submerged.

"We're trespassing," Pop says, after she's being respectful again. "Whatever helps us blend in is worth doing."

One of Pop's dark moods is coming on. During those times, he doesn't want to be around people, and thinks they're all out to get us —but the people who live in the valley already know where we're camping, especially since we had to have Ricky's help, and she isn't the secretive type. The whole dye thing is stupid, but I don't want to get hit for saying so.

The dyed clothes turn awful mottled shades between green and brown, streaky and patchy and altogether horrible. Going to Hanalei School for fourth grade in homemade camouflage clothes is going to be social suicide—as if my red hair and freckles haven't doomed me enough.

"This will help us hide," Pop says as Mom hangs the clothes on a line to dry out. We don't say anything. Staring at the sad sight of the ruined clothes dripping onto the grass, I suspect that we're pretty weird.

I'd forgotten this, since we left La Jolla, because I haven't had to be in school. Embarrassment and disloyalty at the realization make my stomach hurt.

After we complete the move out of the store house and into our secret camp, we withdraw from all of our friends in the valley, pretending we aren't squatting in a jungle-covered vacant lot in the middle of town.

The very first week we're in our camp, the Tai Hook family goes by on the river next to us, fishing from their dinghy with its little outboard motor. We duck into our green tents in our green clothes, dousing our lamps in the waning light of evening.

"Eh, howzit! We know you're in there!" one of them singsongs in pidgin. "You silly Wilsons, you think you hiding!"

"I told you it was ridiculous," Mom whispers to Pop as we wait for their boat to go by in the gloom of the tent.

It's the beginning of summer when we move into our camp, which is pretty in Wainiha Valley and not too rainy. Pop builds a canoe out of a piece of aluminum roofing tin folded in half. He crafts a floaty *hau* bush outrigger to stabilize the canoe, and a couple of seats from boards. He finds most of the materials at the Hanalei dump, and it looks homemade—but it makes the river our playground. We can roam anywhere now.

To try out the canoe and explore a river we've always wanted to see, our whole family, with Knight along for the ride, puts our canoe on top of the Rambler with its surf racks, and drive to Kalihiwai, a deep valley just south of Hanalei.

The Kalihiwai River is wider and deeper than Wainiha, but no one lives in the valley lined with *hau* bush, buffalo grass, and a few gigantic shading albizia trees. We've only ever seen the river from way above on the graceful bridge that spans the magical-looking valley, or at the mouth of the river, where we love to jump in and ride the rapids on inner tubes into the ocean, haul them out, and do it again.

Quiet drifting and absorbing the sounds of nature in a meditative way are usually the only way Pop likes to do things, but having Knight along infuses an unusual degree of noise and excitement into our family adventure. Knight, Mom, and I paddle with mismatched paddles, Bonny sits in the bow, and Pop steers in the stern. We are able to make good time up the river, and our humble tin canoe glides easily through the water.

White egrets fly overhead, and blue herons stand like sculptures in the shallows. A *shama* thrush sings a liquid song, punctuated by mynahs scolding. The skin of the river seems solid, like jade-green Jell-O, until my paddle strikes it and breaks the surface. Watching the sun gild water striders sliding across the surface, and the way the water turns gold as my paddle slices into it, I get distracted and lose the pace Knight is setting.

"Hup, ho!" Knight grins, white teeth flashing over his tanned shoulder like we're a real Hawaiian canoe team. I laugh and we get back in rhythm, speeding up.

We slide under the high span of the bridge, cars overhead a distant whir, and on and on out of view of it. Pop heard there's a waterfall at the end, but none of us have been there, and it seems like we're the river's first explorers as we paddle on.

The channel gets narrower and shallower, *hau* bush clotting the banks with twisted, reaching branches. Pop steers us around protruding logs and clumps of pili and buffalo grass, and finally the canoe, loaded with people and riding low, runs aground on the muddy bottom. We all get out, and working together, haul the canoe up onto the overgrown bank.

We proceed on foot, finding a faint cattle trail dotted with manure that runs along the river. The valley narrows between steep green cliffs, makes a turn, and it gets even more overgrown. We walk for a mile or so, pushing through heavy buffalo grass and brush alongside the river which was now a stream—and then, around a clump of concealing trees, we find the Kalihiwai River's headwaters.

An eighty-foot silver plume of falls pitches in levels off a fern-covered cliff into a beautiful pool. A rainbow arcs above the splashing water. The swimming hole is sheltered by Java plum trees covered in dangling vines, and wild ginger sweetly scents the air. We stand, taking in the beauty, and it seems like we are the first people ever to find this place.

Knight climbs up onto a boulder and gives a Tarzan yell, beating his chest, and leaps into the pool in a cannonball.

I glance nervously at Mom and Pop, but they're both smiling—they like Knight. His energy and boldness are such a part of him and, by association, Darren, whom Pop admires. Since Knight is noisy and getting away with it, Bonny and I whoop and holler, jumping off the rocks into the pool.

There's nothing quite like being hot and sweaty and leaping into a cool mountain stream after such effort to get there. I love the feeling of plunging into the water, the way the chill smacks the breath out of me, and all the shades of green there are to be seen when I open my eyes underwater.

We climb up the cliffs and jump into the pool from higher and higher, and Mom and Pop swim below us, taking turns dipping under the waterfall and watching and cheering us on. Happiness bubbles inside me, so strong that I'm afraid of how I'll feel when it's over.

After an hour or so of playing, we're ready to go. "Can we swim back down the stream to the canoe from here?" Knight asks. "It's shallow, just sliding over the rocks."

"That's fine," Pop agrees. "We'll walk back on the trail and meet you kids there." *Another miracle.*

I'm not sure if it's because Bonny almost drowned, or Mom had her accident, or even something about the flood—but these days, Pop doesn't like us to take chances doing new things. He's cautious and paranoid, like making us dye our clothes.

The three of us slip 'n' slide downstream, slithering over algae-covered rocks as we follow the river between its narrow, overgrown banks, ruining already worn-out bathing suits. We bump, bruise, and shriek with glee, catching freshwater prawns with our hands and throwing rotten, waterlogged guavas at each other as we make our way down shallow rapids to eventually reach the canoe.

This adventure would never have been the same without Knight. Side by side, sliding over the rocks and laughing, I forgive him for the death of the toads.

CHAPTER EIGHTEEN

CAMPING DAYS

Wainiha camping

Age: 9, Wainiha vacant lot, Kauai, 1974

I make friends while we're camping that summer with a girl named Tita. Her mother, Bunny, lives way back in the valley with a surfer friend of my parents. Tita and I are crazy for horses, and our favorite games involve pretending to be horses, keeping elaborate horse society rules.

We can't talk. We can only speak in horse, snorting and whinnying. We take turns being the stallion or the lead mare, galloping along the shallow water of the river inside the sand bar beside the flood debris, kicking up water with our hooves. We become mates, an ordeal involving a good deal of biting and snorting as we act out pictures from The Big Book of Horses, growing mold from the damp in my tent.

I'm terrified that someone will see us neighing, tossing our manes, or rolling and pawing the sand. Somehow, that never happens.

We lie on our stomachs near the hot sand of the sandbar, legs floating in the lazy green river just down from the sun-bleached mountain of flood debris. We're playing with handfuls of tiny black tadpoles, herding them into pools hollowed into the sand bank. "Do you think we'll ever get real horses and be able to ride?" I ask.

"Definitely," Tita says. "I'll do anything to get a horse." Tita has round green eyes, long curly black hair, and a pointed, triangular face like a cat. I don't think she knows how pretty she is, and I'm afraid for her. Beauty like that just means someone might take you to the bushes and make you do sex things with them.

I suspect Tita already knows about sex, which Mom and Pop told me about after Mom got pregnant. It seems gross and weird to me, and I can't understand why grownups like to do it.

Tita won't talk about home. I've spent the night at Tita's house and heard her mom fighting with her current man. I wish Tita could come live with us in our camp on the river.

I chase a few more black tadpoles with my hands into one of our little ponds. Unlike thumb-sized, green frog tadpoles, these tiny black ones stay small and emerge as perfect little toads when they're ready, the size of a pinkie fingertip.

"I have to go back to Hanalei School at the end of the summer. Mom says we can't afford more Calvert School, and she's not up to doing it this year." I've told Tita about the bullying at Hanalei School and that I'm scared to go back.

"It'll be okay. I'll look out for you."

Tita's tough and speaks pidgin most of the time, and she scraps dirty when she has to. She's Portuguese, almost as good as a local, and no one gives her any crap. Minka's still around, and I look forward to seeing my old friend—but Minka still gets hassled.

Tita rolls on her back and I do, too, and we glance across the river at our campsite. The only way you can tell it's there is a little gleam off one corner of the plastic roof, where one of the branches Pop put up for camouflage blew away.

"I hope you guys find a house by the time summer's over," Tita says. "You don't want to be camping in the winter."

"I know." The Big Flood is never far from our minds, and even if that doesn't happen again, winter in Wainiha would be terrible in a canvas tent.

I COME HOME FROM PLAYING WITH TITA TO FIND MOM LYING IN bed in our parents' tent. Pop's in Hanalei fixing toasters and vacuums. She's moaning and crying, rolling back and forth with her arms over her belly. Bonny's with her, eyes big in the gloom of the tent, sucking on her finger with fright.

"It's the baby," Mom gasps. "Go get Ricky."

Ricky's a good friend of Mom's, a petite dark-haired single mom with a little girl, Malia. Malia's a year younger than Bon and plays with us a lot. I run to Ricky's house and, jumping and babbling, manage to convey that Mom's sick and it involves the baby. Ricky comes without question, hurrying after me down the short path from her house to our campsite, the green water hose from her house marking the trail beside us.

"I think I'm losing the baby," Mom says to Ricky, weeping in a way that twists my guts into knots.

Tears sting my eyes like bees. A great sob stuck inside my chest cuts off my breathing. *Losing the baby?* We all want it so much. Mom's four months along, and we've already looked at a book on pregnancy and can already imagine our little brother, shaped like a bean, with his rebellious name Francis. Bonny's crying, tears making her eyes bright green as she snuffles around the plug of her finger.

Ricky's voice is firm but kind. "Why don't you girls go up to my house for a while? Play with Malia."

"We don't want to." I let out the sob, a rasping cry, and wrap my arms around myself to keep from hugging Mom, who I can see is in too much pain to be touched. "We want to help."

"You can't help her with this." There's finality in Ricky's voice.

"Go!" Mom screams, and we run away up the path holding hands.

I try to play with the younger girls and stay distracted at Ricky's house, but I can't stop thinking about Mom, in pain. Eventually Ricky comes back, pale and shaky, her black hair escaping from her ponytail. "I think she's doing a little better. You can go back now."

Mom's still in bed, no longer crying—just staring at the tree silhouettes on the wall of the tent in a way that reminds me of when the crazy started, which squeezes my chest with a new feeling—*fear.* I get in bed with her, and Bonny does too, and we sandwich her between us, stroking her arms and hair until Pop gets home.

We're too worried to eat much of the simple rice-and-veggies dinner Pop makes, but Mom says the cramps are better and she's not bleeding very much, so after our evening reading by kerosene lamp-light, we go to bed as usual.

I wake up to the sounds of moaning and crying. I jump out of my sleeping bag and unzip the tent.

Mom's illuminated in the light of a lamp that's hanging from the tent pole. She's sitting on a white paint bucket, hunched over, her arms wrapped around her waist. Pop is rubbing her shoulders and stroking her hair as she moans in deep pain. She weeps when the pain passes.

This seems to go on for hours. We're all scared by the amount of blood in the bucket, and Pop sends Bonny and me back to our tent. They finally decide to go to the hospital.

Pop's holding a small Diamond Strike matchbox. He brings Bonny and me close in the lamplight and pulls the box open. "This is Francis."

Lying inside is a tiny baby about the length of Pop's thumb. He doesn't have a big head or look funny—he's proportioned just right, like the little plastic baby that I got for my Barbie. His eyes are closed, his mouth turned up in a smile. His hands and feet have ten digits. He has tiny hairs on his head, a trace of eyebrows, and transparent eyelids show us blue eyes. He even has a tiny penis.

I could stare at my brother's face forever.

I expected him to look like a tadpole or something, but he's utterly perfect. He doesn't seem dead; he looks like he's sleeping there in a little bed.

This is the only brother I will ever have.

I don't know how I know, but I know it's true. My eyes fill up with tears so that I can't see him anymore. My chest hurts so bad I can't breathe as Pop closes the matchbox. I swallow the big hard lump of grief down from my chest to my belly so I won't make things worse for Mom, who looks pale and sweaty as she packs paper towels into her panties to catch the blood. Pop has to half-carry her to the car. I'm afraid she'll die, but I don't let that out either.

Following Mom and Pop's staggering progress down the trail, we go to Ricky's house. Ricky turns on the porch light and whispers to us to go sleep with Malia. Bonny and I sneak in to snuggle together with Malia in her little bed as Mom and Pop drive to the hospital, over an hour away.

Pressed between the younger girls, breathing their little-girl smell, feeling their warmth, I'm comforted. Malia's gentle and beautiful with big brown eyes and wispy chocolate-colored hair. She has one hand with the fingers fused together, and tonight I hold it as she sleeps. I like to feel how soft her special hand is. Somehow it makes her even prettier.

Our parents come back to the camp the next morning. Mom's still white looking and shaky. Pop tucks her into bed under their quilt, and she turns away from us toward the wall of the tent. The sun's up now, and the trees make dancing shadows on the canvas, and she watches them. She's not speaking but not crying either.

She didn't die, which would be the worst, but now I'm terrified of the crazy coming back.

"Bonny and Toby." Pop's as serious as I've ever seen him. His green eyes are red-rimmed, his face full of wrinkles I've never seen before. "Let's go bury your brother."

I look at Mom, but she makes a shooing gesture from her nest of quilts. "I can't come. I said goodbye already."

Pop picks up the shovel we use for burying our poop and walks into the jungle with the matchbox in his hand.

Bonny and I hold hands as we follow Pop. Bonny's crying in loud gulping sobs, so I can too, and it's a relief to let the pain in my chest out in tears and snot as my great big feelings overwhelm me noisily. Pop picks just the right spot under a Java plum tree facing the river. He lets us hold the matchbox to look at Francis while he digs a hole with the shovel.

When we open the box, Francis has become just blob, a melted pinkish outline.

"What happened to Francis?" My voice comes out squeaky with horror. "Why is he melting?"

Pop keeps digging, but he says, "Babies his age are so delicate that as soon as oxygen touches them they begin falling apart."

I can't cry anymore; it's too awful. Bonny and I lean against each other and close the box, holding it in both our hands.

Francis would have been a beautiful baby. A sweet boy. A capable, kind, intelligent, handsome man. Somehow I know these things about him.

We put the matchbox in the hole when it's good and deep. We cover it with rich black soil from around the tree's roots. Bonny and I press it down with our hands, and leave our handprints deep in the dirt. The earth is a blanket and we are tucking him in; that makes me feel a little better.

Pop holds our dirty hands, and we stare down at the fresh black pile of soil. "Francis has gone back to heaven," Pop says. "We don't know why, but we know he lives on and maybe he'll pick another family near us to come to next time. We might even see him again, in another body." Mom and Pop believe that we have many lives, and that children are in heaven, choosing families to come live with to work out their karma.

I don't feel comforted by this, because Francis is not going to be working out his karma as a part of *our* family, and I so wanted him to.

Back at camp, Pop gets out his guitar. He's kept playing since the Forest House and is studying slack-key, a Hawaiian sound with a relaxed plucking technique. The guitar has a circle of black resin and inlaid abalone, and a neck of dark rosewood. Pop sits in his canvas folding chair and plays, rocking gently back and forth, one ankle over the other knee to hold the guitar.

I wrap my arms around my legs and rest my chin on my knees, watching the way his big fingers move among the strings and coax beauty out of them.

He plays. And plays. The notes cover us softly, drifting feathers brushing us, touching us like the coins of light falling though the trees.

Mom lies in bed and stares at the wall of the tent, and we all eventually climb in bed with her. We press our bodies against her until darkness covers us, and the day we lost Francis is finally over.

CHAPTER NINETEEN

RIVERSIDE WINTER

Age 9, Wainiha River, 1974

A fog of sadness settles over our campsite next to the river. Pop drives into Hanalei early in the mornings so he can surf and then check what fix-it jobs he has at the little store. Mom cooks our morning oatmeal mush on the camp stove, then goes back to bed, and Bonny and I start at Hanalei School.

We pretend we came from one of the houses out by Knight's, and are picked up by the school bus in front of the old red gas pumps by the Wainiha Store, which still isn't open yet but is now always full of busy carpentry sounds.

Baby luaus are a big Hawaiian tradition left over from ancient times, because if a baby made it to one year old, it had a good chance of living to maturity. A baby luau is a time to celebrate and revel as much as a wedding. Henry Tai Hook, who lives next to the store, gives a baby luau for his first grandson and it's the biggest Kauai has seen: there are five *imu* pigs, a hundred pounds of *poi*, a lake of beer, and five hundred rowdy guests from all over the island and Oahu who overrun Wainiha. The family takes boats out on the river, and they fall drunkenly out right next to our campsite, carousing and celebrating into the wee hours.

We're invited, but not attending luaus or big local parties is our family policy. I wish we could go have fun too, but so far, the family policy of lying low has kept us out of trouble. Pop says that this is because, as the evening wears on, people drink too much, things turn aggressive, and someone usually thinks of scrapping with the *haoles* for entertainment. "Hate Haole Day" can be declared at any time.

Tita sticks by me at school. Her protection helps things go better, but Kira Yoshimura hasn't forgotten that she hates me. She's much the same: pretty and popular, and nasty as a small blue centipede. She gets my old nickname, Haole Crap, going again.

Bonny's in first grade, and she makes friends with Kira's little sister. Bonny's easy nature and good looks keep her from having the hassles I've had. At least, that's what I tell myself when I see Bonny playing with kids I can't even talk to. That bad, jealous feeling I had at the ballet studio in La Jolla sometimes makes me mean to Bonny when we're alone.

I keep an eye on Mom all of the time when we're at the campsite on the river, worrying because she is still not right after losing Francis. She reads a lot on a wood pallet platform that Pop sets up next to a birdbath shrine with statues, crystals, and incense on the spot where Francis is buried. It's comfortable out there, with a futon and a flowered bedspread.

Both Mom and Pop are reading the Bhagavad Gita and studying Yogananda's teachings. *"The wise do not indulge in grief for things that are inevitably changeable and evanescent. Those who always weep and complain that life is filled with bitter things reveal the narrowness of their minds."* Mom writes down her favorite Yogananda quotes on a curling 3x5 card tacked to the Java plum tree in our kitchen area.

Bon and I like to lie out there and read our books, too, with Macadamia Nut, Bonny's kitten, tucked between us. We're all comforted by Francis's nearness in his spot under the Java plum tree.

One day a beautiful glossy black bird with a reddish breast and a white rump comes to the birdbath, which is usually just visited by mynahs, doves, and cardinals. The shama thrush, a songbird brought to Kauai in 1931 from Malaysia, makes his visits a regular thing, singing intricate melodies and sipping water above Francis's grave. He even sings to Pop's guitar music, enchanting us all.

"I think Francis's spirit is visiting us," Mom says. She and Pop decide that Francis has picked up an interim body in the form of the shama. I'm skeptical, but it seems to comfort them, so I don't say anything.

Macadamia Nut has been a great cat at the camp. She stalks prey all day, keeping our campsite relatively mouse-free, and sleeps in the tent at night with Bonny and me. Now a sturdy, gray-striped teenager who goes everywhere with Bonny, Macadamia Nut draws a bead on Francis in his shama thrush bird form—and thus, Mom and Pop decide the kitten must go.

Pop takes Macadamia Nut to the dump, where all unwanted things end up. The dump is a cliff over a gulch, and people pull their cars up and throw stuff off the edge. They leave anything potentially useful on the side for others to pick through. We can also approach from below and look through the trash pile down in the gulch. Most of our household items have come from the "Hanalei Department Store."

Bonny is as hysterical and devastated at losing her kitten as I was about Argos. I feel her pain as she screams and cries, totally unlike her usual mellow self. Our parents' peace is disturbed, so they leave to go visit Ricky.

I hold Bon as she sobs. "Macadamia Nut'll be okay. Someone will fall in love with her at the dump and take her home. She's so pretty and sweet."

This only makes Bonny cry harder. I can't take the place of her kitten or make it okay, and she cries herself to sleep. But Macadamia Nut is a survivor, and I hope she'll find a new home from someone who picks her up at the dump.

We continue pretending we aren't living in the vacant lot, and with the lack of rentals, it's fully December when we finally hear of a house to move into. We're more than ready by then for a real house. Half a year in the campsite with mud, mosquitoes, and centipedes that keep trying to get into our relatively dry tents have worn down even Pop's enthusiasm for outdoor living.

We get a commitment from some landlords that we can rent their house in Haena, a few miles away and a lot drier area—but there's a catch. The owners, who live in Canada, come spend the summers in the house every year, and we have to agree to move out when they return. Next June seems like a lifetime away, so Pop agrees and we sign the lease.

The day before the house is available to move into, we're awakened by a roar like a tidal wave coming in, and the stench of diesel fumes.

A backhoe and tractor are attacking our lot—the owner is clearing it for building!

The trees scream and moan, chainsaws wail, and our hidden homestead is exposed: shabby, mildewed, and tattered after a long six months. It feels like standing in front of a crowd, having your dress ripped off your body.

The shame and embarrassment are almost worse than the pain of what's happening. Not quite, though, because the shama is gone. Our birdbath shrine is crushed, and Francis's grave is annihilated as the Java plum tree falls, its leafy crown landing in the river.

Pop waves his arms and runs out to stop the tractors as they get close to the tents.

"We'll have a house tomorrow," he says. "Just let us pack up and sleep here tonight. Please."

The local guys driving the tractors look down from the machines like they feel bad when they see Bonny and me and Mom, clutching each other in front of the tents. I can tell they didn't know we were there.

"We'll go up to your tents today." The foreman won't look at us.

"But you gotta be out tomorrow. Anything you leave, we goin' tear down and clear out."

We throw everything into our sleeping bags in panic, hauling it past the backhoe and tractor to Ricky's house. As before, she takes us in without question.

"Someone should have told you those backhoes were coming!" she says. "They should have warned you, given you time to pack up."

"Everyone knows we're here on the river. Those assholes wanted to crush us in our tents just because they can. I swear they only stopped the tractors because of the kids," Pop rages. "I can't believe no one told us that lot was getting developed. Fucking off-island *haoles*!"

I agree with everything he's saying, even while aware of the irony that we were once off-island *haoles* ourselves, and have been secretly trespassing on someone else's land. Still, six months of living there has attached us to this little bend in the river. This wasn't the way we wanted to leave: everything we own bundled in sheets and trash bags filling the Rambler, crashing at Ricky's house on the floor.

The parents get drunk and high that night as Bonny, Malia, and I play Barbies in her room and pretend we're okay—but I'll never forget that moment of standing in front of a house made of cloth in my nightgown while a tractor advanced.

The minute we pack up the last of what we can carry, the tractors drive forward and our campsite is obliterated. There's nothing to show that we were ever there, as they scrape away the mildewed tents and our kitchen area. Raw red gashes of track in the dirt wipe out our camouflage paths and secret glade, and a woodchipper's scream follows us as we drive the Rambler, loaded to the ceiling, to our new rental.

CHAPTER TWENTY

THE JOSEPHSON HOUSE

Me napping

Age: 10, Haena, Kauai, 1975

The Josephsons' seasonal summerhouse, our new rental, is the nicest place we've ever lived on Kauai: two stories, carpeted, with vaulted ceilings and a great big deck around the whole second story. Bonny and I each get our own room. The house even has a fenced yard with a *kamani* tree, and a tire swing with such an immensely long rope that riding on it feels like flying.

Mom and Pop are excited because the house will pass muster with Gigi and Grandpa Jim, soon visiting. Pop has given up his fix-it business and got a job cooking at The Anchorage again, the steak-and-seafood restaurant within walking distance.

"Just in the 'Nick' of time," Pop says, making a pun. "Crack out the jeweled corks!"

This phrase arose because Bonny asked our parents, back in La Jolla after one of those endless "lady lesson" country club dinners, "What do ladies do when they have to toot?"

Pop's answer, "They wear jeweled corks in their butts," has become an ongoing joke. It's funny, but I feel a little bad. Gigi doesn't "get" us, but it seems like she cares in her bossy way. She's never stopped sending packages and presents. Her last gift, a giant box of Crayolas, got eaten by cockroaches at our camp. She would not have found it funny like Mom and Pop did when they saw brightly colored cockroach droppings all over the tents and the cooking area.

We buy non-camouflage clothes at the thrift store and settle into the strangeness of hot showers and flush toilets. I have trouble sleeping in a real bed without the sounds of the river and the trees all around me. I'm haunted by the drowned baby, by Francis's crushed grave, by the way the tractors woke us up that last day, and I sneak in to sleep with Bonny night after night.

I make a new friend in our neighborhood, Melanie Adams. Melanie's the first girl I've met on Kauai besides myself to have red hair. We compare our colors: hers is a thick, wavy dark auburn. Mine is a straight, fine strawberry blond. And freckles: hers are big and patchy, the size of peppercorns and dimes. Mine, tiny as sand grains. It feels great to not be a "carrot top ginger freak *haole*" alone.

Mel's a little chubby and doesn't climb trees or go fishing, but she has a great set of Barbies to play with in her family's immaculate condo. Her mom always shoos us out, though.

"Go outside and play!" she scolds. "Get a little exercise, Melanie!"

There are no kids Bonny's age nearby, so she tags along with us as we find ways to stay entertained outside. Melanie decides we should sneak into the Anchorage restaurant where our dad works and hers is the general manager.

"I'll show you how to get in," Melanie says. Bonny and I glance at each other. Bon's eyes, which vary depending on her mood, go as green as new leaves. I wonder what color mine are, and I suspect they're almost as bright as hers at the naughtiness of this idea. We'll get in so much trouble if we're caught! But Melanie is the manager's daughter—she can probably get us off.

It's morning, and the restaurant doesn't open until eleven-thirty. Melanie leads us around the back of the restaurant past fruity-smelling, fly-buzzing dumpsters, to a gray metal door. The three of us squat, plastered against the back wall. Melanie looks around like Inspector Clouseau in polyester, checking to see if anyone's around. I'm imagining my cloak of invisibility as Melanie reaches up and turns the doorknob. It turns easily, and the door swings open. It's heavy, and she actually has to hop up and stop it from banging into a concrete block wall. She sneaks into the dim interior to look around; after all, Melanie can always pretend she's looking for her dad, but we've already been told by ours we aren't allowed to go over to the restaurant and bug him.

She pokes her head out and gestures. "Coast is clear."

We scuttle inside. Dim and shadowy, steel counters and unfamiliar equipment gleam silver in the low light. The floors are covered with strange raised rubber flooring, full of holes, that sticks to our slippers. We follow Melanie's plump square bottom through the cavern of the kitchen into the dining area.

The space looks vast to me, the tables little islands of resined wood surrounded by chairs. In the distance, framed by plate glass windows, the ocean ripples like restless turquoise silk, trimmed in bright yellow beach and shaded by ironwoods and coconut palms.

"I like to take sugar packets," Melanie whispers. "But there's other stuff too." She shows us where these goodies are stashed in the waitress station. We stuff our pockets with sugar packets, saltines, tiny plastic vats of grape jelly, and foil-wrapped butter pats.

My mouth is watering. We're still on a strict no-sugar, no-refined products, no-meat diet. I've never really believed that these things that taste so delicious are *badforyou*. I wolf down the school hot dogs "chopped processed meat leftovers from a death factory" and the cubes of Jell-O "artificially colored horse hooves" with no difficulty.

We sneak back out the way we came, rustling with stolen loot under our shirts and in our pockets, and sprint from the back of the restaurant into a nearby *kamani* grove. On the other side of the strip of majestic trees with their large, paddle-shaped leaves is a sandy-dirt road leading to a row of rich-people houses. Flushed with the rush of burglary, the three of us hunker down in the wide roots of one of the trees to enjoy the spoils of our raid.

My favorite order for the sandwiches I construct is a saltine cracker with butter smeared on it, sugar sprinkled on the butter, and then another cracker with grape jelly on top of that. Silence reigns except for the crackle of the wrappers and the smacking of lips and licking of fingers. We eat everything we stole until there's nothing left but the sugar packets, and then we rip the corners off those and pour them down our throats.

Thoroughly bloated, we look around for what to do next. Melanie pulls a fistful of cardboard Anchorage Restaurant matchbooks out of her pocket. "Let's make a fire."

"That's dangerous," I say automatically. After all those months camping under trees with a camp stove, I know fire is not to be played with.

"Oh, come on. Don't you want to see how these leaves burn?" Melanie holds up a red and brown leaf the size of a small skillet and fans herself with it. "Don't be chicken."

I can never resist a dare. "Okay. But we have to clear an area around the fire so it doesn't spread." We make a pile of the leaves, scraping them together and leaving a six-inch leafless dirt circle around the pile.

We each get a matchbook and light a leaf or two. I enjoy

holding the stem of one of the leaves, holding the flame to the edge and watching the sharp and sour smoke curl up in graceful ribbons. I'm so busy lighting each leaf and watching it burn that I don't realize the main leaf pile has exploded into a merry blaze until it's too late.

"What did you do?" I yell, as the flames leap and crackle. It's so hot I can't get close enough to scrape the dirt ring wider.

"I just lit it," Melanie says, her broad speckled forehead wrinkling in a frown. "I guess we should have brought some water to put it out."

"Or something to smother it." I stomp on a finger of flame that's made it into the surrounding leaves that form a thick mat under the trees.

Bonny has withdrawn against the trunk of the tree. Her finger's in her mouth where it goes when she's scared, and her eyes are wide. I focus on running around the fire and stomping on the escaping flames, but my heart is thundering with terror. Melanie doesn't seem to know what to do at all. "Stomp out the ones that are getting away!" I yell.

It's not working. The fire's spreading, jumping over our narrow dirt band, so I rip my T-shirt off my head and start beating the flames with it. "Knock them out before they can spread!" I yell at the other girls.

Just then a pickup truck pulls up beside us on the road and stops. Knight's dad, large, intimidating surfing legend Darren Richardson, jumps out. He grabs a gallon jug of water and a beach towel out of the back of his truck.

"What the fuck are you girls doing?" he bellows in his booming voice, beating out the fire with the beach towel and throwing the water on the rest. Melanie and Bonny burst into tears and that means I can, too.

"We didn't realize it would get so big." I put my T-shirt, burnt and holey, back on as I sniffle with the aftermath of fright.

"You girls are in big trouble," Darren says, putting his hands on his hips. "If you were my boys, you'd be getting lickins."

We all cry harder. Darren puts us all in the cab of the truck when he's sure the fire's out. He takes Melanie back to her mom first.

Her mom, wearing pedal pushers and curlers, is shocked. She shoves Melanie inside, then turns back to face us. Hands on her hips, she declares, "I knew you hippies were a bad influence!"

Melanie doesn't say a word about how it was all her idea, and I give her a stink eye squint. I doubt her mom will let us play together any more.

Darren drives us back to our house. Bonny and I get spankings with the back of Mom's hairbrush, and lectures about fire too. I know we deserve it, and I'm glad that at least no one knows about us breaking into the Anchorage.

MOM AND POP NEED TO GO INTO LIHUE FOR SOME ADULT STUFF, so they take us to their friend Ginger's house at the remote back of Hanalei Valley to be babysat. I'm annoyed about this, but after the Fire Incident we aren't allowed to roam unsupervised as much.

Ginger lives with her son Kala in a ramshackle dwelling across the street from a pasture with the smooth, olive-green eel of the Hanalei River on the far side of it.

Tiger Espere, the Hawaiian surfer who taught Pop to throw net, is Kala's dad, which automatically makes Kala cool. He's a wiry black-haired boy Bonny's age, full of energy.

"Kala, show them around." Ginger's busy washing dishes. She's a tall blonde woman with a big smile. "Go play."

"Let's go see the river," I say after we've looked at Kala's room and I've verified that there's nothing much to do there. TV still hasn't come to Kauai because of its remoteness and rugged mountains, and Kala's trucks and blocks don't interest me. I'm hoping to see if there are fish in the river.

"We gotta cross da pasture. Get cows in there." Kala speaks pidgin, which we aren't allowed to at home. I can speak it, but don't do it much because I think it sounds lame for *haoles* to speak pidgin, like we're trying too hard.

"We'll take sticks," I tell him. So, armed with some stout lengths of *hau* bush, we set out across the pasture.

Halfway across, we see one of the cows, a shiny black one, acting funny. It trots back and forth, tosses its head, snorts. It's acting like Ferdinand, the main character in one of our favorite picture books. We drop the sticks because they aren't big enough to swat a fly on the cow's shiny black flanks.

"Let's hurry." I grab Bonny's hand. Kala grabs her other one. We jog, headed for a line of trees by the river. Whatever this cow's problem is, we should be okay over there.

The animal drops its head, snorting and pawing the ground.

It's not a cow at all. It's a bull, and it fires out of the corner like a sleek, thundering, two-ton missile, aiming right for us.

"RUN!" I yell. Coward that I am, I let go of my sister's hand and run as fast as I can, making for a single tree in the middle of the field. Bonny stumbles and falls with a cry. I'm horrified that I let go, and turn to look, but the bull runs right over her and keeps coming after me. Kala falls to the ground, too, and now it's just me, running for my life, with the bull right behind.

I reach the tree, a sturdy guava, and jump into the branches, hauling myself up just as the bull rams the trunk with his head, shaking it so hard I almost fall out. I cling like a monkey, and glance back expecting to see my sister's mangled corpse—but she and Kala, hand in hand, are running back and reach the fence, scrambling through.

The bull makes another run at the tree, ramming it. He snorts, paws the ground, stomps back and forth. I try to climb higher, but guavas aren't tall trees. The branches are barely above the bull's head and I can't get any higher because they're too thin. I hang on tight as the bull takes out his wrath on the slender trunk. All of the tree's guavas fall into the grass, shaken loose by the ramming.

Kala and Bonny have reached the house, yelling for Ginger. Ginger comes running out, carrying a section of two-by-four.

"Help!" I scream, as the tree whips back and forth under the bull's latest assault.

"I'm coming!" Ginger runs across the pasture, waving the two-by-four at the bull. "Shoo! Get lost!"

I'm sure I'm about to watch a scene twice as grisly as the pig killing in Wainiha, as the bull swings around to face her and shakes his head. His stubby horns are still lethal enough to leave scars on the guava tree. He paws the ground, rolling red-rimmed eyes at her.

Ginger never slows down as she runs across the pasture toward us. "Get!"

Ginger whacks the bull on the rump with a smack like hitting a home run in softball. The bull gives a startled, indignant snort. She hits it again, and it yelps this time. I didn't know bulls could yelp. "Get out of here!"

The bull snorts one more time, then gallops away to join the rest of the cows in the far corner of the pasture.

Ginger is an Amazon, a Viking conqueror, and an avenging angel all in one. She'd look good in a helmet and chain mail. My imagination turns the two-by-four into a battle-axe.

I'm awed by her.

"Come on down, honey. What were you kids thinking of, coming out here!" Ginger scolds and admonishes as I climb down out of the tree. We walk, holding hands, toward the fence.

I keep a wary eye on the bull. Once I'm on the safe side of the fence I'm ashamed of my cowardice and burst into tears. "I feel so bad. I left Bonny and Kala behind to get trampled."

"He chased you so the little kids were okay. You led the bull away from them," she says, kindness in her light-speckled blue eyes. "Never run away from bulls. Face them, yell loud, whack them if you can. He went for you because you were running out in front."

This sounds like good wisdom, for both bulls and bullies.

CHAPTER TWENTY-ONE

LILIKOI SUMMER

Tita, Bonny, and me at the Estate

Age: 10, Haena, Kauai, 1975

Bon and I are playing in the yard on the swing when Knight and his much shorter buddy, Chris, come walking by. They're armed with sticks and whacking everything in their path. Knight and I get along fine at school, but I haven't had any adventures with him since our trip up the Kalihiwai River, which seems like forever ago. Now that I'm ten, I've started to notice boys in a different way, and want them to like me.

The boys whisper a conference and come over to our fence.

"Hey, Toby. Come play with us," Knight commands.

I glance at Bonny. She gives a little headshake, but I ignore that. "Sure."

I follow the boys out of our gate and down the unpaved, sandy-dirt road. We talk about school and how terrible the teachers are, and how there hasn't been much surf lately. The boys are being nice, and we've reached Bunker Spreckels's house, a cedar sprawl with a big spreading *kamani* tree in the yard. Bunker is a rich young guy who only lives there sometimes, and all of our parents have been to his crazy giant parties.

"Looks like no one's home. Let's check it out," Chris says. I'm nervous about getting caught trespassing but follow the boys into the yard. They roam around and seem to be looking for stuff to take.

"I have an idea. Let's play rescue," Chris says, holding up a length of rope he found under the big house.

"Sounds lame." We're getting older now, and I'm too savvy for any variations on Tiger Hunt.

Chris narrows his eyes at me. He's one of those boys who's never going to grow very tall and is angry at everyone about it, pushing harder and being meaner to prove something. Knight is still looking around the house, his back to us.

Chris persists. "You're going to be taken captive by a tribe of hostile Indians."

"Hell no. I don't think so." I get ready to run, turning toward the gate we just climbed through.

"You're not in much of a position to argue. It's two against one." Chris snaps the rope between his hands.

I can run really fast, but Knight's bigger and faster than either of us. If he thinks this idea is stupid, it won't happen. *Oh, Krishna Buddha God, please don't let it happen.*

Knight walks toward me, smiling—and it's never good when he grins like that. "Yeah, Toby. You're a captive. And we'll come rescue you."

I bolt for the fence, and the game is on.

Knight catches me easily around the waist and hauls me, with Chris pinching and slapping and whooping in an Indian brave imitation, back toward the tree.

I don't fight them because I'll get hurt worse if I do. I'm hoping the rescue part will be more fun than the captivity part. Our parents are friends, and Darren will give Knight lickins if he's so mean that I have to tell on him. After our fun adventure on the Kalihiwai River, I hope Knight's still a friend, even if I know Chris isn't.

All these thoughts flicker through my mind in an instant.

They tie me to the big *kamani* tree. I let them do it.

"Not too tight. Don't want to cut off her circulation," Knight says. He doesn't plan to hurt me. Lighting a fire at my feet to burn me at the stake has already occurred to my overactive imagination—now *that* would be bad.

"We'll be back soon to rescue you," Chris says, with an evil grin, and he and Knight lope off down the sandy road.

I wait. I test my bonds. I wait some more. I glance around. The wind rustles in the *kamani* leaves overhead. Something rattles in the empty, deserted party house. The bark of the tree is harsh and scratchy on my bare legs and arms.

"Hey!" I yell. "Any year now!" I inject my voice with sarcastic vigor. "This is lame, you fuckers!" I use really bad words, hoping to lure them out of where they're hiding, waiting for me to cry and beg. "Pricks! Assholes! Sissy rug munchers!"

I wait some more.

Slowly, it dawns on me that they'd never sit around waiting for me to cry this long—they'd get bored. Clearly, Chris and Knight aren't coming back.

I try to pick at the knots but can't reach them. One of the boys must have been a Boy Scout because I can't get them loose, can't twist my hands around. I can't bend enough to chew on the ropes either.

I'm going to be stuck here forever, unable to sit down or pee, my legs throbbing with pain from standing immobile.

But there are other houses back here. Surely someone will drive along and find me.

Time passes, and I eventually work the ropes down a little lower so I can squat.

By the time a passerby on the dirt road sees me, dark is approaching. I've screamed myself hoarse, calling for help.

I don't know the kindly woman driving by who finds me. She really has to work to get my knots untied, and her exclamations of horror make me hysterical. I'm shivering and can't stop crying when she finally gets me loose. She wraps me in a towel and drives me the few blocks home.

Bonny has been telling Mom and Pop that something's happened to me with those boys, but they aren't looking for me yet since it's not quite dark. Dark is our curfew.

Mom gets me into a hot bath, and I cry more because the rope burns sting my wrists and ankles. I hear Pop talking loudly into the phone to Darren about what Knight did.

I hope Knight gets lickins. I really do.

MOM TELLS ME THAT KNIGHT GOT LICKINS, BUT NO AMOUNT OF beatings is enough to make his betrayal okay. Our families don't hang out anymore, and now we ignore each other at school.

Chris's mom is a waitress who works all the time and "can't do anything with him," so Chris continues to roam the neighborhood looking for trouble and doesn't get punished that I ever hear of.

THE JOSEPHSONS COME BACK FOR THEIR THREE-MONTH SUMMER

stint just when it feels like we've adjusted to living in their house. Other people plan things differently, but I'm not surprised when my parents handle the disruption by saying, "No problem! We'll just camp!"

After the ordeal of Wainiha, I'm not looking forward to camping. I've gotten used to hot showers, a flush toilet, and a mosquito-free, soft bed. I'm grumpy and slow packing up my stuff to move to our campsite in a vacant lot overgrown with huge *kamani* trees a block or so away from the Josephsons' house.

The new camp area is dry and smells of the sweetness of summer leaves. The tropical sunshine blasts down above, but here under the vast, spreading *kamani* trees, it's cool and dappled.

Pop sets up a campsite on top of a carpet remnant, with plastic over our tents and an open cooking area. Bonny and I have acquired guinea pigs by then, wonderful squeaky friends named Guin-Guin and Mr. Fuzzy that we bring over from the house. We build "habitats" for them out of rocks and logs and play with them constantly.

The Josephson family is really nice, and their twin sons, Leif and Eric, are a little older than me at thirteen. I'm nervous at first that they will come up with evil plans, but the boys seem happy to have some other kids to play with, and they don't mind that we're younger and girls. Bonny and I take them across the street to the ocean, and we go spearfishing with my three-prong.

I'm good at getting fish with that spear, called a three-prong because the head has three points that spread open. The end of the spear has an attached loop of rubber tubing, and to hit fish, you wind the tubing around your hand and twist and stretch it up the shaft of the spear. When you let go, the spear flies out and nails the fish. Usually, I follow up by driving the fish into the bottom and pushing the spear all the way through so it can't get off the prongs.

You have to get really close to fish to hit them with a three-prong, though, and I teach the boys my tricks, like hiding behind a coral head and scratching on the reef so the fish come check it out. They both bring in their first fish and are stoked.

Leif and Eric have been coming from Canada to Kauai every

summer since they were little, and they know our vacant lot well. When we're not at the beach or playing with the guinea pigs, we play tag and hide-and-seek.

One day while doing that, Eric disappears. The three of us search, and search, and search. Finally, I yell, "Come out! We give up!"

We hear him laughing—somewhere way above. I tip my head back and look up. Eric is grinning down at us from a mat of vines on the very top of the tree we're under, at least forty feet up.

"Come on! It's solid up here!" Eric bounces on the vines to demonstrate. A yellow lilikoi falls at my feet with a thwack, but the vines don't move, and he doesn't plunge to his death. Eric's bronzy eyes are gleaming with excitement. He reminds me of a mongoose, a creature they have on Oahu—all sinewy brown motion. Leif is tall, blond, and better looking, but I like Eric's attitude—he's daring and funny. "You scared?" he challenges me. Somehow in the order of things, Eric and I are the leaders.

"Ha! No problem." I start climbing. I'm not particularly fond of heights. I wouldn't call it fear, exactly. It's more of a breathless dizziness when looking down. So, I don't look down, which is really the secret to climbing anything.

Eric yells directions from above: "On your left, there's a branch. Then you have to go out a bit . . ."

Near the end, I have to shinny along a narrow branch thrusting up through the canopy. It's slender, and bounces as I slide along with my legs on either side, not looking down. Bonny and Leif shout encouragement, waiting their turn. Eric widens the entrance hole in the vines for me, and I pop my head and shoulders out into the sunlit sky.

The vines billow off into the distance in mounds and dip like a scarf tossed down over the tops of the trees. Monarchs, white cabbage moths, and a small blue butterfly flutter in sunlight so bright it stabs my eyes. The air is filled with the sweet/tart scent of lilikoi blossoms, round white spaceship-like medallions dotted across the green sea of vines.

"This is exactly like the part in *The Hobbit* when Bilbo climbs to the top of a tree to find his way out of Mirkwood," I exclaim, enchanted. Eric looks blank—he clearly hasn't read the book. He goes down a few notches in my estimation.

"Is it safe?" Leif hollers far below us.

"Let me check it out." I yell down into the gloom, and climb off the branch fully onto the vines. I spread myself out and go slow as I crawl over the thick mat of vines on the treetop, checking for holes, my heart pounding with a feeling that I'm pretty sure is joy. Eric is bouncing on the vines, testing them with me. I can see that the vines are laid down in layers—each year, a new layer, and the growth is at least a foot deep.

"I never knew this was here all these years," Eric says, bouncing. "I can't believe I never knew about this."

"Me neither." I wish I'd found this when we first moved into the neighborhood. Knight would have been so impressed. He wouldn't have tied me up and sold me out if I'd found this and showed it to him. I still feel weirdly sad about what happened, that we can't be friends anymore.

I make my way back to the hole and peer down. Leif's and Bonny's white-blond hair seems to glow in the dim, their faces as pale as a deep-sea fish looking up at me through forty feet of space. "Come on up, you guys. You won't believe it up here," I say.

Thus, begins my happiest summer ever.

The Josephson boys are adventurous and fun and not a bit mean. The four of us become inseparable. We get so comfortable on the treetops that we run across the vines, playing tag and hide-and-seek. No one falls through, though a few times we fall partway, dangling an arm or leg into space.

None of our parents know about our treetop escapades—they're just glad we're out of their hair.

Pop is still working at the Anchorage alternating lunch and dinner shifts. Both Mom and Pop surf most days, but they usually leave Bonny and me at camp and drive to Tunnels or Hanalei to go out. During the days, Mom reads a lot while Pop plays guitar, or she walks the beach picking up *puka* shells and stringing them for the necklaces she sells to tourists. They both still drink and smoke *pakalolo*, but I'm not as worried about them as I was. They seem happier than in Wainiha—and I have friends and freedom now that take me out of our little world.

When we feel like swimming, the four of us kids get into suits and grab towels and trek down the dirt road to the ocean, going snorkeling and diving for fish on the reef near the Anchorage. Other times, we walk the beach, foraging for shells for Mom. The whole time, we stay in the characters of endless games of make-believe: pirates and crusaders, knights and Viking explorers, cowboys and Indians.

We're so happy together it seems like it can't end—but it does. At the end of the summer, the boys tell us they have to go back to Canada. We start packing up the camp, getting ready to move back into their house. I'm so sad that they're leaving, but I'm also looking forward to plumbing again.

One day, right before the Josephsons leave, Pop returns to camp, loud and bright with excitement—he's got a new job as the caretaker of the big Wilcox estate in Hanalei.

Kauikeolani Estate is right on Hanalei Bay, a sprawling, white, plantation style mansion, surrounded by acres and acres of lawn with ponds, coconut trees, and decorative plantings. It's owned by an old-money *haole* family descended from missionaries, the Wilcoxes. Instead of returning to the Josephsons', we're moving into a cottage on the Estate, part of Pop's salary package.

Eric and I climb up to the vine mat on the top of the trees to say goodbye. I feel sluggish with sadness. He's been my best buddy all summer, and his friendship has gone a long way to heal me after the meanness I've had from others.

Popping our heads up out of the hole, we stare out at our summer kingdom. Our heavy play has trampled and damaged the vine mat, wearing it thin. There are few lilikois and hardly any leaves. It's going to be another year before it grows back.

"The vines will be ready for us to play up here again by next summer," I say.

"Right," says Eric. His usual banter is missing. We climb up through the hole and lie on our backs and look at the big arc of sky. There are just a few clouds up there today, feathers drifting on the blue.

"Hey," he says.

I turn my head and look at him. He's lying on his side, facing me and very close, his hands folded under his cheek. His golden-brown eyes, slightly too close together, are intent on my face. I feel a fluttery feeling in my stomach that I've never felt before.

"Can I kiss you? To say goodbye?"

"Okay," I whisper. He puts his lips on mine for a long moment, just resting them there. They're warm, and his breath smells like Crest. I like it and wriggle a little closer, and he wriggles a little closer, and he kisses me again, a soft smooch that makes me tingle.

He picks up a handful of my hair, sifting it through his fingers so it drifts down over my face. My hair's the palest gold it ever gets from all the summer sun, but I still wish it was thick, blonde, and shiny like Bonny's, and that I didn't have all these freckles.

"I like your hair. I wish I could take some with me," he says. "To remember this summer by."

"My hair? Sure." I yank out several strands, making my eyes water, and hand them to him. Now I turn on my side and watch as he very seriously wraps the golden hairs around each other, twisting them together into a coil.

He puts the little circle in his pocket. "You're going to be here next year, right?"

"Yeah. I live here, not like you poor tourist lame-asses who have to go back to the mainland every year."

"Hey!" he says. I jump up and run away across the thinning, trampled vines, and he chases me one last time.

CHAPTER TWENTY-TWO

WORKING FOR THE DESCENDANTS

Age: 10, Kauikeolani Estate, Hanalei, Kauai, 1975

"Albert Wilcox, offspring of missionaries, built up a fortune through growing sugar. He married a Hawaiian woman, Emma Kauikeolani Mahelona, and named their estate for her," Mom tells us as we unpack our stuff and carry it into the two-bedroom plantation cottage that's our new home. "Carol, my high school friend, married Gaylord Wilcox, a descendant of Albert, and they have three little girls. Carol and Gaylord need help cleaning the big house and babysitting, as well as keeping the grounds tidy and mowed. We're all going to help with the work."

I'm so excited to live in a beautiful place like this, right next to Hanalei Bay, that I don't care what we have to do to keep it.

The whole place's official name is Kauikeolani Estate, but everyone calls it the Estate, and the white mansion where the Wilcoxes live is the Big House. Our caretaker cottage was built for servants around the turn of the century and, along with four other cottages and barns, is separated from the Big House by a huge, impenetrable green wall of ironwood hedge.

The cottage is tin-roofed, and has creaky, painted wood floors.

Nobody's lived in it for years, judging by the dust, mold, and mounds of gecko poop on every surface. Two bedrooms, a big kitchen, a small living room, and a front porch make up the floor plan. The bathroom at the back has a deep, claw-footed tub with a shower on a rod.

Pop's full-time caretaker pay is three hundred a month, plus the house, which roughly equals the same money he made at the Anchorage but for a lot more hours of work. Mom says we definitely still need food stamps to get by. Taking a look out at the rolling lawn in front of the house, she says, "First thing we'll do is put in a garden to supplement our food."

Mom and Pop have noticed that Bonny and I don't bicker as much when we have our own rooms, so I get my own bedroom, and Pop sections off a portion of the living room with plywood to make a bedroom for Bonny. Gigi and Grandpa Jim, thrilled that we're going to be in an actual house again, offer to buy paint and materials to make it nicer. Mom unpacks her sewing machine from the stuff we stored in the Josephsons' garage while we were camping, and buys fabric for every window to sew curtains and pillows.

We all tackle painting the kitchen and living room white, with sunny yellow trim. The kitchen is the biggest room in the house, and we paint all the way down to the galvanized tin counter and deep, battered, iron-and-porcelain sink. When Mom adds a yellow checked curtain to cover the open area under the sink, and a ruffle above the window looking out at the back yard, the kitchen becomes as cheerful and charming as she's tried to make everywhere we've lived.

My room is already painted a powdery sky blue, with old-fashioned sash windows trimmed in white. I love it just the way it is. We put a rag rug down on the red-brown painted floor. Pop builds Bon and me each a twin-size plywood platform bed, and I choose a light cotton fabric spattered with fat, pink, old-fashioned roses for the curtains.

Lying on a foam pad on a raised bed in the reflection of those blue walls, I feel like I'm inside a flowery cloud.

It's utterly perfect. I shut my eyes and wish and hope we get to live here longer than six months.

The lawn around our cottage and the Big House goes on for acres and acres. A pond, shallow and green with algae, fills the back area. Half of it is in the mowed lawn, and the other half is in the fenced cattle pasture peppered with coconut trees that's also part of the Estate's land.

Standing on the grassy bank looking at the pond, I'm shocked to see a huge fish's dorsal fin cutting through the water. Other surges and jump patterns in the water show fish that are way too big for a normal backyard pond.

I yell for Pop, pointing at the fin cutting the water. "Looks like an *ulua*, a jack," he says. "Gaylord told me the pond used to be connected to the Hanalei River, so a lot of small fish and even a turtle got in here. When they closed the pond off, the trapped fish grew huge. But you aren't allowed to fish in here."

"Not allowed to fish?" My eyes bug out. "What? I want to catch that thing!"

"Nope. Only the family from the Big House are allowed to fish in the pond, and they save it for guests from the mainland and their friends."

My shoulders sag with disappointment.

"Get over it," Pop snaps in the grumpy way he has since he started the job. He takes off his sweat-soaked ball cap and wipes his forehead on his arm. He's not used to putting in a full forty hours a week at something so physical as the yard work of this giant place, and I can tell he's having second thoughts about taking this job. I hope he doesn't quit. I already love it here.

Bonny and I continue our exploration and discover a deserted boathouse with an attached classroom filled with old wooden desks.

"Looks like they had their own school here," I tell Bonny, running my finger over a deeply grooved *KIMO* carved into the desk.

We find a big barn filled with shadowy rusting tractors and farm equipment and an abandoned greenhouse, overgrown with neglected orchids. We're poking around inside the greenhouse when I hear a kid's voice call from the door.

"You aren't supposed to go in there. Broken glass." I turn to see a petite dark-haired girl. She points at broken glass inserts of the glass roof overhead. "The glass is all over, and our parents don't let us inside." The girl looks a little older than Bonny. Behind her stands a younger girl, big-eyed, with wispy brown hair.

"We just moved into one of the cottages. We didn't know about the glass. We just wanted to see everything," I tell her. "I'm Toby. This is my sister, Bonny." We pick our way carefully out of the broken-down greenhouse to face her and her sister.

"I'm Nicole. This is Darcy. And this is our place." She makes an arm gesture that encompasses the whole area. These must be the kids from the Big House that we heard about. "Our other sister is too small to play out here with us, but we can show you everything." Nicole grins, and it takes up half her face.

I'm glad she isn't snooty about living in the Big House. She and Darcy seem really happy to have some other kids to play with.

Over the next weeks, while Mom and Pop adjust to working a whole lot more than either of them are used to, we crawl around, under, and all over the sprawling wedding cake of a mansion. We collect antique trash from under the house: tiny colored medicine bottles, bent silver spoons, and even a gold pocket watch with rusted innards which I'm lucky enough to find under our cottage. We take over the pond's boathouse as our fort, and make a "store" out of all the junk we collect, where we trade with each other and haggle over items for our individual forts.

When that gets boring, we play "school" in the abandoned class-room at the battered desks. We take turns being the teacher, writing on the crumbling natural slate blackboard with stubs of chalk. We invent elaborate treasure hunts, with clues and tasks that I orches-trate for the younger girls.

I sneak in some fishing because I could say the girls wanted to, and they're part of the Big House family. But the girls are grossed out by the fish, so I have to throw back what I catch—and I never hook any of the really big ones.

The best thing about the whole situation is where the Estate's located: right across the street from Hanalei Bay.

Hanalei Bay is a great deep arc in the island with a beach that runs its entire length. There's no reef to spoil the swimming except at the surf spots, way outside. Our whole family is thrilled to be so close to the best beach on the island, all sparkling water and smooth sand bottom, with great surfing just a paddle away.

When the chores of the day are over, Bonny and I and the Wilcox girls throw on our suits and run to the beach for hours of swimming and jumping off the pier into the crystalline water below —and we share this joy with the local kids. On the pier, everyone gets along.

Mom and Pop go out to surf the Bay every day. Mom rides one of the first Morey Boogie bodyboards ever to arrive on Kauai, and Pop rides a variety of boards depending on the wave size.

This location is the first time we've had easy access to beginner surf spots, and Pop decides to teach us surfing. No other girls our age are surfing, but he wants us to learn, and like most sports I've tried, I want to master it. We already know ocean safety, like how to spot a rip current, get out of it, and read the ocean. At first, Pop goes with us to help us learn, putting Bonny and me up on a longboard at the *keiki* spots next to the pier and the Pavilion a little way down the beach.

"Getting waves is all about positioning and timing," Pop says. "Observe a wave from the beach, and see the point where it breaks consistently. Then position yourself in front of that peak. From there, choose a "lineup," a reference point on shore. That way, no matter where the current or conditions are moving you, when you paddle back out you can always get to the right place by finding the lineup object on shore."

We pick a reference point to line up with and I get that, but I'm not so good with the timing part. I either start paddling for the wave too soon and it breaks on top of me, or too late, and then the next one lands on my head. Still, I love the feeling when I do finally catch a wave—the breathless excitement, the speed, the responsiveness of the board to turn the way I lean. Pretty soon, I'm able to go out on one of Pop's boards by myself.

THE ONLY DOWNSIDE OF OUR MOVE TO THE ESTATE IS THAT POP IS working really hard, and it makes him super grumpy. The yard work of the big Estate is never-ending, and he hates the long boring hours of mowing. He's exhausted in the evenings, and has begun drinking at least a six-pack a day.

Mom tries to encourage him. "You're getting in shape!" She pats his arm muscles, which are definitely bigger. He doesn't seem motivated by this.

Mom is happy, though, always busy with projects. She's putting in a gigantic garden plot in the middle of the yard. Making it into planting beds requires backbreaking hours from all of us shaking dirt out of chunks of the former lawn. When she's not gardening, she helps Carol at the Big House with cleaning and continues to make her *puka* shell necklaces.

One Saturday morning, Mom and Pop sit us down at the kitchen table for a "confab." Confabs are family meetings where "changes in policy" are laid down. I've come to dread confabs—the news is seldom good.

Mom tells us they've decided to divide up Pop's work hours so he's not so tired. "I'm going to do fifteen a week, Toby will do ten, and Bonny five. That way, your dad will be able to surf and be in a better head space," Mom says. I work this out mentally—with all of us pitching in, Pop will now be working about half as much as he's supposed to.

Ten hours a week is a lot. I cringe at the boredom of so many mindless hours raking leaves and grass clippings, which I've already deduced will be my function. "Don't most dads work full time? Is it right for us kids to do work when you're getting paid? Do the Wilcoxes know?"

Pop gets mad, ballooning bigger and turning red before my eyes. "Enough of the lip. That'll be a barrow of manure." This is Mom and Pop's favorite new punishment: sending us into the pasture with a wheelbarrow and a shovel and having us fill the barrow with cow pies for Mom's composting on the garden.

"It doesn't seem right." I fold my arms and frown.

Pop stands up, his face dark and neck veiny. "Make that five more barrows! And if you keep it up, I'll add on work hours too!"

I shut my mouth with difficulty. If I keep talking back, I'm going to get lickins with a hairbrush and more work. I don't like Pop so grumpy, that's for sure. Since we moved, he's edgy and that dark mood hovers around him like a fog. I got used to him being mellow, like he was while we were at the Josephsons' and camping. Working a few days a week at the Anchorage Restaurant left a lot of time to sit around, playing guitar, and smoking *pakalolo* after surfing.

It's probably a good thing for us all to help Pop stay in a good head space as Mom calls it, and having time to go surfing is an important part of that. He's growing some new pot plants in the bathroom, but the leaves are soft and only waist-high, and there aren't any buds. I wish the *lolo* was ready now, so he could take the edge off.

So, I do two hours a day of yard cleanup, and it's just part of my chores.

On flat days with no surf, I take my mask and snorkel and cruise around the pier's pilings checking out the fishing situation, which is good for *papio*.

In the dark water there, spread-eagled and floating, I see my first hammerhead shark; a baby only three feet long. Its T-shaped body weaves along the sand bottom like a metal detector searching for treasure. I hold myself still and it undulates beneath me, moving on down the sun-rippled shadows cast by the pier.

Pop retrieves our old canoe from Wainiha, and Bonny and I take it out to explore a whole new terrain. The pond goes on awhile, deep into pastureland rimmed with reeds and punctuated by wild palms heavy with coconuts.

The sea turtle rumored to live in the pond is sleeping on a muddy beach area where the cattle drink. Turtles are endangered in Hawaii, and I've never seen one up close. It's roughly the size of our kitchen table. We pull the canoe up next to him, and I get out to investigate.

"Be careful. He has a big mouth." Bonny sounds worried as I tiptoe over and squat down next to him.

The turtle's head is the size of a football, and his bill looks wicked sharp, his closed eyes wrinkled gray coin purses. Dull shades of green and brown, with circles and shapes on the surface like the rings on a tree trunk, pattern his algae-covered shell. I set my hand gently on the shell; it's hot from the sun and feels like a horse hoof.

He startles awake and opens an eye that reminds me of dragons: brown and black, shot with gold phosphorescent rays. He whips his head away and heaves his giant body around, paddling his massive flippers, trying to get back into the water.

Bonny shrieks as I hop back into the canoe and push off with the paddle. I sit in the bow and position us as he drags his bulk around on the muddy bank and launches into the shallow pond. "Get ready! He's going to pull us."

"No!" Bonny exclaims, but I'm already reaching for the turtle as it thrashes past. I catch the rim of the shell behind its head. We're both yelling with terrified excitement as the turtle tries to get into deeper water.

I've leapt onto a bucking bronco, and I drop the paddle, hanging halfway out of the canoe, holding onto the shell with both hands. The turtle heaves and thrashes, lifting the front of the canoe with his bulk, but my grip on his shell prevents him from submerging. My arms are yanked almost out of the sockets, but I don't let go. He's so big that, like a gigantic outboard, he tows us out into the center of the pond.

"This is so awesome!" I yell back at Bonny, who's managed to catch the paddle I dropped and is grinning at me.

The reeds, palms, and muddy banks slide by, nesting coots and herons watching as we paddle past them on turtle power. The great reptile seems tireless, but I'm not, and I finally let go of his shell as we come out of the pasture area into visibility by the lawn, where we could be spotted from the house.

From then on, we like to visit him in his resting spot and bring him veggies from Mom's garden. We don't make him tow us again—we could tell how scared he was.

Now that we're in Hanalei, with flat roads and everything accessible, I get a rusty old banana seat bike at a garage sale and ride to fifth grade at Hanalei School. Bonny's staying home and doing Calvert, so I'm on my own this time. I'm delighted to find that my old friend, Tita, and her mom have moved to a house right across from the Wai`oli Hui`ia Church in the center of town. I swing by her place in the mornings, and we bike the couple of blocks further to school.

I need money now that I have a place to spend it, with Ching Young Store a mere bike ride away. Doug, our neighbor in one of the cottages and technically the Estate's handyman, is a heavy-browed man whose name, dark demeanor, and main occupation have lent themselves to the nickname "Drug."

"Bring me all the magic mushrooms you can find when you're out in the pasture shoveling that cow shit," he tells me. "I'll pay you a dime for small ones and a quarter for the big ones."

This seems like a great deal when sugar-laden candy bars sell for a quarter. I'm still scared of cows after the Bull Incident at Kala's house, but the cattle are usually in the pasture across from the pond, so on my manure pickup runs, I check each cow pie for mushrooms before shoveling it out of the grass and into the barrow.

"Magic" mushrooms are small modest umbrellas of almost transparent silver-gray. They're delicate, and get crushed if put in a bag, so I bring along a glass artichoke jar with a wide mouth for collecting. I've known that grownups like to get high and trip out on these since the Forest House, but I've never been even remotely interested in trying them myself. I'm scared of being out of control like I've seen people acting: silly and giggly, or staring into space seeing things that aren't there—and with my imagination, who knows what I might see?

Shrooms grow from spores, so I encourage that. If I find an old or dried-up looking cow pie, I'll sometimes squish a mushroom up and rub it into the surface, leaving it so more can grow.

This goes on a while, and one day I take my jar of shrooms to Drug's cottage.

"Doug?"

He's frowning and looks like a pirate as he comes to his screen door in loose surf trunks, scratching his hairy belly. "Whaddaya want?"

I keep my eyes on his face, away from the bearlike pelt of his chest and below. "Your shrooms. Got some big ones in here."

Doug takes the jar from me, stirs it with a finger. "I'll count them and get back to you."

"I already counted them. There are eighteen. Six are the big size."

Doug narrows cold brown eyes at me, and I squint back. I don't trust Drug not to cheat me out of a quarter or two.

Doug slams the door and walks back inside. I cock it open and peer in after him. He opens a large wooden box, and a powerful wave of *pakalolo* reek rolls out to greet me. Clearly Drug's got a major stash, but even when I squint, I can't see what's in there—I don't see well long distance.

Doug comes back and puts two crumpled dollar bills and a dime into my hand. "I need about twice that many to make any money," he says. "Get me more."

I stick the money in the pocket of my worn cutoffs. "I'll bring you all I can find."

"Let me show you what I'm selling so you understand." Doug gestures for me to follow him inside. I'm wary of getting cornered with men, so I keep an eye on the door and bet my fast feet can get me out of there if I need to. He leads me into the surprisingly neat kitchen, where he's got a row of empty spice jars lined up and a big can of honey beside them. "I put the shrooms in the honey. The chemical in them that makes people trip seeps out into the honey and gets stronger. I can sell one of these jars for fifty bucks, but I need about twice what you brought me to fill just one bottle."

I can do the math. "So, you'll give me four bucks and you make fifty?"

"You've got a smart mouth, you know that?"

"I guess. I'm just wondering how that's fair."

"I have to buy the jars and the honey and sell the stuff. You can't go into business and undercut me in this town, in case you're thinking of it."

"I'd never do that." I stare down the dealer who lives in my back yard. "But I want a quarter per shroom, no matter the size."

A long pause as he takes my measure. "Done. Now get out of here."

I don't need any further encouragement.

The next afternoon after school, I take Tita to Ching's Store and we buy a pile of forbidden sugary treats with my two dollars and ten cents in shroom money. Loaded with tasty loot, we ride our bikes to the county repair yard across from her house, and out of view, leaning our backs on the mountain of gravel used for town pothole repairs, we eat Nutty Buddies and Sugar Daddies, Snickers, and Paydays. We finish off our feast by sipping grape Fanta while chewing wads of Bazooka gum. As a finale, I bought us each a box of Tomoe Ame Japanese candy, delicate pink chewy bliss wrapped in edible rice paper with tiny toys that come in a separate section of the box.

"Thanks for sharing your money, but I think you should save it for a horse," Tita says, hard to understand through her bulging cheeks. She plays with the plastic charm she got in her Tomoe Ame box. "You can get a horse for just a couple of hundred dollars, or lease one, and you could just keep it in the Wilcoxes' pasture by your house."

"You think so?" A couple of hundred is still a shit-ton of money, but I've been asked to babysit the girls at the Big House and some other kids by Mom's friends, and I can get a whole dollar an hour babysitting.

"Yeah." Tita has joined 4-H, and she's deep in the riding scene. "You can lease a horse at the stables for only forty a month or so."

"That's still a lot of money."

"I help my mom clean houses, and I babysit so I can pay for the horse I'm using. I want you to get into it too so we can ride together."

Riding real horses with Tita? I'd do anything to make that happen. That day I resolve to start saving for a horse. Between shrooms and babysitting, it shouldn't take long. When I announce my goal, Mom smiles. "Good to have something to save for, that way you don't spend all your money on candy."

She flicks a piece of chocolate off my lip but says nothing more. My face goes hot with embarrassment. I know how she feels about sugar and processed foods.

Mom tells us that evening, chopping Swiss chard from the garden to go with our beans and brown rice, that she's pregnant again.

"I wanted to wait three months before I told you, until we were sure the baby was okay," she says. Her smile glows. Bonny dances around clapping her hands, and I throw my arms around Mom's waist, hugging. She has a tall, sturdy body that feels strong enough to have a dozen more babies, and she's only thirty-one. Her hair's long and streaked with blonde from the sun, her skin the deep tan of polished coconut shell. Like Pop, she's been getting in shape working on the yard and boogie boarding at Hanalei every day.

"I can't wait to see my baby brother or sister." I remember Francis's tiny perfect face. Whoever's already in her tummy is already almost as big as he was when we buried him.

CHAPTER TWENTY-THREE
TIDAL WAVE ESCAPE BOXES

*Grampa Jim, Bonny, Toby on Keiki, and Gigi with Baby Anita at
Estate*

Age: 11, The Estate, Hanalei, Kauai, 1976

Mom and Pop have a radio in the house where they listen to the
news, and there's nothing good happening in the outside world.
With gas rationing in effect, we can only buy gas on certain days of

the week, so we only go to Lihue once a month in the Rambler. "Hawaii is too dependent on shipped-in food and supplies," Pop says. "We have to be prepared to survive if we're cut off. Nuclear energy, Big Oil—they're all in bed together and anything could happen." With Barking Sands military base on the south side of the island, being a target in some world war seems like a real possibility.

Concerned about this, every time our parents go into Kapa`a or Lihue, they buy extra nonperishable food in case of The End of the World. Big bags of rice and lentils, boxes of powdered milk, dried fruit and nuts, honey, and vats of organic peanut butter from the co-op are all stored in one of the outside barns in big plastic paint buckets with lids so the rats and insects can't get in.

School is going okay so far. Mr. Nitta's a tidy Japanese man who wears short-sleeved, button-down shirts with undershirts beneath, something I haven't seen since living with Grandpa Jim. He has a head of thick black hair he plasters into a helmet shape with stiff and flowery-smelling goo. The fifth-grade classroom is a big, airy wooden room with louvers that admit a nice crosswind. My new teacher is not one for a lot of decoration, so unlike my other classrooms, the walls are bare except for maps and a chalkboard. I find it restful, easier to concentrate in the simpler décor. I'm having trouble seeing and take a spot right at the front with Tita at a shared desk.

To add to my worries about nukes and the Gas Crisis, Mr. Nitta tells us about tidal waves. These huge waves are caused by underwater earthquakes. They suck back the whole ocean from the floor of the sea, leaving all the fish flopping around, and then surge back in, high as a house, and mow down everything in their path. Hanalei has a few rusty sirens around, set up since the 1965 tidal wave, but "every family should have an evacuation plan and a bag packed for escape," Mr. Nitta tells us. "Make a list of all the things you would take to escape and pack your bag ahead of time. Hanalei is a very vulnerable zone."

Maybe because of the stockpiling at home, or the disaster drills we've been having at school, I begin to worry nonstop about tidal waves.

I go home and pack my emergency bag—an old pillowcase. I put in my gold locket from Gigi, my precious drawing pens and paper, the rusted gold watch I found under the house, a change of clothes, a spare toothbrush. I try to assemble the Family Escape Box Mr. Nitta has recommended—five gallons of water, food for a week, candles, and a flashlight with batteries.

There's no food for a week that could be transported to high ground. We either eat fresh food, or food that needs a lot of prep, like beans or rice. I can't find a single can of Spam or box of Hamburger Helper like Mr. Nitta suggested. I settle for a washed-out milk jug of water and bag of dried figs.

That night, I have a dream that we are all annihilated by a wall of water and can't run away from it. I wake up with tears on my cheeks, and go to my parents' bed to burrow between their sleep-smelling bodies, something I haven't done in years.

"We have to pack an Escape Box," I whisper to Mom in the dark. A little wind stirs the hand-sewn curtains. Pop snores beside her, oblivious.

"Okay, you can tell me about it in the morning," she mumbles—but in the morning there's no time to pack anything, and with her pregnancy, she's still in bed when I get myself on my bike and off to school.

Mr. Nitta wanted us to bring in examples of what we put in our Family Escape Boxes, so I wait for everyone to leave for recess before I put my bag of figs on his desk.

"We don't have an Escape Box," I tell Mr. Nitta, "But my parents are very worried about the Gas Crisis so we have a lot of beans and rice and other food stashed. I think we will be okay if we get a tidal wave."

He peers at me through square black glasses and lets a beat go by, as if trying to understand what I'm saying. "I could call them."

"Oh no." A call from school would freak Mom and Pop out. I'd have drawn attention from The Man. "I will get something together. I just brought the figs in to show you that if I had one, it would be a very nutritious escape box."

"I can see that." His eyes twinkle a bit, but he doesn't mock me. Mr. Nitta has a way of cracking jokes and teasing that makes class fun, and he has already picked up on Kira's hassling me and put a stop to it—at least, whenever he catches her. Kira and I mostly ignore each other now; I stay out of her way and try not to attract her attention. Kira reminds me of Pele, the vengeful volcano goddess. Even when things appear peaceful, she's boiling underneath and waiting for a chance to blow up.

The bell rings ending recess, and Kira is the first one back to class. She's followed closely by my friend, Samson, one of the Chandler boys who I suspect might have a crush on me—but because of Kira, he just quietly slides his cookies over to me at lunch.

I don't want Kira to see the figs, so I give the bag a little push toward Mr. Nitta. "Can I leave these here until the end of the day?"

"As long as you pay the tax." Mr. Nitta opens the bag and takes out a fig, biting into it with a flourish. "There, you paid it. Thanks."

I leave his desk and take my seat. When everyone is back, Mr. Nitta calls out. "Who's having trouble getting their Family Escape Box together?"

Several hands go up, and Mr. Nitta organizes kids into teams to do a "scavenger hunt" at various families' houses around town to gather the basics so everyone can have one.

"You just want to sleep well at night knowing you're prepared," he says. This perfectly echoes my dream of the night before, but I wonder if an Escape Box will really help if a tidal wave comes. It seems like it's better for afterward than during. During, nothing will help but getting to higher ground.

Mr. Nitta makes a list on the board of the suggested contents again. I squint because, even sitting in the front row, I can't see the board well enough to read it. I finally, reluctantly, reach into the slot in the table, take out my glasses, and put them on.

I've been having trouble with my vision for a couple of years now. We can only afford the glasses Welfare will pay for. There are four frame choices, each uglier than the last, and this pair was the best of the options: lenses shaped like stop signs in thick purple plastic.

FRECKLED

I'm not only a redheaded, hippie bookworm, but I wear cheap, ugly glasses.

A few days later, I go for yet another eye checkup an hour away in Lihue with old Dr. Yee, who's been upgrading my glasses to stronger every six months since I was nine. This time, he pulls my mom aside for a whispered discussion. I frown, looking at them through the giant metal lens contraption I'm still stuck behind.

"What's going on?" I say.

"Nothing, honey. We just need to see a specialist," Mom says, and there's a funny tightness in her voice that puts me on alert. On the way home, we stop by Kapa`a Library. I've pretty much read everything in the place, and I'm working my way through adult fiction alphabetically now. Mom parks under an ironwood tree and sends Bonny and me in alone.

"I need a break," she says. "The baby is making me tired."

She looks pale and closes her eyes, leaning back in the seat as we wind down all the windows in the Rambler so the breeze passes through. The faithful old car is quite rusty now, the upholstery on the roof blooming in gray mildew patterns.

At the checkout, my old friend the librarian, Mrs. Rapozo, eyes me over her half-glasses as she opens a stack of books topped by Erica Jong and James Joyce, since I've got to J by now. "Fear of Flying. Hmm. Does your mother know you're reading this?"

"Sure. She doesn't believe in censorship."

Mrs. Rapozo tightens her lips, and I know I'm in for a good one. I've already devoured the Jackie Collins section, in spite of Mrs. Rapozo's audible sniffs and attempts to catch my mom's eye.

Mom starts the car when we get back in. We drive home, the windows down. There's no radio reception in the car because Kauai's too small to have its own station, and the steep mountains prevent reception—the same reason there's no TV on the island, either.

I lean my face on the window frame and watch the ocean stream by, the flashing columns of coconut trees, the swishing cane fields, and corduroy rows of pineapple. I do my favorite driving daydream.

The car is pulled by six galloping black horses, and I alternately stand on the hood and drive them, or climb onto their backs and urge them to go faster, cracking a rawhide whip over their heads. Sometimes, I lean down to unhitch one of them and let Bonny drive the team while I drop to the horse's back and gallop out in front.

I can feel everything about the daydream: the surge of the horse's muscles, silky under my bare legs; the wind cutting my eyes so I have to squint; the way the leather straps squeak with the strain of our speed. I breathe the warm perfume of horse that surrounds me and love the way the animal pours on more speed when I bend alongside his neck and whisper "Go!" in his ear.

"I'm having a confab with Pop when we get home." Mom still has that funny note in her voice. "And then we have to talk."

Confabs are rarely a good thing. I can't get the daydream going again after that.

After the evening routine of dinner, baths, personal reading, and homework, I listen as hard as I can to Mom and Pop's confab from my side of the wall, but I can't make anything out but their muffled voices.

I turn off the light and take off my ugly purple glasses, setting them on the dresser. Immediately my world goes fuzzy. "Impressionistic" is how I like to think of it. Silver moon luminosity lights the cabbage roses on the curtains from behind.

Mom knocks on the doorjamb, then flicks on the light and comes into my room carrying a kitchen chair. *This can't be good.* I sit up in alarm as she sets the chair beside my bed. Pop follows her in and parks beside me on the bed.

"Toby, we have to go to the mainland to see a specialist. Dr. Yee thinks there's something seriously wrong with your eyes and . . . that you're going blind." Mom chokes on the last words, and Pop puts his hand on her shoulder. This just makes her cry harder, and she reaches out to pull me into her arms.

I can't take it in.

I've just started surfing, riding the little waves next to the pier—how could I surf, blind? I love my drawing and art. I love seeing everything! I think in pictures. There's no one who likes seeing more than I do.

"I would rather die than be blind." I push away from Mom's arms. My throat is closing off my air. My chest won't lift to breathe until I tell it to.

Mom sobs harder.

"Maybe Dr. Yee's wrong. He's not sure, that's why he's referring you. Gigi is going to pay for you and Mom to go to the specialist, and you can visit her in La Jolla, too." Pop tries to make it sound like a treat.

They're trying to comfort me and I recognize that, but my skin is cold, my chest constricted, my body turned to wood. I wait stiffly for them to leave, and they finally do, shutting the door. I hear Mom crying some more through the thin wall connecting our rooms.

I get out of bed and drag my plywood bed frame, scraping the painted floor in long gashes, over to the window. I push up the sash and lie there with my face pressed against the screen, staring out at the moon. I blink, and squint, and that delicious white lozenge like a mint in the sky won't come into focus.

My whole body contorts with pain, and the tears burst out. I muffle my sobs in my pillow so I won't stress out the family any worse.

I'm terrified of a world without light. My hidden cowardice pounces, mauling me like a lion, making me think of dying rather than be stuck in a world I can't see. I tick through the methods I could kill myself.

Drinking Pop's insecticide.

Too risky, it might just make me sick.

Drowning.

I already know how my lungs burn like inhaling fire when the seawater gets in. I'd never be able to make myself do something like that on purpose.

Cutting my wrists.

Would hurt my family too much to do it that way. So gross.

Hanging.

Not sure I know how.

Guns.

I don't know where to get one or how to use it.

I decide on jumping. I already like jumping off the waterfalls, and jumping requires just one decision and then you can't take it back—plus I could make it seem like an accident so my family isn't so sad. Maybe I'll jump off the cliff into the dump, where all unwanted things end up. If I survive that, there are lots of other cliffs with rocks at the bottom.

I cry in great heaving spasms into the pillow. Finally, I'm exhausted, and rest my face on the window frame, staring at the fuzzy moon.

There's an angel descending from the moon, drifting down toward me.

Or something like an angel. I blink repeatedly, and squint, but I can't see it clearly.

Maybe it's Jesus. I've heard about Jesus from Gigi who's a Catholic and believes he's the Savior. Mom says he's just a great teacher, like Buddha.

This angel has a Jesus vibe, but I can't see it well enough to be sure. But there's definitely a radiant, glowing white figure right outside my window, and it's not going away.

I hear a voice like a bell in my head: "Don't worry. It's going to be okay."

The silvery-white presence glows, rising and falling gently as if the air were water it's floating in. The constriction around my chest releases, my breath comes easier. My heart pounds with a new excitement—I'm being visited by a supernatural being!

I sit up and open my mouth to call Mom, Pop, and Bonny so they can see—and the angel fades, disappearing.

It's gone.

But it told me not to worry, and that everything would be okay.

Snuggling back down into my sleeping bag left over from the camping days, I press my cheek against the screen, my face turned up toward the night sky. I fall asleep that way.

All through the hurried arrangements to fly to California for a second opinion, I'm unfazed. I've been visited by an angel—it doesn't get any more reassuring than that. My dad, his green eyes unfamiliar with the shine of tears, hugs me goodbye. Bonny cries openly, both at the news and at my departure, and I cry because she does—as usual. But I'm not worried anymore.

We get on the plane and take our seats. Mom holds my hand. I smell the fear on her, an unfamiliar tang of stress, and in that moment I know how loved I am: by my parents, by my sister, even by my grandparents.

They pick us up at the San Diego Airport in Grandpa's big floaty-suspension black Cadillac and take us straight to Macy's for new clothes. This is La Jolla—I can't see the doctor in my thrift-store getup.

"We have The Best Specialist lined up." Gigi pats my hair, her fluttery birdy-hand a-jangle with gold bracelets as we sit down at the La Jolla Beach and Tennis Club for lunch.

"Whatever it costs, don't worry about it," Grandpa rumbles, piercing blue eyes almost hidden under craggy dark brows. "We're taking care of this."

"Thank you so much," Mom says meekly. She's wearing a new pin-tucked maternity smock from Macy's, my grandmother's idea of appropriate clothing, and she picks at her salad.

"Thank you," I echo, resisting the urge to scratch at the seams of jeans so stiff and new that they feel like they could walk on their own. I'm still not worried, even though all of the adults are.

We take the Cadillac to the doctor's office in a high-rise building. I'm a Kauai bumpkin enough to enjoy the long ride up in the elevator—I haven't ridden one of these since the last time I was in La Jolla.

The Best Specialist is a kind middle-aged man who jokes a bit to put me at ease. We go through the usual lens fittings with the big black metal lens contraption on the moveable arm. He gives me eye drops and pretty soon I can't see at all. He puffs air into my eye, and it stings. He looks at it with a light, for a long time, and says "hmm." I hold my chin in the black plastic cup and keep my eyes open so long they water until he takes a picture, a burst of light that feels like my brain exploding.

So far it's nothing different than what Dr. Yee does, except that this man's breath smells like the peppermint Chiclets I see peeking out of the white pocket of his jacket, instead of the faint cigarette smell Dr. Yee has.

He sits down with Mom and me when the whole thing is over.

"You aren't going blind," he says to me. Mom covers her mouth with both hands and her eyes well up. "You have severe astigmatism, which is a malformation of the lens of your eye. You'll have to get new glasses every six months until the degeneration slows down after puberty."

I look down at the slightly painful nubs just beginning on my skinny chest—that could be a while.

Gigi and Grandpa pay for the visit and a pretty new pair of glasses with delicate gold frames, then take us to the Country Club on the hill for a celebratory dinner. I remember to let the valet open the door for me this time.

Mom doesn't participate in the bottle of champagne they order, but they let me have half a glass. I hold the slender flute, watching the bubbles stream up from the bottom through liquid the color of fresh-cut pineapple. It tastes cold and misty, and the bubbles tickle the inside of my mouth.

"I knew The Best Specialist would get to the bottom of this," Gigi says. "That quack on Kauai put everyone through an unnecessary scare."

"Dr. Yee. Sounds Asian," Grandpa says, with a snort. He has low opinions about Asians, Jews, blacks, and pretty much anybody who doesn't belong to one of his clubs.

Mom bites her lip. She doesn't believe racism is okay, and it's hard for her not to challenge their comments. I know she's keeping quiet for me, to make sure I get the pretty glasses that will be mailed to us on Kauai soon, and my heart swells with love.

"We appreciate the support in getting a second opinion," she says carefully.

The next day, Mom borrows Gigi's cream-colored Thunderbird, and we drive a little north of La Jolla to Yogananda's ashram, the Self-Realization Fellowship, a big walled compound on the cliffs in Encinitas. Mom gets excited when she hears there's a summer yoga camp for kids my age.

"Wouldn't this be a great camp to go to, Toby?" She gestures to the fanciful buildings with swirly gold-plated tops like cupcakes, gracious plantings, and Hindu statuary dotting the grounds.

I worry about being made to fast on lentils and water while doing meditation and yoga all day, but after my recent divine visitation, I should give something back. "It would be good for my meditating."

Mom's been showing me how to meditate, but I suffer badly from "monkey mind" and have difficulty sitting still. I've only been able to do fifteen minutes so far.

"We'll see if Gigi will pay for it," Mom says. We glance at each other and laugh. Gigi loves to send Bonny and me to camps—dance camp, art camp, tennis camp—but I wonder how a yoga camp at our guru's compound will go over. Without her sponsorship, we don't have money for anything like that.

"Let's see," Gigi says about the yoga camp. "I think the country club is doing a nice tennis camp this summer that would be right across the street and might be more appropriate." I nod eagerly at the same time as Mom shakes her head, and the topic is shelved.

Back home at the Estate, we settle into a routine. Pop works, mostly doing the mowing while we do a lot of the other stuff around the edges. Mom's belly gets bigger, and she spends a lot of time working the garden. The hundreds of barrows of cow manure Bon and I have hauled help her grow some of the biggest vegetables anyone in Hanalei has ever seen—her Chinese cabbages are the size of basketballs.

I babysit the Wilcox girls after school and other kids on weekends, and I hunt for magic mushrooms early in the morning before the sun can wither them. I stuff my future horse money away in an envelope hidden in my dresser.

In January, a month from when the baby's coming, Mom says,

"We have a surprise for you. There's a Shetland pony for sale in Hanalei town, and he's three hundred and fifty dollars with his tack. If you pay half, we can get him for your birthday."

"Yes! YES!" I jump and clap my hands and do some cartwheels in front of the house. I can't contain my excitement and let out those big loud feelings in whooping, hollering, and dancing around. I've actually saved a hundred and fifty dollars, and even though that's not quite enough, Mom and Pop have scraped up their part, too.

The next day, when I get home from school, Keiki is standing in the pasture.

He's a golden palomino with soulful brown eyes, and he swishes a thick white tail that's a lot like Bonny's long blonde hair. He's too small to be intimidating and just the right size for me at my current height of four feet, eleven inches. I fall in love instantly.

"Pop brought him here for you." Mom waddles after me in her maternity muumuu as I put rubber rain boots on with my shorts and bound into the pasture. "It wasn't easy. Keiki was staked out next to the Laundromat, and your dad had to lead him all the way here, so you better tell him thanks."

"Thank you, thank you, thank you!" I embrace Keiki's shaggy neck. He swings his head and snaps teeth big as piano keys at me, making me jump back.

Despite all my horse fantasies and reading, I've only actually ridden a couple of times—trail rides with a guide at my grandparents' house in Palm Springs. I feel a qualm of doubt. I don't really know how to proceed, and Keiki seems a bit grumpy even if he's cute.

"Where's Pop?" Gigi and Grandpa Jim owned a ranch when Pop was growing up. He knows how to handle horses. "I want to thank him."

"He had to go back to work."

"Okay, I'll ride over and find him." I picture chasing Pop down on his drive mower from the back of my gorgeous palomino pony. "Where's the tack? I want to ride!"

They've put the tack in a shed behind the house. I lug it to the fence: a great little Western saddle, bridle, and Mexican blanket.

There's even a rubber pail with brushes and a hoof pick. I'm grateful for the Basic Horsemanship book I've borrowed from the library. "If you can read, you can learn anything," Mom always says, and so far, that's been true.

Keiki's staked out to a metal loop Pop pounded into a stump, and he steadily walks away from me as I approach, resulting in a comical circular chase until I wise up. Using a banana as bait, I get the halter on him and tie him to the fence. I'll groom him first, clean his hooves, then figure out the tack.

That's when I realize there might be a reason Keiki was for sale.

He stomps tiny hooves instead of letting me pick them up. He swishes his tail with mean accuracy when I brush his hindquarters, and gets me in the eye with the whiplike strands. Mom tries to provide ideas, but is too pregnant to really help, and what should have taken a few minutes turns into an hour of struggle. Finally, he's tacked up as best I can figure out. Still wearing my shorts, T-shirt, and rubber rain boots, I put my foot in the stirrup and swing aboard. I'm on my pony! I lean forward and tighten my legs and give a little cluck, like the horsemanship book says.

Keiki just stands there.

I kick him, and say, "Giddyup," which sounds as ridiculous as I thought it might.

No response.

"Maybe I should lead him." Mom takes his bridle and he walks, very slowly, as if his joints hurt and he's constipated. She opens the gate and leads him out of the pasture.

I'm less than thrilled with the experience so far. "Let go, Mom. I can handle it."

The feeling is like being at the top of the boulder-strewn path at the forest house on my first two-wheeler, learning to ride a bike.

Only this bike won't go.

Keiki stops again as soon as Mom lets go of the lead rope. I kick him, then whack his shoulder with the loose end of the reins. He puts his head down and begins eating grass. I pull on the reins to no avail.

"I'll walk him a little more," Mom says. I'm mortified to have my mom, the size of the Goodyear Blimp, leading us around.

"No, let me do it," I say, but Keiki won't move unless she leads him. We proceed at turtle speed along the fence.

Suddenly Keiki pricks his ears, and I feel a new vitality go through his sturdy body. "Let go, Mom! He's ready!"

She lets go. Keiki picks up his walk to a trot, moving along the fence, his head up, mane blowing in the breeze. I bounce in the saddle, listing from side to side, but *I'm riding my own pony!*

We reach the end of the pasture fence. Ahead is the long driveway that leads to our house from the main road. I pull on the reins to turn Keiki, but he pays no attention.

He has spotted the road, and he remembers walking all the way here to this strange pasture with these strange people, and *now he's going home.*

I know this as suddenly and totally as if I'd just had a Vulcan mind-meld with his tiny Shetland pea-brain.

"Whoa!" I yell, bracing my feet in the stirrups and pulling back—which the Basic Horsemanship book assures me is the proper procedure.

In reply to this, Keiki tucks his head and picks up speed, going from a trot to a canter to a full gallop down the long sandy driveway toward the main road. Mom clutches her belly, trying to run after us, yelling something. I'm too busy trying to stay on to listen.

Without slowing down or checking for cars, Keiki careens onto the two-lane asphalt road leading to Hanalei town, and gallops down the double yellow stripe in the middle of the road.

I hold onto the horn with both hands for dear life—and then, horror of horrors, discover I haven't tightened the girth enough. By agonizing inches, the saddle begins to rotate to the side and me with it. Sensing weakness, the devil in palomino heads straight toward a telephone pole with intent to scrape me off.

By clutching his mane, I manage to haul the saddle back upright and only whack my leg on the telephone pole, but now Keiki has a plan to rid himself of me. He gallops straight for the next pole. I know I can't make it past another one, and I let go of the mane. The saddle swings to the side and I'm dumped, rolling, onto the side of the road.

Keiki gallops on toward town, the saddle under his belly, his head up and ears pricked, his tail flying like an Arabian stallion.

I lie on the side of the road, winded, and finally sit up, checking for broken bones. A surfer friend of my parents, racks piled high with boards, stops his pickup truck in the road across from me. "You okay? That your pony I passed back there?"

Air's still having a hard time getting into my lungs, so I just nod. The guy's having a hard time keeping a straight face. "That pony sure knows how to run. Want a ride to go get him?" The guy's chin is still twitching suspiciously.

I stand up, thinking over my options. There's an oozing scrape on my leg from the pole, and I feel jangled and sore, but otherwise okay. Just then Mom pulls up with Bonny in the Rambler. She greets the guy in the truck. "Eh, howzit, Bob!" They chat as I get into the battered old sedan, head hanging with mortification and disappointment.

"That was awesome," Bonny pokes me. "You really showed him who was boss."

"You okay, hon?" Mom asks when Bob finally drives off.

"Yeah." I fold my arms over my sore ribs and stare morosely out the window as we drive into town. Sure enough, Keiki is grazing unperturbed in the vacant lot next to the Laundromat.

I've lost my confidence about riding, so we put the saddle in the car's trunk. I sit in the back seat holding Keiki's reins out the window and lead him home that way as Mom drives slowly. Thankfully, there are no other cars on the road.

Later, I ride my bike over to Tita's house. She tells me we should start Keiki out on a "lunge line," and that I need riding lessons, but she'll help me at first.

"Shetlands are brats. It sounds like he hasn't been ridden in a while." This pronouncement from my expert riding friend consoles me somewhat, but I soon discover that my beautiful little palomino is just as stubborn as I am.

Putting the saddle on, Keiki blows up his belly so the girth loosens later. Every time I mount, Keiki whips me with his tail or snaps his teeth, though I get good at jumping out of the way. His mouth is tougher than shoe leather, and my arms grow stringy with muscle from fighting for the bit. My riding choices are walking with an adult holding the lead line so he doesn't run away, or perambulating the enclosed pasture, where he drags his feet as if every step is torture.

Eventually more confident, I take him outside the pasture alone. Twice more he runs away "home" to his vacant lot by the Laundromat, throwing me off in creative ways along the side of the road.

I'm not going to give up, no matter how battered, road rashed, or concussed I get, and eventually we come to something of an understanding. Using treats of papaya and chunks of coconut, I begin to win his black, treacherous heart.

One day I ride him across the street, fulfilling my fantasy of riding on the beach. All is glorious as we clop across the lawn to the beach. The ocean glimmers aqua perfection in the distance. The steep green mountains that define Hanalei are as glorious in the distance as a painted backdrop. A light breeze cools my brow and blows Keiki's blond mane across my freckled hands, and the tightness of perfect happiness expands my chest.

The minute Keiki feels the warm sand of the beach on his hooves, he squats and pees immensely. I'm still chuckling at this, thinking how warm sand makes me feel the same way, when he takes a few more steps and drops to his knees.

"No, Keiki!" I shriek, and kick out of the stirrups, launching off his back just in time as he drops and rolls, almost crushing me.

He eventually gets up, grunting happily, and shakes the saddle loose. Sand packs every nook and cranny of the tooled leather. I tighten the girth, hop back on, and we proceed a little further. He tucks his head, a telltale sign trouble is ahead, and forges into the surf up to his neck, ignoring my yelling and pulling, soaking me and the saddle.

On the way out, he throws me off and rolls in the sand again. My tack is almost ruined and takes hours of cleaning and oiling to restore. I don't take him to the beach anymore.

I'm determined to master him, though. Within a few months I can, with the aid of a sturdy crop and a heavy spade bit, pretty much ride him. He stops returning to the Laundromat, and now, when he runs away with me, he gallops to his feed bucket on the fence by our house.

I finally decide to ride him on the beach again, but bareback with my swimsuit on, now that I have him managed better. We cut across the yard of the house directly across the road from us, as I did last time. There's a chain draped across their driveway but open grass on either side. With his telltale chin tuck, Keiki heads for the chain at a trot.

"Keiki, no!" I bellow, thinking he's going to jump over it. I've fallen every way there is by now, and I know that a bareback wipeout will be painful in my suit on the neighbor's asphalt driveway. With new arm muscles I've developed, I lever Keiki's head to the side, trying to turn him, but it's too late—he bolts for the chain with a surge and yanks his head free of my grip. Instead of jumping it, he dips his head under the chain and cleverly uses the heavy metal links to scrape me off. I land hard on my tailbone in the driveway.

Keiki gallops across the yard onto the beach, bucking and kicking up his heels, gloating over his victory. Reaching the beach, he drops to the sand for a good hard roll, grunting with pleasure. I get up, straighten my bathing suit, and walk carefully toward him.

"Hey boy," I say in my best "good pony" voice. "Whoa, Keiki."

He rolls an eye back at me and leaps up. He gallops away down the beach, tail high, farting with joy.

CHAPTER TWENTY-FOUR

HULA LESSONS

Pop's birthday in Hanalei

Age: 11, The Estate, Hanalei, Kauai, February 1976

Mom and Pop bring Anita Leilani home from the hospital. I've just

turned eleven, and maternal instincts I never knew I had are acti-
vated by my adorable, ten-pound, green-eyed baby sister whose
silver-blonde hair sticks straight up. I walk Anita around in the
kitchen after she's been fed, enjoying the warm, milky-smelling heft
of her even when she cries, which sounds like a kitten mewing.

Mom had a rough time with the birth and lies around a lot during
the day, keeping the same rhythms as Anita.

She calls her mother to tell her about Anita's birth. Maga's a tall,
blue-eyed redhead with a big personality, and Mom says I got my red
hair from her. Maga, her new husband Egidio, (formerly an Italian
policeman, now a Fuller Brush salesman) and their teen daughters
Patricia and Nancy, live in Santa Barbara, California.

"Your milk must be so rich," I tell Mom. Bathing Anita in the big
kitchen sink, we have to be careful to soap around all her pudgy rolls.
She has one on the back of her neck that, as it gets a little sun on it,
looks exactly like a marshmallow. I like to kiss it and breathe in her
sweetness.

The baby seems to stress Pop out because she's in their room and
cries at night. He's the least happy of us even though we share his
work hours—withdrawn and grumpy, even after smoking *pakalolo* and
drinking more than ever. I avoid him as much as possible, put in my
ten hours a week, and try to stay quiet and help with the baby.

It's all I can do. I really love it at the Estate, and I don't want
anything to change.

"We should understand and participate in Hawaiian culture
more," Mom's decided. She's made friends with some Hawaiian
ladies over the years and has learned *lauhala* basket weaving, a
lengthy process that involves harvesting the long, spiny *hala* leaves
from the Dr. Seuss-like native trees, stripping off the thorns, drying
and processing them, and finally the weaving itself.

We don't have any Hawaiian language or customs taught in
school, and Mom hears about some hula lessons in the church hall in
Hanalei. She asks Gigi to pay for me and Bonny to go, and Gigi
agrees and says she can't wait to see us do hula on her next visit.

I'm excited arriving at the echoing wooden stage of the circa 1841 church hall where they hold the lessons. I heard shells are used in hula, and Bon and I each bring two large spotted cowries Pop found diving. We left them on an anthill for a month to get the innards properly cleaned out.

The *kumu,* teacher, is a sturdy Hawaiian woman with large brown eyes and the most amazing waterfall of shiny black hair threaded with gray like silver streamers. She tells us we need two cowries, a pair of *uli`uli* feathered rattles, a small *ipu* gourd and a pair of *pu`ili* bamboo sticks. We can buy what we don't make ourselves from Kumu.

Kumu directs us into rows on the stage.

I'm the only *haole* girl in the group except for Bonny and Nicole, who's tagged along at the last minute. I feel like a rice grain in a bowl of poi, and it's not a good feeling. My tummy tightens with dread as I spot Kira Yoshimura, my old enemy, and she gives me stink eye. "Whatchu doing heah, Haole Crap?" she hisses.

Kumu opens with a short chant in vibrating Hawaiian so Kira has to shut up and pay attention. I awkwardly copy my neighbors as we begin a simple hula using the cowries to gesture, clicking them together.

"Pu pu
Hinu hinu
Pu pu
Hinu hinu e . . ."

I mess up, and Kira pinches the back of my arm, her favorite torture spot, making me yelp.

"Kira!" Kumu's voice snaps Kira's head around. "Since you already know these dances, why don't you stand in front of the new girls so they can watch you."

She puts Kira right in front, under her eagle eye, and I stand just behind her. Kira can't give me humbug right in front of Kumu. I focus hard on getting my footwork and graceful hula hands just right, and Bonny, Nicole, and I muddle through the class.

After, when I'm putting our borrowed hula equipment away in the musty-smelling supply closet, Kira comes up from behind and pinches the back of my arm viciously. "Ow!" I jump and rub what's already turning into a blood blister.

"You don't belong here, fucking *haole*," she snarls. "Go home to the mainland." She's extra mean because I'm on her turf, and Tita isn't there to run interference.

"What's your problem?" I turn to face her. "I nevah did notting to you." I speak pidgin and try to stand taller—after all, I'm bigger than she is, and I was recently visited by an angel. I remember what Ginger said about bulls—*yell loud, never run, and whack them if you can.*

"You so stupid for ask dat!" Her dark eyes flash, her voice vibrates with rage. "Haole Crap!"

"You look more Japanese than Hawaiian to me, so no talk shit, Kira Yoshimura. I don't hear any Hawaiian in *your* name, either."

We give each other a long glare in that dark closet, and finally she whirls and stomps off. I don't savor any victory—in fact, I know I'm in for it now. Kira's greatest power has always been her ability to rally other kids to do her bidding.

The hula lessons become an ordeal because of Kira's unrelenting campaign to drive me out. She trips me, pulls my hair, pinches me, and gets the other girls to do it, too.

In front of Kumu she's all smiles. "You like me show you how?" She's petite and lovely and does hula perfectly, and her voice drips sweet venom which Kumu misses.

Bonny and Nicole drop out, but I'm determined to continue. I enjoy hula—like ballet, it's a physical challenge, and I like physical challenges. I like the percussion of the *ipu*, the rhythm of the chant, the good feeling I get when we are all coordinated as a group.

After class one day, Kumu puts her hand on my shoulder and tells Mom, "Toby's picking it up really well. She's got a feel for it, and she works hard."

Mom knows it has been difficult socially. She says cautiously, "Toby doesn't feel like the other girls accept her."

I want to look down and hide, but make myself look at Kumu. I need to know if she thinks the hassling from the other girls is okay.

Kumu's expressive black brows come down in a fierce frown. I like watching her mobile, golden-skinned face with its wide nose and fine-cut, plump lips. You always know exactly what she's thinking, and I like that. "Who stay giving you trouble?" she asks me.

Complaining about the bullying is being a rat and only makes it worse. *"The nail that sticks up gets pounded down,"* Mrs. Harada says in my mind. *"Keep your head down and don't draw attention to yourself, and maybe they'll forget we're here."* Pop's version.

I'm still trying to make that approach work. "Nobody, Kumu. It's okay."

"You tell me if anyone gives you hard time. I want you to keep dancing," Kumu says. I'd do anything to make her smile like she does, looking at me.

A few weeks later, we stay late rehearsing one day for our first performance. I help Kumu pick up the hall, offering to sweep the stage for her. Kira has been calling me "suck-up" and "brownnoser", but the closer I stay to Kumu, the less likely I am to get pinched.

After Kumu locks up the building and gets in her rusty old pickup, I fetch my bike and push it across the grass in front of the beautiful green church next to the hall.

Kira and a group of kids from school come out from where they've been waiting for me, out of sight behind the building. When locals come for you, there's never just one out to beat your ass. They call it "mobbing," and they do it in a group because it works.

"Fucking *haole* crap, I told you to go home." Kira's swinging a spider lily bulb the size of a grapefruit, ripped out from the ground beside the church. She has two boys with her and two girls from hula class. I know every one of them, and how much they hate me for the color of my skin.

I jump on my bike and try to blast out of there, but they grab me before I can get up speed on the grass. They knock me off the bike. Everything is a blur of hitting with lily bulbs, hair pulling, punching, and kicking. I'm curled in a ball on the ground with my arms around my head, waiting to die, when they finally finish with me.

"Now you get the message, Haole Crap?" Kira says. "Don't come here again."

They jog away, high-fiving and laughing.

I lie there until the coast is clear, then get up slowly. I'm aching all over, covered with soil from the roots of the bulbs. I spit dirt out of my mouth, and it's ground into my hair. Even my nose is filled with dirt, and every inch of my body feels bruised. My scalp stings from losing chunks of hair. I get up, wobbling and staggering. I jump on my bike with a burst of adrenaline. Pedaling through town, tears I couldn't cry during the attack pour down my cheeks.

Mom renders first aid, puts me in a bath and to bed. I even get two pink baby aspirin, a rare treat for pain. She calls Kumu on the old rotary phone, and of course Kumu wants the names of the kids.

I won't give them up. Kira's hatred will spread even further if I tell. Being *haole* is my crime and my punishment.

I refuse to go back to hula. I refuse to go back to school. I get hysterical every time they tell me I have to go, running away into the pasture and climbing up into the trees where Mom and Pop can't reach me. I don't feel safe anywhere alone. I have bad dreams about tidal waves almost nightly and keep ending up in bed with Bonny, like when I was a little kid.

The only time I really feel good is riding Keiki, and he's my constant companion.

Mom eventually caves. She orders another set of Calvert curriculum and pulls me out of public school, telling Mr. Beck it's because of the bullying. Now Bonny and I are back to the routine we had in Wainiha—lessons in the morning followed by work hours, followed by free time.

Calvert is actually a lot harder than the work I was doing at Hanalei School, with Latin, pre-algebra, and composition writing added on to the normal subjects.

With a little help from Pop, Bonny and I build a tree fort out in the pasture in one of the ironwood trees. It's an old door resting on the branches, just a platform really, but up in the tree with its hidden handholds to climb into, I feel safer. I go there often, by myself, with a pillow and a book. Reading continues to be my best escape, a magic carpet of adventure ready to take me away any time I open those big stiff covers with their delightful musty library smell.

During our free time, Bonny and I invent elaborate games with make-believe characters, dressing up and speaking in accents. I get so good at riding Keiki that I can ride him without a saddle or bridle. My favorite game is being an Indian brave and chasing and shooting homemade arrows at Bonny, the hapless white settler, from Keiki's back.

Bonny and I are together too much, and I'm mean to her. I don't know why. She's my only real friend, but I pinch the back of her arms and cheat her out of Gigi gifts with bad trades, since I know the value of things better than she does at only seven. I don't know why I do it; I hate that I do it—and I can't seem to stop.

CHAPTER TWENTY-FIVE

THE HOKULE`A

Christmas family picture with Sarah the goat at the Estate

Age: 11, The Estate, Hanalei, Kauai, 1976

The Hokule`a, an authentic sixty-foot replica of an ancient double-hulled sailing canoe, is crewed by Hawaiians replicating the migration to Hawaii from Polynesia without anything but star navigation. It's a historic day when the sailing canoe lands in Hanalei Bay.

Our family, along with half the town, crowd along the old pier in the middle of the Bay as the huge canoe with its triangle sails makes its way slowly to tie up. A conch blows, greeting the vessel. Eager hands catch the ropes and pull the huge canoe in to the pier, securing it, as a *kahu* priest chants a *pule* prayer of blessing and greeting. The crew comes up onto the pier to applause, hugs, and greetings, and mounds of ginger, plumeria, and ti leaf lei.

We hang back and watch, proper etiquette for *haole* outsiders. We can't press in through all the locals and Hawaiians in the middle of such an important cultural event. Pop keeps his hands on our shoulders, and the warmth and strength in them feels reassuring. We may not be able to go greet the crew, but we're here, too stubborn to leave.

When the crew, dressed in traditional garb of *malo* and *kihei*, are properly buried under lei, the performances begin. Several *halau* chant and dance in the ancient style, stomping, whirling, and chanting in Hawaiian.

The sun's hot, beating down on our heads, and I can feel my perpetually sunburned nose crisping yet again. Finally, it's time to go to the park for a potluck luau under the ironwood trees.

The park's picnic tables groan with traditional Hawaiian food: *kalua* pig baked in an underground *imu* oven, succulent *laulau* wrapped in *kalo* leaves, *lomi lomi* salmon mixed with chopped tomatoes and onions, vats of rice, tubs of *poi*, bowls of *opihi*, teriyaki chicken, salty *limu* salad made of edible seaweed, guava sponge cake, lilikoi meringue pie, and delicious coconut *haupia* pudding.

Mom has brought a dish to share, too—a great big won bok and mixed vegetable salad, grown in her garden, with soy sauce and sesame seed dressing.

Standing in the food line, with my cardboard *luau* plate with the square sections, the chatter of pidgin, delicious smells, and music of ukuleles filling the air, beer flowing and everyone cheerful, I enjoy a feeling of belonging. I haven't really had that feeling since the days after the Wainiha flood. I've been a witness to something that will be remembered in song, dance, and literature for years to come.

We're too shy to approach the crew at the welcome event, but the next day the canoe has been moved, anchored inside the calm waters of Hanalei River's mouth. Mom makes a huge plate of chocolate-chip oatmeal cookies, rich with butter and brown sugar, and sends Bonny and me to the river to give them to the crew.

We're feeling still shy, but the burly Hawaiian guy on deck when we arrive grins big. "Come check her out, kids!"

Encouraged, I hand up the cookies to him. "My mom baked these for you folks. She said to tell you they're from our family." Mom made me repeat to her that I was saying they were from *our family*, the nuance there being that we're *haole,* but that we want to honor the Hokule`a too. "She said to tell you we're very proud to see you on your journey."

"Thanks! The cookies look so *ono!*" The crewman takes the cookies and gives me a hand up the rope ladder onto one of the hulls, Bonny ascending close behind.

The canoe is being used as a floating teaching school about the Hawaiians' means of travel and navigation, and I'm impressed with its size until I look at the living area, a tiny shelter that's dauntingly small for a crew of more than ten members. Everything is tidy and stowed, and there isn't a nail or bolt anywhere—the entire craft is held together with six miles of rope lashings.

On the way back to the Estate, less than a block away from the Hanalei River, Bonny and I skip and jump with excitement that we gave something from *our family* to that pioneering crew. Our bare *haole* feet touched Hokule`a's historic wooden deck, and we felt welcome.

CHAPTER TWENTY-SIX

AN EPIC BATTLE

Me, Mom, and her giant homegrown cabbage

Age: 11, The Estate, Hanalei, Kauai, 1976

Our world gets smaller and stranger as Mom and Pop drink and smoke more, hoard more supplies, and invent rules and rituals for the family as we withdraw more and more. I've seen enough by now to realize it's happening, but I can't do anything because I'm trapped in the bubble of safety that is life at the Kauikeolani Estate.

Mom budgets severely. I think it's because Pop's drinking so much beer that he's using up the food budget. We eat a lot of veggies from the garden, beans and rice combined as a protein, and drink Brewer's Yeast for nutrition. Mom mixes a tablespoonful into water for each of us in a mug. The yeast is the color of deli mustard, has a mealy texture, and tastes like raw mushrooms. Breakfast is a shake made with papaya and bran mixed together "for digestion." The papaya shakes thicken very quickly to a pudding texture if not drunk right away, and I hate the texture. One day I end up sitting at the table with a shake in front of me for an hour because it has thickened and I can't drink it. I'm not allowed to leave the table until it's gone, and eventually I get it down, gagging all the way.

"I'm glad you're away from that germ factory," Mom says, referring to Hanalei School. Getting sick in our family is no fun. If we're sick, in order not to pass germs along, we get an individual set of dishes to use, are isolated to our rooms, and given fruit and water to eat for the duration. I understand why but it feels like punishment, and both Bonny and I try to hide any symptoms of being sick for as long as possible.

Worst of all are Mom's health "colonics." She administers weekly enemas using a big red rubber hot water bottle and a white tube with a nozzle inserted into the rectum. "Did you know that the average person has five pounds of undigested meat rotting in their intestines?" she says, with that gleam in her eye that reminds me of the crazy. How could we have meat in our bowels when we don't eat any? Still, she insists the colonics are good for us and will keep us healthy.

We lie on the bathroom floor on a towel with the enema bag hanging on a hook on the wall, gravity-feeding water and an herbal mixture into our innards. My sphincter never learns to relax, and I hate the bizarre full feeling and the frenzy to reach the toilet in time in order to spew it all back out.

I think it's gross and weird, and I try to refuse. I end up getting so many wheelbarrows of cow manure and work hours as a consequence that I cave and go along with it. My mouth continues to get me into trouble—but I just can't see colonics as "normal." And I badly want to be normal.

Bonny and I bicker more and more now that we're thrown together so much. Everything she does irritates me, even though I know she's not trying to. She's still prettier and sweeter than me. Mom and Pop and the kids at school like her better. It's never been fair that way.

We still play Barbies with elaborate societal and dramatic rules. In an abandoned garden patch next to the house, we build a city for the Barbies, with roads, houses, and Breyer horses to ride. One day, feeling powerfully evil, I tie her favorite Barbie to a stake.

"Poor blonde settler woman. She's been taken captive." I'm continuing our drama in the pasture with the Barbies. "And now she's being sacrificed."

"No! Stop! No!" Bonny cries. Her eyes well up and she sobs as I pile sticks around Barbie's feet and light them with a wooden match from the big red box Pop keeps by the stove. The doll melts gruesomely, and the plastic stinks as it burns. I check to make sure Mom and Pop are nowhere around. Bonny smears the tears away and scowls. "I'll get you for this."

"I'd like to see you try." I'm still a little bigger, but she's a tall eight-year-old with long legs that promise a height that I won't have. I walk off and leave her there crying as she pours water on her melted Barbie.

Something in me feels a vicious satisfaction but shame, too, like I ate something bad, and the feeling churns in my stomach. I hate all the feelings I'm having. Some part of me knows how wrong it is to hurt my sister like this, but I can't seem to stop myself.

I go into my bedroom and escape into the Black Stallion series, which I'm rereading. As usual it instantly takes me to somewhere better. I lean alongside the Black's straining neck as he gallops across the desert. I *am* Alec.

Bonny comes into my room. She's carrying a big, round rock the size of a breadfruit that Mom brought home from the beach. She hoists it overhead.

"I'm going to smash your face." Bonny's deadly serious. Her blue-and-yellow eyes blaze. Her arms tremble with the strain of holding up the huge, heavy rock.

I sit up on my bed. I'm only a little nervous. "You wouldn't dare."

She steps closer. "I'm going to."

"Yeah, right."

She heaves the rock. It hits me square in the face and knocks me off the bed, stunned, my glasses bent, my forehead bruised.

I'm totally shocked that she actually did it.

I come roaring up off the floor like a berserker and chase her through the house. We make it all the way outside. Next to the compost pile I catch her around the waist. I throw her down on the ground, and it's a frenzy of hitting, kicking, hairpulling, biting, with us rolling in the dirt.

Somehow Bonny ends up on top, sitting on my chest. She wrenches my glasses off my face and holds them aloft.

"I'll break them," she threatens.

"Not the glasses! Not the glasses!"

They're the nice, gold-framed glasses Gigi bought me from the specialist in California. If they break, I'll have to go back to the purple plastic stop signs I had from Welfare.

"You stop being mean to me!" she yells, spit flying.

"Okay! Just give me the glasses." She hands them back. I put them on, panting with fright at almost losing my precious specs.

"Don't mess with my Barbies." Bonny is still sitting on me. "And I'm not being the settler woman anymore."

"Fine."

She gets off me and we both stand up. We go back in the house and help each other clean up in the bathroom with peroxide and bacitracin. I crack a few cubes of ice from the aluminum ice tray and put them in a paper towel, holding the ice to my swollen forehead. "I won't tell if you won't tell," I say. It's a frequent mini-conversation.

"Fine."

She's bested me physically, and it marks a turning point. I stop treating Bonny badly because she's going to hurt me if I do. I suspect, somewhere dark and half-known, that I've been acting out on her all the tortures done to me. Every time that thought tries to bubble up, I deflect it with something happier I'd like to imagine.

I'm good at not knowing things I don't want to know—like what is happening in the cottage behind us when the couple who've moved in back there scream at each other.

I can hear the sound of the man hitting his wife and her cries of pain and fright, but I shut my ears, wrapping a pillow around my head, and open a book. I pretend everything's okay until it is. The next day, I see the neighbor woman, limping and bruised. She smiles with her distorted mouth and says "Hi," and I wonder how she got hurt.

When I read, there's nothing going on for me but the story. Reading is a feeling like diving into warm water and staying under for as long as I possibly can. I savor the feeling of anticipation when I've got a new book from a favorite author, like Anne McCaffrey with her intelligent spaceships and tiny, friendly dragons. Adjusting my glasses and leaning close, a pillow rolled up under my arm, I open the book and submerge. The horror, grief, pain, and rage of people on the page are much more tolerable than any around me.

CHAPTER TWENTY-SEVEN

A GOOD GURU IS HARD TO FIND

Age: 11, The Estate, Hanalei, Kauai, and SRF Compound, La Jolla, California, 1976

Mom and Pop are still seeking a religious trip that really resonates with them. So far, Paramahansa Yogananda's teachings have stuck the longest, but the Krishnas have been visiting and evangelizing in Hanalei in their orange robes and marigolds. A family we're friends with, the Bryans, get involved. The Krishnas are building a temple outside Kapa`a, and the Bryan family invites us to a "love feast." I still feel a special fondness for Vinnie Bryan for rescuing Bonny so long ago, and I remember having fun with Kenny.

Social opportunities of any kind have become rare due to home-schooling and Pop's paranoia, so I'm excited to go check out the love feast. We pile into the Rambler and go to the Bryans' house first. The parents greet each other and light up joints on the porch to get in the mood for the evening's festivities.

Their two boys, Kenny and Paul, are around the same age as Bonny and me. Kenny has a long craggy face that might be handsome when he's older, and Paul looks like a younger, dark-haired

Vinnie. Bonny and Paul go inside to investigate his toys, and Kenny and I go explore the *hau* bush woods behind their house.

We squeeze into the dense *hau* growth. *Hau* bush is more like a giant woody vine than an actual tree, twining in a dark, sidewise-growing mosquito-ridden mass that we climb through and over for something to do. I think of Mirkwood Forest from *The Hobbit* again. This would be a great place for giant spiders to live.

"What do you think of the love feasts?" I ask. "Everybody keeps their clothes on, right?" I worry about having to see a lot of icky penises and boobs. Kenny shrugs. I can tell he's embarrassed by his parents' religion by the way his neck gets red. "It's okay. The chanting's boring."

"Chanting?"

"You know. *Krishna, Krishna, Hare Hare, Rama Rama.* It goes on a long time."

Now I know why the parents are getting stoned, and wish I could too. I've breathed enough secondhand smoke to know it makes you mellow.

Back at the house, Kenny's mom gives Bonny and me tulsi bead necklaces, which we drape around our necks for the feast. "You chant the Hare Krishna using the beads," she says. "One bead per chant."

"I know how to do that. It's like the rosary."

Kenny's mom pinches her mouth tight, but nods.

Gigi's Catholic, and showed me how a rosary works. You say *Hail Mary full of grace, deliver us* on each jet bead, and the Lord's Prayer when you get to the silver cross with the agonized Jesus on it. The tulsi beads look like the same idea to me.

We drive to the newly built Temple. The grounds are still muddy and trashed from bulldozing, and the newly planted palms and plumeria trees list about trying to get their roots settled. We meet in an open tent for a lecture—sitting cross-legged, we listen to the Krishna guru talk about oneness and karma and the interconnected nature of all things. I'm mildly interested, particularly in karma and how it deals with bullies. After that, they light bowls of incense and the chanting begins.

"Hare Krishna, hare Krishna, Krishna Krishna, hare, hare. Hare Rama, hare Rama, Rama, Rama, hare hare . . ." It goes on a very long time.

I glance over at Kenny and catch his eye. We almost burst out giggling, and Mom elbows me. I try to look spiritual and close my eyes and chant with the tulsi bead necklace like I'm supposed to.

Finally, the food. We were all supposed to bring something, so Mom brought one of her famous salads: veggies from our garden chopped up fine and topped with a pouf of homegrown alfalfa sprouts in a big wooden bowl.

We rearrange ourselves in a big circle on the *lauhala* matting floor of the tent. Orange-robed monks, just regular *haole* guys from what I can tell but with shaved heads, lay banana leaves down the center of the circle, and set the food, in bowls, on the leaves.

"Om. Shanti shanti, Om," everyone chants. Then we fold our hands and bow to each other, saying, "Namaste."

Big smiles everywhere. It really does feel loving. This must be the "love" part of the "love feast."

I'm starved by then. All the potluck food is in a row of bowls with serving spoons, and we're each given a smaller bowl but no utensils. "We eat with our fingers," Kenny whispers, miming a three-fingered scooping gesture.

The Hawaiians eat that way too, but with them, it's real—it's their culture. This seems silly, almost pretentious, like trying too hard to be exotic. I fiddle with my beads and keep my sassy mouth shut.

The adults take the food out of the center and get it circulating. We serve hummus, chuppattis, couscous, beans, guacamole, steamed veggies, and Mom's salad into our bowls. I'm so hungry I don't mind the finger food thing even though it's messy, and discover that someone has brought bowls of clear water, set near every two or three people, to rinse our fingers with. After the meal, the adults do meditation and we kids are allowed to run around.

Kenny and I explore the grounds where the Temple will be, and put flower and leaf offerings in front of the various blue, mauve, and many-armed statues sprinkling the grounds. I'm soon annoyed by all the mosquitoes and go hang out in the meditation area because they have mosquito punks lit. The smoke from these mosquito retardants swirls around, mixing with sandalwood incense and forming a strange odor—but it does keep the skeets away.

I endure about ten minutes of meditating before Anita, who's been mellow in a backpack on Pop's back, begins to fuss and it's finally time to go.

On the way home in the Rambler, Mom says, "I'm not sure about the Krishnas. Let's try the Bahá'ís next. We'll know where we're supposed to be when we find it."

I'm not sure what religion my angel was from, and I'm still looking, too.

I NEED MONEY FOR MY 4-H HORSE ADDICTION, AND SO ADVERTISE babysitting services around town with handwritten flyers: *"Responsible childcare in your home by a big sister—extra fun for kids, and I'll tidy your house, too!"* Mom tells her friends, and my little business gets off the ground. If the family's houses are in Hanalei town, I ride to them on my bike, and if they're further away they pick me up in front of the Estate in their cars.

I enjoy babysitting for the most part, and have a knack with kids from babysitting Anita and playing with younger kids so much. I don't tell the parents I'm only eleven; with my hair braided and my glasses on, I look at least thirteen or maybe fourteen. I build up a list of "regulars" and they rave because I not only play with their kids, but I wash their dishes and run the vacuum around, too. "Find a way to add value to whatever you do and people will keep coming back," Grandpa Jim would say with his bristly eyebrows aquiver at imparting one of his business gems.

I get a call from a new family, far enough away that the dad picks me up. They have a party to go to. After me and the kids, aged two and four, wave the parents off, we make forts and boxed Mac & Cheese for dinner (which I love for its forbidden processed orange fakeness), play Candy Land, take a bath, read stories, and go to bed.

After the kids are in bed, I indulge in the real reason I like babysitting.

I like to find out all about my clients—that curiosity I've always had has only gotten stronger. I want to know everything about how other people live their lives. I begin my investigations in the kitchen, sampling and inventorying their food choices. This family is loaded with *badforyou* junk; I snack on Cheez-Its, chocolate chip cookies, and pork rinds.

After bingeing carefully on food that won't be missed, I move on to the bathroom cupboards. They have some multi-vitamins and sleeping pills, and an off-brand of toothpaste and floss. For a well-off family, they're skimping on the essentials.

The mom's diaphragm, stored in a shell-shaped pink case in the bathroom cabinet, is missing. That means she's planning to have sex tonight, probably after the dad takes me home. Mom showed me her diaphragm one time, but not the gel that goes with it. I squeeze a bit of the spermicide out of a wrinkled tube and rub it between my fingers, smelling it.

It smells like Windex. Gross.

I try to imagine what goes on with this thing during sex: you fold the springy dome loaded with goo in half and shove it up into your vagina, so some man can stick his penis in there and hose it all down with sperm. Mom's explained it to me in agonizingly mortifying detail. "Sex is a beautiful act between people who love each other," Mom says. I've caught my parents in that act twice and didn't see the beauty.

On to the bedroom I go. Closets are jam-packed with clothes, a lot of dark heavy garments apparently left over from the Mainland, because they'll never wear all that wool and quilted down over here. A row of leather shoes, mildewing in the Hanalei damp, attest to the fact that this *haole* family hasn't yet fully adjusted to life in Hawaii.

I save the best for last—the bedside tables. In the drawer on the mom's side, a vibrator that looks like a pink flashlight and a copy of what I've already read, *Fear of Flying*. On dad's side, a Penthouse and a few oddly shaped implements I suspect are sex toys, and a black leather case.

The case looks important. I sit down, put in on my knees, and press the little catch with a keyhole in it. It pops open, and lying in the foam is a revolver with a black plastic grip. I take it out. It's heavy and smells like machine oil. It's probably not loaded because there's a row of bullets sitting in a channel in the foam, but I feel like I've been naughty just by touching it. I put the gun back, close the case, and put it away. I curl up to read Penthouse with a bag of Cheez-Its until the parents come home.

I hear the crunching of the car on the gravel a long way off, and put the magazine and snacks away in plenty of time. I'm washing the dishes, looking virtuous, when the couple comes rolling in.

"Ready for a ride home, cutie pie?" the dad says. *Oh great.* It's gonna be one of those. I look at the mom to intervene, but she's already staggering down the hallway.

The dad weaves as we drive, bumping from side to side, and thankfully the road is deserted. I hold onto the sissy handle and check my seatbelt, praying to get home without ending up against a coconut tree.

"Are you a natural redhead?" he asks with a grin. "I love redheads."

"What do you mean?"

"Does the carpet match the drapes?"

I don't know what he's trying to say, but I bet it's something nasty. I've seen which Penthouse pictures he folds the corners down on. "I don't dye my hair, no."

"How old are you?" He puts his hand on my leg.

I take his hand off and put it back in his lap. "Eleven."

"Jesus!" he exclaims. "I thought you were older."

"Most people think I'm thirteen."

He doesn't reply to that.

At our driveway, he peels off a twenty, way too much money. I don't offer change, just stuff it in my pocket and trot off into the darkness, mentally striking their name off my list of clients. A dad like that might be harder to fend off next time.

With the success of my babysitting business, I'm able to pay for the food for Keiki and fees for the gymkhana and riding classes I take. I even buy a goat, a registered Toggenburg named Sarah. Pop helps me fence a little pen in the corner of the yard, and we build a stall for her when it rains. Sarah becomes very attached to me and follows me around like a puppy, bleating whenever I leave her.

It also feels good to have money to loan the family when we come up short at the end of the month. They always pay me back, and I like helping.

Pop's still drinking too much, and his dark mood comes and goes. It seems like I'm always on the verge of setting him off these days—everything I do annoys him. Now that I'm not in school, Pop thinks the best use of my time is helping with his work hours.

I totally get why Pop hates his job. I hate it too. Except for the drive mower, which I enjoy, it's boring. There is no easier way to do some things, which is so frustrating, and it's physically tiring. I rake up big, paddlelike *kamani* leaves from the lawn of the beach house that's a part of the Estate, doing yet another hour of yard work for some comment he thought was sassy. The *kamani* leaves, for instance, are each the size of a dinner plate and the shape and heaviness make them hard to rake. We can't use them on Mom's mulch pile because they take too long to break down, so I'm stuck raking them, then loading them into a wheelbarrow and pushing it across hundreds of yards of lawn out to the pasture, where I dump them with the other non-composting yard waste into a giant pile with coconuts, palm fronds, and tree branches that also don't break down easily.

I usually take Sarah with me to do my yard work. Sarah is curious and interested in everything. Her yellow goat eyes with their slit pupils are kind of spooky, but she can't help that. She likes to nibble on my hair, and she has silky lips that feel like gentle tickly kisses.

No matter what I'm doing, if Sarah's along it's more fun. I get lonely in my corner of the giant yard, working, but she's good company.

Bonny's been bitten and thrown enough by Keiki to decide she doesn't want him now that I've outgrown him, so we find a new home for my beloved Shetland. A family buys him who has a boy a little younger than Bonny. They promise to take good care of him, and I give him a goodbye ride around the pasture without saddle or bridle—he listens to me perfectly, but now my feet dangle well below his knees. He's been a great first pony, and I'm confident on bigger horses now because of the hard knocks Keiki gave me when we first started out.

I hug him and whisper "I love you" in his fuzzy ear, and they cart him off in a rented trailer. I mope for days, even though I knew it was time.

Summer rolls around, and Gigi has agreed to pay for Yoga Camp at the Self-Realization Fellowship compound.

"Grease up your jeweled cork!" Pop chortles, in a good mood at the prospect of getting rid of me for a while. I fly alone to California, enjoying extra macadamia nut packets and a silver United Airlines pin from the stewardesses watching me through plane changes.

Gigi enfolds me in her powdered-chemical-flowers hug at the airport, and after that I press my cheek against Grandpa's golf-sweatered chest. He's a big man, well over six feet, and his two-tone loafers are enormous.

"Let's get you outfitted." Gigi jingles her gold bracelets with anticipation as we get into Grandpa's black Cadillac.

"I'm fine, Gigi, I have the clothes you bought when I came for the specialist.'"

She eyeballs me. "We'll start at JCPenney's."

Gigi's shopping trips, mandatory at every visit, have begun to be agonizing. She brings ruffly, scratchy, and over bright clothes to my dressing room, loading me up in a never-ending stream until I start saying yes just to get it over with—and then, she circles around when the clothes are on, saying, "Hmm," and patting my hips.

"You need a bra," she tells me, pinching my hip as she adjusts the back waistband of the pants, her way of telling me she thinks I'm getting fat.

"No," I say, crossing my arms over my still-flat chest—and feeling the hard, painful nubs that have begun to poke out my T-shirts.

"Yes. Your—um." She gestures. "They're visible." Gigi would never say nipple.

In the end I leave Penney's with a training bra, several pairs of itchy polyester "slacks," and a couple of ruffled blouses. I do manage to get one pair of denim shorts and a T-shirt out of it, which are the compromise items I get to keep for letting her pick the rest.

We have a "lady lesson" dinner for old times' sake at the Country Club, complete with a review of Grandpa's achievements in front of his portrait, but I've memorized my manners and don't need any reminders. As a reward, I'm allowed a trip to the dessert table.

I'm stocking up for asceticism at yoga camp and come back with a heap of sugary sweets that makes even Grandpa's brows go up. He pats my wrist in rare approval, shutting down Gigi's protests. "Girl's fine the way she is. Let her eat a few desserts."

The next day, my grandparents, looking a little uncertain, drive the Cadillac into the Self-Realization Temple between entrance pillars topped with giant golden lotuses. I say goodbye for a week, and walk off with a saffron-robed woman who takes me to a large, airy dormitory.

The grounds are huge, and the other kids are surprisingly normal. I even like the yoga and meditation classes, and especially the silent "self-reflection time" we have in the afternoon when we are supposed to journal and think about things. I like journaling and thinking about things. Sitting on my little red pillow in the meditation room, I cogitate on what's been happening in my life.

It feels like the tidal wave I've feared has engulfed me with feelings—powerful feelings that buffet me about like the waves I like to surf in Hanalei Bay.

Anger at the kids at school who bullied me or stood by watching while it went on. *Jealousy* of how things are easier for Bonny, and that she's prettier. *Jealousy* of the Big House kids, and all they have, like

Nicole's beautiful horse, Huni, who's getting fat from not being ridden. *Fear* of what's happening to our family as Pop gets more unpredictable and Mom's wrapped up in the baby.

In fact, there isn't much going on in my life that makes me happy except riding and my goat, Sarah.

The meditation teacher, a beautiful older Indian lady, wears a sari and a dot on her forehead. She tells us to let go and observe thoughts and feelings, to distance ourselves from them. Her twittering, bird-like voice is enhanced by her accent. "Yogananda has said, 'If you permit your thoughts to dwell on evil, you yourself will become ugly. Look only for the good in everything so you absorb the quality of beauty.'"

This truth spreads through me like a tea bag in hot water, releasing color and flavor. I look out at the glass-framed vista of the gardens with the ocean in the distance. I feel the beauty soaking in—and Kauai is the most beautiful place of all.

But I already carry ugliness inside of me—ugliness that's been put on me and done to me, and now is a part of me. I'm mean, jealous, selfish, greedy. *Ugly.*

I don't know what's going to happen in my life, to my family. I'm still just a kid, and I can't control anything. I can't stay ahead of what's coming, prepare for it, or figure it out. But I *can* be in this moment, right now, and fully experience it.

Through meditation practice, I learn to sit quietly in my head, tolerate my dark feelings, and be okay in spite of them. I learn that exercise and being in nature help me feel better. And I begin to write as a way to sort it all out, using words to understand myself and the world through journaling.

The food is as I suspected: sugar, meat, and artificial-free. I crave sugar the first few days but come to appreciate the sweetness of beet salad and the fluffiness of couscous, though I'm never going to be a fan of lentils. We're still eating them with every meal at home because The End of the World didn't happen, and they were getting moldy.

Yoga class is taxing, even for someone my age. We hold the poses until muscles are trembling, and I do my first headstands and splits. It feels good to master my body, along with a measure of control over my mind and emotions.

On our last day at camp, we tour Paramahansa Yogananda's opulent former living quarters. I'm startled by the luxury and feel a little betrayed, as if finding out my favorite TV evangelist drove a Rolls—which Yogananda did, too.

At the end of the tour, we form a line and head toward an altar that holds a pair of leather shoes set on orange velvet draping. "The *prana* of the Master is concentrated in his shoes," our teacher tells us. "We kiss them to partake in his energy."

I shuffle forward with the rest of the kids, trying to tell myself I believe this—but I don't. Shoes don't have energy. They have foot odor, and germs, and kissing anyone's shoes feels like slavery, not freedom.

I finally get to the shoes.

I really look at them. They're leather slippers, arranged on an orange cloth with a few other mementoes: a lock of dark brown hair, a watch and pin, a fresh, plump marigold.

I won't kiss anybody's shoes. It's just not my nature. I'm too stubborn, stiff-necked, and proud, the Guru would say.

I guess I need a few more turns on the wheel of karma.

CHAPTER TWENTY-EIGHT

LOSSES HURT

Me, Anita, and Huni the Horse

Age: 12, The Estate, Hanalei, Kauai, 1977

I want to go visit Keiki at his new family's house in Moloa`a. The family had said I could, and in spite of having a leased horse and Nicole's Huni to ride, I miss my fuzzy little palomino rascal-buddy.

241

"Can we stop by their house on our way home from town next time we go?" I ask Mom one day.

"Toby." Mom gets serious, switching plump Anita to her other hip. "I didn't know how to tell you this, but...Keiki died."

My face feels frozen, my eyes open too wide. "What?"

"You know how he loves coconut." Keiki's favorite treat was a whole coconut, smacked in half with a pickaxe. He'd put his little muzzle into the open coconut half and chew it out with his big yellow teeth. "The dad broke open a coconut for him, and he ate a piece of the shell. He choked to death."

The horrible picture my overactive imagination creates makes me recoil. I want to vomit, can actually taste it in the back of my throat. Mom reaches out to hug me, her hazel eyes fogging, but I can't stand to be touched. I'm gasping with pain, hyperventilating.

I run to my room and grab my pillow, blanket, journal, and current library book, a four-inch-thick promise of mental escape called *Dune*, by Frank Herbert. I scramble through the fence and run across the rough, tussocky pasture barefoot, all the way to my tree fort. Up the hidden handholds I go, awkward with my burdens. Up on my platform in the swishing branches of the big ironwood tree, I make a nest and cry for my lost pony, face in the pillow and blanket over my head.

I feel like I'm crying for everything I've ever lost and never had.

I'm crying for the end of my childhood, for all the silly, lovable, naughty ponies in the world who have to die someday—because we all do. Everything good always ends.

I cry until I'm hollowed out, great gouts of tears and snot soaking my pillow, my throat raw with howls of grief.

I've never been a pretty crier when I really let go, and the best place for emotional storms is out in nature. I'm just another small wounded animal, briefly here, suffering, and soon forgotten. Nature can handle my storms, even if other people say I'm too intense, that I feel too much. Nature can take it all, even when I worry that my feelings are so strong that they'll break me, and I'll go crazy like Mom did.

When I'm done crying, I sit up, close my eyes, and get into the lotus position. The chatter of mynahs, the funny beeping call of the Hawaiian coots in the turtle pond nearby, the wind in the branches of the ironwood tree, shushing, swishing—all these sounds soothe me. Flakes of sunlight fall though the branches onto me, and the breeze dries the tears off my hot face. Calm and emptiness fill me, and that's a relief. I'll stay out here all night, and fast without food to honor Keiki and all he meant to me.

I open *Dune* and escape into a world of intrigue and giant sandworms.

But like that other time I ran away grieving for a lost pet, mosquitoes and my empty stomach eventually drive me back to the house. Skulking into my room after dark, foraging for a snack in the rusty refrigerator, I'm ashamed of my weakness.

Keiki deserves at least a full day of fasting to honor what he meant to me, but I can't master my body or my emotions. Eating cold brown rice with a spoon from the leftover pot as I stand in the light emitted by the refrigerator, I worry that, along with ugliness, I'm seeded with crazy.

MOM AND POP DECIDE TO CELEBRATE THEIR ANNIVERSARY BY taking a three-day hike along the Na Pali Coast to Kalalau, leaving me in charge of the house and my sisters. They've been fighting lately, angry whispered rumblings in their bedroom. Pop's still hating his job as the groundskeeper. Mom's still working up at the Big House, cleaning and watching the girls when Gaylord and Carol go out. They're both feeling frazzled and overworked in spite of morning surfing.

Mom tells me more than I want to know, as usual. "We haven't had any really good sex since Anita was born, and we really need to reconnect." She's also worried about Pop's drinking because I see her counting the beer bottles in the recycling box by the back steps.

"You're such a good babysitter, I'm sure it will be fine. We'll have some people poking their heads in to check on you girls."

The three of us kids stand on the porch and wave goodbye as they drive off in the Rambler.

The adults looking in on us consist of a hippie chick friend of Mom's named Twig, a skinny high-strung woman who makes us nervous. Anita cries just looking at her. Surfer friends, Tom and Cheri Hamilton, who currently live in their van, are really nice— Tom has a rumbly voice that's reassuring and I've never seen him anything but mellow, and Cheri is a strong, tall woman with long, ripply blonde hair and a practical manner. Both sets of friends drive up the first day, come into the house and see that we're alive and have food in the fridge, and leave, saying, "Call us if you need anything."

Anita has a bout of diarrhea and fusses for hours at bedtime. She gets sicker and runs a fever. Halfway through the night I remember I'm still just a kid, but I don't feel like one, walking her and heating her bottle of expressed breast milk, dunking and swishing her slime-coated cloth diaper in the toilet, and worrying that we'll run out of clean diapers and have to call someone for a ride to the Laundromat to wash the hideous contents of the ammonia-reeking pail.

I'm so exhausted from not sleeping and being stressed out that I think of calling Tom and Cheri, but they don't have a phone; maybe they'll stop by, maybe they won't. Twig has one, but I can't imagine how she'd be helpful. So, I assign Bonny and me shifts carrying and entertaining fussy Anita.

Anita's heavy as she rests her hot head on my shoulder. Her plume of white-blonde hair tickles my nose as she wriggles uncomfortably in my arms, and I know I don't feel right to her. I'm too small. My shoulder is hard and bony, my chest flat, my arms stringy around her solid plumpness. Her green eyes are sunk in pouches of red from crying, and her little pink cowrie mouth is turned down.

My imagination, always so powerful, is my enemy. Every time I set her down in her crib, I imagine she's dead when I come back to check on her. I can see everything about it: her ashy, limp body lying there. How I try to do CPR and accidentally crush her ribs, like the health nurse at school told me can happen. I can feel the rubbery touch of her dead lips as I try to blow life into her. The pain I felt when Keiki died would be nothing compared to the grief of losing Anita, and everyone would blame me for letting her die.

I'm terrified, and yet calling 911 is out of the question unless Anita is in a coma or something. The ambulance will come, and it will cost a fortune, and The Man will be alerted. They might even put all three of us in a foster home for being left alone without a parent.

I try everything to soothe Anita: a bath, which she usually loves but now shrieks at, taking her for a walk in her stroller, even dosing her with baby aspirin which finally gets her to sleep. That break means Bonny and I have time to wash and scrub the disgusting diapers in the kitchen sink, wringing them out by hand and hanging them out to dry on the clothesline outside, where sunshine and palm trees mock me.

I'm never having kids. It's just too scary when they get sick.

Anita is feeling better by the time Mom and Pop get back late the next day. Their faces are lit with "reconnecting," which I imagine consists of skinny-dipping and having sex while dropping acid or eating some of Doug's honey-soaked magic mushrooms. Anita's already reaching for Mom with her chubby hands as I hand her over. "We survived. Please don't ever do that again."

"Yeah," Bonny says. She has her hands on her hips. "Toby was so bossy! She is not the mom!" Her voice accuses Mom of leaving us too, and I'm glad of the support even though I'm the bad guy. Pop ignores us all and goes into the house.

"It's a mess in here," he grumbles from inside. "Smells gross." I tremble with rage, thinking of the mountain of diapers I washed, of the sleepless nights, of my fear and responsibility.

"Didn't Tom and Cheri and Twig help you?" Mom looks glossy and tan, smiling and happy. She's not taking us seriously. She thinks it was okay to leave us, and I can tell by the gleam in her eye that she's already planning her next escape.

"No. There wasn't anything they could do. Anita was really sick."

Mom doesn't care how we feel.

I know something new: for Mom and Pop, we kids don't really exist as people with needs that matter. Other parents sacrifice to give their children education, lessons, opportunities. But not our parents. We're there for them, not the other way around.

I wonder why it took me so long to notice this.

CHAPTER TWENTY-NINE

THE CUP INCIDENT

Age: 11-12, The Estate, Hanalei, Kauai, 1977

The afterglow of Mom and Pop's Na Pali Coast hiking adventure doesn't last long. Pop grumbles constantly about his twenty hours a week. He sits in his room after work every afternoon, playing guitar, sipping Primo beer, and smoking *pakalolo*. His angry depression is a black cloud that I can almost see and definitely feel. We all give him a wide berth and try to stay quiet because his temper explodes at random intervals into yelling, stomping, and door slamming.

I join Mom in monitoring the beer bottles by the back door. He starts drinking at noon now. Mom tries to keep everything calm. She's worried because he's literally drinking our food budget away. I feel bad for her because the three of us kids are never quiet enough, and he snarls and stomps around the house before he leaves for the eternal mowing.

Our world gets even smaller. Trips to town are fewer and fewer, and even trips to Hanalei. Adults stopping me and asking, "Why aren't you in school?" has made me feel like there's something wrong with what we're doing, and Mom and Pop don't want to draw attention to the fact that Bon and I aren't attending. Between the bullying attack at hula and homeschooling causing comments, I stop roaming town on my bike.

Homeschooling gets sketchier. Mom just hands me the Teacher Guide and says, "Follow the assignments." We stop mailing our tests and bigger assignments to Calvert for grading. "Too expensive. We don't need those extras," Mom says.

We have a very lean Christmas, with a tiny Norfolk pine in a bucket as a tree, and handmade ornaments. Gigi's longed-for boxes don't get to us in time to open, and presents under the tree are a plastic Pokey for me and a Gumby for Bonny, with walnuts and store-bought oranges in our stockings.

"Christmas is so commercial, anyway," Mom says, fixing corn bread for breakfast as a treat. "It should be about love."

I feel ashamed of my disappointment, and I can tell Bonny feels the same by our guilty glances at each other.

Doug, our mushroom-selling neighbor, gives us our nicest presents: a horse care book, new hoof pick and hoof ointment for me, and a good quality pocketknife for Bonny. We are thrilled with these.

We're invited over to the Big House on Christmas afternoon for cookies and to play. Bonny and I goggle over the massive Norfolk pine our dad cut down and installed in the vast living room of the Big House for the family, dressed with colored lights and glass balls. We eat gingerbread cookies and watch the girls ride their shiny new Big Wheels all around the giant porches of the Big House, and wait for our turn to ride when they get tired of them.

Standing there, picking the Red Hot eye off a gingerbread man Carol Wilcox baked, I realize we're poor. Really poor, and we're servants. It's not a good feeling. It makes me want to hide from the world even more. Because we aren't really poor—we're here this way because Mom and Pop have chosen this life on Kauai. They could have had the "normal" life Gigi and Grandpa Jim tried to give them. But we're here so they can live in Hanalei and surf every day, without thinking about how it feels to be standing in a doorway on Christmas Day, looking at plenty.

Anger blooms in my heart. I do my yoga breathing and try to be present in the *now*, like Yogananda says. But all I feel is jealous of the abundance in front of me that I can't have, and shame because I don't want to feel that way. I want to be proud and throw the ginger-bread man in the trash, but I am too hungry for the sugar and sweet of it. Shame and anger tie my stomach in a knot and I sneak off, climbing into my tree fort with the cookie and my book, where I escape into a reread of the Lord of the Rings.

Books are my escape and comfort, a world I can disappear into whenever I want, where battles are epic and enemies are clear.

MY TWELFTH BIRTHDAY'S IN JANUARY, AND AS A BIRTHDAY present, Aunty Jan, my mom's youngest sister from her first family of four, pays for me to come visit her in Honolulu. She's a single woman working for a big Oahu corporation, and she wears business suits and her hair is in a severe blunt cut, even in Hawaii. We've had a special connection since I was five, when Mom and Pop left me with her for a week when they took baby Bonny on a camping trip.

Aunty Jan meets me in the open-air Interisland Terminal at the Honolulu Airport with its wafts of plumeria flowers and jet fuel. I'm so excited I'm almost hopping as she leads me to her little Honda Civic at the Honolulu Airport. Her zippy little car is the end-all of groovy.

"You look like you could use a treat." Aunty Jan has a female version of Grandpa Garth's booming voice that makes me smile and a big laugh that tickles the air. She doesn't agree with a lot of Mom's health food opinions. She takes me to famous Napoleon's Bakery, and we eat sugary treats and I drink my first cup of coffee, liberally laced with cream. I'm so hyper after that we take on Ala Moana Shopping Center, one of the biggest malls in the whole United States now that it's 1976. The floors and floors of stores, from ritzy Liberty House at the top to the Chinese Market at the bottom, are completely overwhelming.

Aunty Jan takes me to the Honolulu Zoo, exotic and smelly under the spreading banyans, the nearby Aquarium, and to the University of Hawaii Manoa. We drive over the breathtaking switchbacks of the Pali Highway to see Kaneohe again, and on the way back we stop at the top of Pali at a lookout, and lean into wind that's so strong it holds us up.

It's a magical weekend, and I come home to Hanalei heady with the discovery of a wide world of wonders just an island away.

Mom picks me up at Lihue Airport in the Rambler with Bonny.

"Did you have fun?" Bonny's face is bright, and I give her thick blonde braid a tug.

"I bought you presents," I say by way of answer. Bonding over the three days we were left with Anita brought us close, and I feel guilty for having done something fun she didn't get to share. Besides, Ala Moana Shopping Center is just too mind-blowing to put into words.

Mom's worry shows in folded-together lips and a frown that won't go away. "You girls need to be quiet when we get home. Pop's cutting back on his drinking, and he's grumpy."

I subside into silence, feeling the newly expanded world I'd just glimpsed contracting around me again. At home, I take Bonny into my room and open my backpack to show her the presents Aunty Jan and I bought her. Mom takes Anita, who's fussy again, outside for a walk.

Pop barely greeted me upon our return from the airport, but now he comes to the door. He's still wearing sweaty work clothes and the black mood is dense around him.

"Bonny, you need to do the dishes."

"Just a minute." Bonny's back is to the door so she doesn't see his thunderous expression. She's opening a wrapped gift from Aunty Jan.

"You better hurry," I whisper as he disappears. She speeds up unwrapping the gift, but she's distracted by the new Barbie she's uncovering and trying to open the box.

Pop's at the door again. "I told you to do the dishes!" he roars.

He reaches in with one long, tanned, muscular arm and grabs hold of Bonny's braid. He gives a savage yank that hauls her right through the door and into the hall. Her hands come up to try and take the weight off her hair, grabbing onto his hand.

I jump up in shock. *This is my fault.* I distracted Bonny so she didn't listen. I brought his wrath on us by leaving the family and not making sure everything was okay. I run after them as Bonny's dragged down the hall and all the way across the kitchen by her hair. "Pop! No! Please, stop. This is my fault!"

I can't hear anything or see anything but Bonny's face, distorted by the pulling on her scalp. Her eyes looking back at me are stark and huge—blue-gray with yellow specks, not green at all. I noticed that a long time ago, but I forgot.

He hauls her to the drainboard and shoves her head into the sink, still holding onto her hair.

"I told you to wash the dishes," he grinds out. He grabs his china mug of yeast water and dashes it in her face.

"Pop, no! You're hurting her!" I yell from the doorway, heading toward them. He's still got her by the hair, holding her dripping face over the sink, but he swivels and his eyes are the exact shade as hers. His face is so red and twisted that I can't even tell it's him.

He throws the mug with a heave of his arm. It hits me in the face with so much force I fly backward.

Everything goes black.

I HEAR A HIGH-PITCHED SOUND LIKE A TEAPOT LEFT ON. AS I slowly come back from somewhere else, it gets louder—it's someone screaming.

Pain accompanies surges of red that have replaced the black behind my eyelids.

If only I could go back to wherever I was.

I don't want to be around for whatever's coming next.

I keep my eyes shut, and that's a good thing because blood fills my eye sockets. I feel its heavy gooey wetness, smell its coppery heat on my twitching eyelids. Mom's yelling at Pop, somewhere overhead.

The hands touching me, putting something that feels like a towel on my head, are Bonny's small light ones.

She was the one screaming.

Mom puts my head in her lap. She's dabbing at my forehead with something wet, and she's crying. Bonny's crying. Anita's crying. Even Pop is crying as he keeps saying, "I'm sorry. I didn't mean to do it."

I feel queasy and sleepy. Eventually, they get me cleaned up. There's a discussion about the hospital because my forehead is nastily cut. I chew the maximum amount of orange, sweet baby aspirin tablets allowed, but my head still really hurts. Somehow, I'm propped up in bed in clean clothes. My bloody shirt is floating in the toilet, where we usually soak Anita's dirty diapers.

"I told you I was sorry," Pop says, sitting on the bed. My eyes are almost swollen shut so it's hard to see him. "You don't want me to go to jail, right? If you tell what happened they'll put me in jail. So, you can't tell or it's the end of our family."

"Okay." I don't want anyone to know this happened. I don't want Pop to go to jail when he's obviously sorry. It was really my fault he lost his temper with Bonny, and as usual I brought shit down on myself with my loud, sassy mouth.

We don't go to the hospital. They put my forehead together with butterfly Band-Aids, and I stay at home until all the swelling goes down in my face, which takes a while. Bonny and I don't talk about what happened, but at night she comes and sleeps with me. All of us lie to anyone who asks and say, "Toby fell off a horse and hit her head."

Mom's been planning to take Anita to meet her mother, Stella, who we call Maga. She calls Maga after the Cup Incident, in spite of the long-distance charges. Mom drags the phone into our parents' room, and I hear lots of whispered confabbing.

A week or so after the Cup Incident, she announces, "I'm taking Anita on a trip with Maga to Guatemala for a month. I need to think about things."

Pop, who's gone to an anger management counselor in Lihue at her insistence, folds his lips shut and doesn't say a word. I'm shocked that he's going along with this. He hates it when she goes anywhere without him, but he's quiet now because he's afraid she's going to leave him.

Yep, she's going to leave us with him, and take off with Anita and start a new life. Bonny and I go for a walk with her, pushing Anita's stroller, to get her alone.

"Don't leave us here with him!" Bonny begs, tearing up. "We're scared!" Bonny hardly ever emotes like this. Mom blinks hard, and I can tell she's feeling bad.

"We don't know what might happen when you're gone." I hang on her arm. "Please take us with you, too."

I've barely got the Band-Aids off my forehead and the scar is still puffy, marking me for life. If the Cup Incident happened when Mom was out taking a walk, what could happen if she's gone for a month?

"He's sorry and he means it," Mom says stoutly. "Pop's not drinking anymore, but he's smoking *pakalolo,* so he'll be mellow. He's going to the anger management counselor. And he knows I'll leave him if he does anything."

That doesn't reassure us.

During one of their confabs, I overheard him complaining about the stupidity of having to go to anger management. "This would all go away if I just had a different job. Like I told the counselor, I hate my job and that's what's making me angry."

"We'd have to move because your job is tied to this house," Mom told him. "Anyway, I need to get away and think about everything. I'll know what we should do when I get back."

I don't think she's coming back at all. This is Mom's way of easing out the door without a big scene. She's afraid of Pop, too. She'll go to California, to Maga's house with Anita, and we'll get a have-a-nice-life letter.

I can't bring myself to say goodbye when she leaves. Bonny and I will have no one to protect us if Pop gets mad—though I do believe he's scared, too—scared of being stuck with us, without her.

I hug Anita goodbye, though, trying not to let her see me cry. She's so sturdy and plump, with the same green eyes Bonny and Pop have and that shiny white hair, and the delicious marshmallow on the back of her neck that I love to kiss. The weight of her body and all the nights I've walked her and carried her have made a baby-shaped impression on my chest and arms.

I tack up Huni, who the Wilcoxes let me ride because he doesn't get enough exercise. I take him out into the pasture to avoid seeing Pop drive Mom and Anita to the airport. I run him around my homemade obstacle course until we're both too tired to feel much of anything.

Pop starts drinking again right after she leaves, but only two or three beers a night. Bonny and I don't let down our guard, but like Mom said, Pop tries to be nice. He's carefully polite, shutting the door when he pees and saying "Excuse me" when he farts. He goes to the store and buys a few special things like cheddar cheese and bread. He even cooks sometimes, though Bonny and I do the other household chores and our usual hours.

One evening, while playing guitar, he calls us into the bedroom.

"You girls need to learn to relax," he says. "Especially you, Toby. Always so uptight." We're used to watching him roll his own joints or pack a bowl, but we glance at each other with wide eyes when he hands us each a joint. "This will help you relax."

"Mom wouldn't like us smoking," I say bravely.

"She doesn't have to know, does she?" Pop smiles, and the squint lines next to his eyes make them look friendly. I know better. His face is chiseled with lines now, the blond hair gone from the top of his head but for around his ears, a few lonely strands brushed across his scalp. He looks older than thirty-three.

I remember how handsome he used to be, how I thought he looked like a Viking god when he chased the local guys away from our camp. I think of him teaching me to fish, and taking me on hikes, and about how much I wanted to be James Theodore the Third, the son he never had. I think of all of that in a flash, and I take the joint from the big square hand that is the original of mine.

He lights my joint and shows me how to drag on it, then hold the smoke in my lungs—hot sweet thick darkness—before letting my breath out slowly to get the maximum effect.

Then he does the same with Bonny, while I take another drag.

We both cough at first, but like every new thing I take on, I'm determined to master this thing I've seen the grown-ups all around me spend so much money and time on. There must be a reason *pakalolo* is so special, and if so, I want in.

I feel dizzy at first, then giggly—but not relaxed. I feel energized, and a bubble of what might be happy, a feeling like Christmas morning when there are presents. A feeling like galloping Keiki down the beach, or taking off on a wave, or leaping off the pier into that turquoise water below. A very good feeling.

I go outside into the yard, where darkness is welling like a rising tide. I leap across the lawn, dancing ballet, which I haven't done since lessons in La Jolla. I sing my current favorite song: "Bye, bye, Miss American Pie. Drove my Chevy to the levee but the levee was dry . . ."

I eventually wind down and go back inside. Pop is plunking his guitar, picking out "American Pie." He smiles at me. "*Pakalolo* made you hyper," he says. "Never heard of that before." Bonny is curled against his side, fast asleep.

"Yeah, but I'm happy," I say, and we both smile. It's the closest we've been in years. But, he won't let me have any more joints after that because me being hyper is the last thing he wants.

We fall into a nice routine. Bonny and I help with the yard work, take care of the animals, do our school stuff. I fix dinner, usually simple soups and biscuits, sometimes tacos. We both clean the house.

In the evenings, Pop drinks his beer, smokes his bowl, and plays guitar. We listen, reading books on the big bed beside him. I lie next to him on one side, Bonny on the other, as he picks out a new slack-key song he's been working on. His hands handle the guitar gently but firmly, coaxing the music out. The afternoon light shines in and lights the blond hairs on his legs, and his skin is the golden-brown of

Keiki's palomino coat. Bonny looks more like him, and it makes me a little jealous. I have his hands and feet, though.

During these mellow afternoons he tells us about himself. "I couldn't be what my dad wanted. I couldn't handle the pressure. Grandpa Jim wanted a son who could follow in his footsteps, and I just wasn't up to it." He tells us he was drafted for the Vietnam War, but at the exam he was disqualified. "Four-F. So many guys were trying for that, and I just answered everything honestly and got out of the draft because my anxiety was so bad." I can tell Four-F means something's wrong with you mentally or physically. He goes on. "I used to get so nervous before Mom and Dad's cocktail parties that Mom would give me Valium. I started drinking when I was about you kids' age. I could handle dealing with people when I'd had a few beers."

I didn't know that about Pop. In all the Wilson family pictures, he's tall and handsome and looks the part they wanted him to play—but really, he couldn't handle much more than surfing and being a fix-it man.

Sometimes after work he takes us surfing by the pier, which he hasn't done in ages, and when we go into town, he takes us to breakfast at the Kountry Kafe, and even to a matinee at the big, creaky old firetrap theatre in Kapa`a. Eating *badforyou* movie popcorn, sitting on the hard-wooden chairs watching the flickering screen, I decide we might be okay if Mom doesn't come back.

But Mom finally does get back. After a month in Mexico and Guatemala, she's lost weight and looks beautiful and tan from hiking and exploring the villages. Anita is all silver hair and gold skin. Both of them look prettier than I've ever seen them, and this makes me scared.

Mom has always had something about her, a mysterious something that's more than just looks. Even as her thighs have gone triangular and her breasts flat from nursing Anita, she's still as sexy as one of those ancient fertility goddesses. Men love her. They like to talk to her, flirt with her, hang out with her, and she with them. I wonder if she met someone in Guatemala and feel guilty for thinking it.

Mom is like a kerosene lamp—pungent and bright, warm and inviting, and always has the potential for explosion. In the times when she's happy and loving, I draw close and want nothing more than to reflect her light. But there's always been an unevenness to how she burns, a flaring so that black soot streaks the glass, and that's her inner crazy.

She finishes a bowl of the welcome-home soup and biscuits I made, and looks across the table at Pop. His eyes are bloodshot from getting loaded this afternoon, like he does every day. Fear makes his hand tremble as he crumbles a biscuit into his bowl.

There's a clear, determined look on Mom's face: her chin is up, her jaw is tight, and those forest-stream eyes are wide and focused. A reckoning is at hand. She is not under the influence of anything, and it makes me realize how often, in the past, she was. Anita chews her biscuit in her high chair, looking on.

Mom takes a breath, blows it out, and sits up straighter. "I took the trip in spite of the Cup Incident because it was already planned, and I needed to think things through. I'm leaving you," she says to Pop. "You need to get sober and get your head and your anger under control. Girls, we're going to visit Maga in Santa Barbara for a while. I already have the tickets."

Mom already has reservations for us to leave? Reservations to the Mainland mean money has been spent. The journey might as well be carved in stone. Bon and I are shocked into open-mouthed silence.

Color drains from Pop's ruddy face. He reaches toward her, pleading. "No. Let's talk this over."

"How long are we going to be gone? What about the animals?" I ask, trying to keep my voice steady as I think of the horses I ride, and my goat, Sarah.

"I don't know how long we'll be gone." Mom won't look at me. "It's up to your dad when he gets himself together. But it could be a while."

Bonny and I glance at each other, connected by invisible ESP. She's feeling just like I do—sad, scared, a little bit happy that we're leaving him, and guilty too. We liked our special times with Pop in the evenings, but we're also breathless with relief that Mom didn't abandon us after all. The scar on my forehead hasn't gone away, even with nightly applications of popped Vitamin E capsules, and it reminds me every day how bad things could get.

After dinner, I carry Anita into my room with me to pack. Anita's sweet and calm like she always is, and I set her on my bed. She is wearing a white Mexican baby dress with bright, elaborate embroidery on the yoke and her green eyes are round as a doll's in her tan face. She pops a finger in her mouth and lies down, snuggling into my pillow and watching as I pull my old suitcase out from under my bed.

The suitcase's got dust on it. It never used to be stashed in one place long enough to gather dust, but we've been here for three years, the longest we've been at any house.

I hear Mom and Pop's voices clearly through the single wall that separates my room from theirs. Mom's voice is high and loud, making declarative sentences. Pop's is a low, sorrowful rumble.

I feel so sorry for him, but I'm mad at him too. I wish I could hate him, but I can't. The mass of confused feelings I have is like a ball of yarn stuck in my throat.

It would have been easier if she'd left him right after the Cup Incident, that innocuous description marking a detonation in our family. If she'd left him then, we wouldn't have had time for this half-healing that's given him hope.

There's silence in the other room for a long moment, and I wonder if they're kissing. They've always had a lot of sex. Sex was what he was hoping for when he showered, shaved, and put on the clean shirt I had washed and dried in the sun for him.

In our years of tents and close quarters, and even this old single-walled house, I've come to know all the different sounds they make. There's the squeaking of springs, of course. The slow moan that sounds like the opening snarls of a catfight. The sharp cry like a seabird. The muffled words. The deep sound of satisfaction my dad sometimes makes, like when you take a bite of a really good meal.

I'd fold my pillow around my head and hum for the duration,

thinking determinedly of other things: horses, usually, or the plot of the latest Andre Norton novel I was reading. Though frequent, Mom and Pop usually didn't take more than fifteen or twenty minutes, and some part of me, while wishing I didn't have to hear, was content knowing that the primary engines of our little train were firmly coupled.

We were safe another day, as long as they were making love.

"No," Mom says clearly through the wall. "I can't stay. I love you, but I'm leaving. Things can't go on like this. You need to get help, and the kids and I need to be somewhere else while you do it."

I sort my clothing and the possessions I've begun to accumulate in three years, as Anita watches, sucking her finger. Packing the suitcase, I'm reminded of my old tidal wave escape kit. The same things, except the water jug, go into my suitcase that were in that old pillowcase under my bed.

CHAPTER THIRTY
THE BUMPY ROAD TO RECOVERY

Age: 12, Santa Barbara, California, 1977

Maga meets us at the L.A. Airport in the giant blue Oldsmobile Vista Cruiser station wagon she's driven since 1968, immaculate inside and out, the upholstery protected with bubbled plastic seat covers. Egidio is fanatical about clean upholstery.

After a short, rough period of getting rid of stuff, finding new homes for the pets, and saying quick goodbyes, we're here, if a little raggedy and tearful.

"Well. That wasn't fun, was it?" Maga greets Mom brusquely, but pulls her in for a long, strong hug—after all, the two of them were together in Guatemala for a month just recently and probably planned the whole departure. Mom must have got the strength she needed to break away from Kauai, and Pop, from those strong arms holding her.

I'm still trying to forget Pop's devastated expression as we left him at the airport.

"Hey, girls." Maga hugs each of us against her wide, deep bosom, and I inhale her sandalwood scent and lean into it.

She's always seemed more like an aunt than a grandma, her attention on her new family and her affection toward us, indifferent. Tall at five eleven, Stella Fenenga Natale has light blue eyes under ruddy, untrimmed brows and a prow of a nose, making her striking rather than beautiful. Her strawberry blonde hair, once the exact shade as that of her youngest daughter Nancy and myself, is ribboned with white through a thick braid hanging down the back of her embroidered turquoise smock. Mexican amulets tangle in a mass across her breast, and she's wearing linen pants and sturdy leather sandals.

Outspoken, educated at Berkeley, liberal, and fluent in three languages, Maga couldn't be more different than my Chanel-clad grandma, Gigi—yet I recognize a similarity in their steely wills.

Maga and Egidio seem to have had as little time to prepare for us as we have had to pack because when we get to their three-bedroom ranch house in the foothills of Santa Barbara, we're not sure where to put our stuff or where we should sleep. There's an awkward period of milling around while Patricia closes her door, the Bee Gees thumping, and Nancy shows me her Barbie collection and Breyer horses.

The house is stuffed to the windowsills with the antiques Maga sells at her little shop, *Yesterday*, downtown, and we move some of the clutter aside to unfold the couch in the living room for Mom, Bonny and Anita. I sleep on a pallet in Nancy's room.

My first order of business the next day is to make a "fort" where I can withdraw to be by myself. I set up my hideout in the canyon under the deck. Using an old carpet remnant, I create a little bedroom for myself amid musty dead grass and old beer cans, slots of brilliant California sunlight streaking my humble domain through the boards of the deck. I move all of my favorite things out there: the few plastic Breyer horses I brought, my journal, and my art supplies.

I miss my animals more than anything. Naomi went back to her real owners, and Pop is still trying to find a home for Sarah.

"Watch out for snakes and black widows under there," Patricia says. She's a sophisticated fourteen and looks the most like Egidio: tall with a high forehead, square jaw, and flowing mane of chocolate-brown hair. She has a poster of Parker Stevenson from the Hardy Boys on her wall and spends a lot of time in the bathroom with a curling iron.

Nancy looks like a younger version of Maga: long-legged, blue-eyed, with a thick riot of strawberry blonde hair and the same proud nose.

Our hair color bonds us, and it's a good thing. I need a friend in this place. Only a year older than I am, Nancy's much more of a teenager than me, but she lets me lie on her bed and listen to the radio. We love the Weekly Countdown Top Forty and watching MASH.

We arrive just before Spring Break when no school is in session, so Bonny and I lie around in the living room, glutting ourselves with Nancy and Patricia on food and TV. My half-aunts feel a whole lot like cousins I'm just getting to know.

Mom is too broke to buy expensive health food, and too distracted by trying to find a place to live and some way to support us, to keep Bonny and me from ravaging Maga's fridge. We eat and eat. The free bananas, coconut, and papayas we ate so much of from the Estate's trees are nonexistent, as are the abundant Swiss chard, won bok, lettuce, and Chinese pea pods from Mom's huge garden. Instead, there's a plethora of junk food in the house that we binge on without restraint. Cookies, ice cream, gallon jugs of whole milk, whole boxes of Kraft Mac & Cheese, and packages of hot dogs and frozen French fries are all inhaled. We lie around eating and watching reruns of *I Dream of Jeannie* and *Gilligan's Island* as we revel in having television for the first time.

Pretty soon, I can't fit into any of the clothes I brought—not that they were right for the Mainland anyway—and I have to wedge my plump thighs into Nancy's too-long hand-me-downs. I'm chubby for the first time in my life, and my body, sprouting breasts and tummy rolls simultaneously, feels as foreign to me as everything else.

I have hardly been doing my homeschool curriculum in the last six months since Mom and Pop stopped paying attention, and I haven't actually been attending school in over a year. Maga insists that we to go to school, so Bonny is enrolled in Cold Spring Elementary in fourth grade, and I get on the bus with my two aunts and head off to Santa Barbara Junior High where I'm in seventh, Nancy in eighth and Patricia in ninth.

I climb aboard the echoing yellow bus where it picks us up, down the steep hill of Westmont Road, and around a couple of bends in Sycamore Canyon Road. It smells of rubber, foot odor, and the Cheetos some ninth graders are eating. Social distribution seems to be by grade from front to back, and Patricia and Nancy suddenly pretend they don't know me and walk to the back of the bus, sitting down with their friends.

I scan for an empty seat with someone who doesn't look scary, and slide in to sit next to a pudgy girl with dark hair hanging over her face, arranged to hide a pair of glasses that look like my last pair from Welfare. She has a book open on her lap, and my heart gives a leap of hope—maybe she needs a friend. "Hi."

She looks up long enough to see that I'm in as bad a shape as she is looks-wise. Her eyes are brown and intelligent. "Hi."

"What's that you're reading?"

FRECKLED

"The Black Stallion Returns."

"Oh, I love that one." I bounce a little with enthusiasm. "What do you think of the Red? I don't like him as much as The Black, even though I know I'm supposed to."

We spend the drive to school discussing Black Stallion arcana. My new friend's name is Laurie, and she lives a few blocks away on Sycamore Canyon Road. I'm hugely relieved. I only need one friend to survive, but I need at least one, and my faithful Tita is far away now.

Nancy reappears beside me as the bus disgorges us in front of a building the size of a city block with that California stucco-and-red-tile look. "Mom said to take you to the office to pick up your schedule." She's talking about her mom, not mine. My mom disappeared that morning with Bonny and Anita to get Bonny registered at nearby Cold Spring Elementary.

Nancy leads me down echoing halls bustling with people, many of them brown, but not the brown I'm used to. At the office, they print out my schedule. Nancy leads me at a run to my first class.

"See you at lunch?" I ask.

The scrunch of her nose tells me that Nancy, while feeling sorry for me, has her own well-established world. "We have separate lunch times. Sorry."

I turn reluctantly and step into the Algebra class.

School is something I've always been good at, so even though I'm completely intimidated, I'm excited too. I set my Santa Barbara Junior High Condors student folder, schedule, and map down on an empty desk and go boldly up to the front of the room to ask for a book.

The teacher, an older Hispanic man with mutton-chop whiskers, hands me a book so battered it's held together with duct tape. Inside, double rows of students' names are followed by the year. The row of names goes back to well before I was born—but I guess algebra doesn't change much.

I ask for a few sheets of paper and a pencil, and return to my desk. I write my name in the book below the others: *Toby Wilson, 1977.*

Writing my name feels like making a statement: *I am here, now.*

The last time I did any math at all was in fifth grade, so I'm worse than way behind. I labor through the class, moving up to sit close to the front so my glasses work well enough to see the board, diligently copying everything, hoping to learn by osmosis.

I don't care how I look to others. I know I won't be popular. I just want to get back to learning, catch up, and get A's again—and as a bonus, not have anyone call me *Haole* Crap.

With that priority, I make quick progress catching up academically but spend miserable days sitting alone in the cafeteria with my homemade peanut butter and jelly sandwich on white bread.

On my way to my usual spot in the corner of the caf with the loners and losers, I pass the Chicana girls at their table. These exotic creatures are totally different from the Hawaiian, Japanese, mixed, and *haole* girl cliques I'm marginally familiar with. The girls' lips are glossy, their eyelids flash jewel-like color, and they wear bright, tight, low-cut clothing. They seem to despise me on sight as I skulk about in my thrift-store jeans, untrimmed hair askew and latest pair of Welfare glasses hiding my rabbity eyes. I never go into the bathrooms because they gather there like a flock of brilliant parakeets, smoking cigarettes and chattering mockingly in Spanish, freezing my bladder too much to pee. "Stay away from them," Nancy warns me. "They can really mess you up."

As I pass one day, balancing an open library book I'm reading on top of my humble lunch bag, I accidentally knock into one of the Chicana girls with my elbow. The chocolate cafeteria shake she's holding splashes down her breasts and onto her white Ditto jeans in a spectacular spill. Chiefess among the Chicanas; the girl is gorgeous —a fall of perfect black curls touches her tiny waist, and big gold hoop earrings brush the shoulders of her low-cut top. That we are even in the same species is hard to believe.

She jumps up and shrieks. "*Madre de Dios*! Fucking *gringa puta!*"

"Oh my God, I'm so sorry!" I stammer, backing away, the library book clutched to my chest.

"Stupid cow! I'm going to kill you!" She yells more in Spanish that I'm happy not to understand. "Get her!" She yells to her minions, and five Chicanas surge up from the table to do her bidding.

I drop the book and my pitiful bag lunch and make a dash for the cafeteria door. The girls, hampered by getting up from the table and stack-heeled strappy shoes, scramble after me, screaming like harpies. I punch through the doors, fleeing past an open-mouthed teacher, and run down the hall full tilt in my old Adidas.

I may be chubby now, but I've always been fast on my feet. I hurtle down the long, echoing hallway and am already banging out into the quad through the double doors by the time the girls, still screaming terrible things, make it out of the caf. Once in the quad, I look around for somewhere to hide, but there's nowhere in the expanse of asphalt peppered by knots of kids, everyone turning to look at my noisy exit in disdain. I bolt for a lone pine tree on top of a little grassy knoll, a spot not occupied by a clique. Worst-case scenario, I can climb the tree—that method's worked for me before. Reaching the tree, I hunker down and peek back around it.

The girls spill out into the quad, looking around, stabbing long colored fingernails into the air as they swear vengeance in Spanish. None of the groups of *haoles* and blacks scattered over the area turn me in, thank God, and finally the Chicanas retreat back to their turf.

A pudgy girl in a hoodie is sitting alone on the other side of the knoll. She pushes the hoodie back to reveal a familiar face. "Toby. What are you doing up here?"

It's Laurie, the girl from the bus, and I drop down beside her. We still ride together, but then part ways and don't share any classes. This is the first time I've seen her during the school day. "Oh, thank God it's you. Do you want to meet me here at lunch from now on? I can't ever go in the caf again."

"Yes." Her eyes, made tiny by the thickness of her glasses, blink happily at me and her acne-riddled skin flushes. "What happened?"

I tell her my tale of woe, and she shares half her lunch with me since mine's abandoned with the book in the cafeteria.

The knoll is a spot none of the popular kids like due to a long uphill trek and the tree's poky, slippery needles. Safe from prying eyes, Laurie and I hide out there, reading paperbacks and playing with a pair of plastic horses she smuggles in her backpack.

Laurie doesn't live far from Maga's, so I start getting off the bus at her house to hang out after school. Each day we trek up the steep driveway to her square modern home, dig the key out from under the mat, and let ourselves in.

The house smells like cigarettes, and the ceiling is sprayed with white sparkle-flecked drywall. A lot of mirrored tile with gold veins in it and beige shag carpet dominate the rest of the place, except for Laurie's room, which is pink and decorated for a much younger child. Laurie's mom and stepdad both work, so we make ourselves white bread bologna sandwiches and settle in to wrangle her herd of Breyer horses and play Parcheesi.

I leave for Maga's as soon as her stepfather arrives. He's a bear-like suit-clad man with a gunshot voice who lights a cig and pours a huge Scotch the minute he gets home, yelling things like, "So, you two chubsters eat our whole fridge yet?"

His loudness and mean comments make me cringe, and I feel so bad for Laurie, who's scared of him. My dad was mean too, but in a different way, and I think it might have been easier because sometimes he was nice.

Pop is "bottoming out," Mom calls it, in the new vocabulary she's picking up going to a group for spouses of alcoholics. He was supposed to keep our scene going at the Estate; instead, he's quit working and is drinking and surfing all day, living in the Rambler and a tent at night. He gave my beloved goat Sarah to a family who tied her out in their backyard—where she was attacked by their dog and killed within a week.

I don't cry over Sarah like I did over Keiki. In fact, I can't even think about what happened to her—my mind just flits over it. It's simply too awful for me to take in. I don't have room for big emotions, for missing our life on Kauai. I'm too busy trying to get through each day.

Someday, I'll have a wonderful family of my own, a house that I own and never have to keep moving from, and a great big yard and garden and room for all the goats and horses and beautiful things I could ever want. I'm smart. I can get all that if I work hard. I just have to keep doing good in school, and get myself to college, and then get a good job. I won't live like this when I grow up—no. Not ever again.

These are the words I write in my journal in my little cave under the deck. This is my manifesto.

Mom sits us down in the living room on the couch where she, Bonny, and Anita are still sleeping each night. "I'm not getting back together with Pop," Mom says. "Not until and unless he gets his shit together."

Churning, guilty-bad feelings make my tummy hurt when I hear this. "We should have stayed. Taken care of him."

"No, Toby. That's co-dependent thinking. It's not your job to take care of your dad—he's supposed to take care of you." Mom has patches of red in her cheeks; she's really enthused about this twelve-step program, and this kind of talk is totally new. "You saying that just confirms how much you need to go to the group for children of alcoholics."

I don't want to go, of course. It's hard to wrap my head around learning that Pop is an alcoholic—his drinking and smoking was so much a part of our lives, just there like gravity. Now it's supposed to be something we object to and need to understand? And what about Mom's drinking and smoking and taking drugs? Really, I just wish we could go back to happier times. Wish I could get a time machine and go back to that summer with the Josephson boys on top of the trees . . .

Unexpectedly, Nancy is interested in finding out what the teen group is about, and that makes my excruciating embarrassment a little easier to bear. The four of us, leaving Anita home with Maga, Egidio, and Patricia, borrow the Vista Cruiser and drive to a run-down church whose basement hosts the meetings.

Mom leads us into the building, and it feels as foreign and nerve-wracking as when we visited the various cults on Kauai. I've already bitten my nails down to bleeding nubs so there's not much I can do with my hands as Mom points me, Bonny, and Nancy at the door of our meeting and heads off for her own.

The room smells as if the dirt from all the feet of everyone who ever attended the church above has sifted down through the floorboards and embedded itself in the nap of the burnt-orange carpet we sit on in a cross-legged circle. I huddle in Nancy's shadow as the adult leader leads us in a chanting prayer: "God, grant me the serenity to accept the things I cannot change, courage to change the things I can, and the wisdom to know the difference."

Kids around our age sit cross-legged, folded in on themselves, or sprawled confidently. Expressions range from wary to blank to bored, and there are other girls with chewed nails hiding behind bangs. My weirdness definitely blends in, and I begin to relax. We go around the circle, encouraged to "share our experience, strength, and hope" with each other.

I'm surprised at how forthcoming the girl next to me is, describing a home where she has to wake up a passed-out mom and cook and clean for her siblings after school. A boy with a dad who used to beat him tells us some of the lies he's used to explain his injuries, and I find myself fingering the L-shaped scar on my forehead.

There are other kids with scars here, some much worse than mine—and John, the handsome blond boy I've been crushing on in gym class is also at the meeting, though he refuses to talk about home. At the end, he says "hi," to me.

Sold. I'm going to those meetings every week.

After going to a few more of her own meetings, Mom tells us that she's realized she's an alcoholic and drug abuser too, but that she's a "periodic," not a daily user like Pop.

This isn't the revelation she thinks it will be. Mom has always seemed to need something— be it a drink, a toke, or the surf—to deal with life. Her moods and appetites are too big for her to contain or manage. Now, without the curbing effects of substances, she is volatile but clear-eyed and energetic. The sober Mom I'm getting to know in Santa Barbara is a different woman than the one from Kauai.

Struggling to find work without any childcare for Anita during the day, Mom tells Bonny and me that she asked for financial help from Gigi and Grandpa Jim. "Jim told me, 'welfare is for people in your situation,' she says, white-faced with rage. "They offered to help us 'get on our feet' if I went back to your dad." Clearly, my grandparents aren't in favor of our parents' breakup. Cash and checks that Gigi gives to Bonny and me in cards and letters, are *Returned to Sender* by Mom.

CHAPTER THIRTY-ONE
MOVING AND MOTORCYCLE GUYS

Sorting laundry for the laundromat

Age: 13, Isla Vista California, 1978

We've definitely worn out our welcome at Maga and Egidio's by the end of the school year when Mom announces she's found us our own place at last. A woman named Tina from Mom's twelve-step program rents us a one-room garage apartment in the college town of Isla Vista, a bedroom community for the University of California, Santa Barbara.

There's no choice: we're moving again.

I'll miss Laurie, and I'll have to start a new school in the fall, but at least we have a carefree summer ahead, and Isla Vista is a great place to explore.

Tina's a funny, raunchy, square-jawed woman who's never seen without a Virginia Slim dangling from her lip. The best thing, besides the fact that we now have a room of our own (even if we all have to share it) is that she's got a daughter, Kim, who's just Bonny's age.

A small, safe town, Isla Vista's flat, and Bonny, Kim, and I go everywhere on our thrift store bikes. We spend the summer roaming, playing Barbies, building forts in the eucalyptus trees at the edge of town, rolling down the dunes of the natural reserve, and smoking cigarettes stolen from Tina.

One day Mom takes me, Bonny, and Anita for a picnic at the Santa Barbara Mission Rose Garden, one of my favorite places. I wander through the rose bushes, putting my face deep into silky, frothy blossoms and breathing in scent. I spot Double Delight, a white and red rose with cinnamon smell that I ordered at the Estate with babysitting money. Getting those roses, packed in plastic and sawdust from so far away, planting them, and waiting for their first blooms to reveal their beauty was one of my favorite things about that three-year stretch of stability in our lives at the Estate. Double Delight was just one of many things I loved and left behind.

I spend a lot of time staying distracted, keeping busy so I won't be homesick for the Estate and our freedom and fun on Hanalei Bay. If only Pop hadn't gotten so bad with his drinking, and those kids hadn't beaten me up . . .

I look up from my reminiscing to see a man getting off a motorcycle parked near the picnic blanket Mom has spread out on the grass. Anita and Bonny are helping unpack the food, but they pause to look up as he walks across the grass to join them.

I squint to see him better—my latest pair of glasses aren't really working anymore.

I've suspected my mom has a boyfriend. She's been secretive, hiding with the phone in the bathroom, giggling as she talks to someone. She's gone away for the weekend on a "business trip" and to an "AA retreat" and left us with Tina. *Could this be the boyfriend?*

He couldn't be more different than our tall, well-built, handsome father. This dude is shorter than Mom and has bowed legs like a cowboy without his horse. Even motorcycle leathers don't make him look cool or intimidating—he has sandy hair and looks like a kid when he takes off his helmet.

What the hell is Mom doing, a woman with three children, dating some young motorcycle guy?

The man walks right up to Mom where she sits on the picnic blanket and leans down to kiss her, straightening reluctantly like he'd enjoy kissing her a lot longer. Mom gestures to the other girls, and he squats to shake their hands, smiling.

A dark tight feeling of protectiveness rises in my chest. No way am I going to let this intruder disrupt our lives! I straighten my overly tight shorts and stalk toward them, my eyes feeling hot. The man stands up and meets my angry stare. "Hi. I'm Greg. You must be Toby."

Mom stands up too, all fluttery. "Greg is a friend from the program. We're spending a lot of time together, and we decided it was time for him to meet you girls."

"I can see what kind of friend he is." I fold my arms over my annoying new breasts. "And I'm not interested in pretending it's okay." I don't want my parents to get back together, but I don't want Mom dating even more.

"Last I checked, it was perfectly legal for two grown adults to spend time together," Greg says. "Listen, I'm not trying to take your dad's place or anything. Got no interest in that. I just care about your mom and want to hang out with her, so I guess you'll have to get used to me." His pale blue eyes are level and calm, his demeanor confident.

"When hell freezes over." I stomp off into the rose garden to nurse my snit.

Greg wears down my resistance over time, and I eventually have to admit that he's a good guy. He may be short and too young, but he's prepared to deal with all of us girls to be with Mom, and that says something about his character. He's kind, funny, great at board games, and he makes Mom happy, even though I can tell by his uneven teeth that he's from, as Gigi would say, the "wrong side of the tracks."

I admit publicly that I like him when he takes care of Mom through a bad cold, bringing her tea and soup, and rubbing her back. Pop would never have taken care of her, let alone any of us, with his selfishness and germaphobia.

Fall rolls around, and I have to start eighth grade at a new school, Goleta Valley Junior High. This time, Mom is required to come in with my school records, and when the office ladies see how incomplete they are, they send the two of us to one of the counselors.

"Wow. This's a lot of moving. And a lot of different schools and educational settings," the counselor says, sorting through the patchy file. She addresses me. "Your grades are great wherever they're recorded. It's a miracle you could do that. You're a brave and resilient young lady."

I sit up straighter, smiling at this praise. Someone sees that I work hard and do the best I can, no matter what else is going on. It's the first time an adult has praised me for being "resilient," or offered any comment at all on our situation.

I glance guiltily over at Mom. Her hazel eyes are wide and dark green with tears.

I can tell this is the first time she's realized that our pattern of moves affects me, that it would be hard for a kid to adapt to the things I've been through. She's seeing me through someone else's eyes, and she looks shaken to the core.

Mom reaches for some Kleenex and covers her eyes with it. "It's hard getting sober," she says through the wad of tissues. "I plan to stabilize things now."

Mom's quiet as we leave the long, low building with my new schedule. We get into the old VW bug that she bought when we were at Maga's house. She leans her head on the steering wheel, then puts her hand over mine.

"I'm sorry." She blinks, looking out the window. "I'm really sorry for putting you through all this. I'm doing the best I can."

"I know you are, Mom, and I love you." I lean on her and she hugs me, then starts the Bug with a rattle.

But even with apologies, Goleta Valley Junior High is another huge, jarring, overwhelming social experience interspersed with academic struggles in math, where I remain behind but determined to stay on the "college prep" track.

Standing in the free lunch line with the blacks and Mexicans to get food I actually need, ignored by both groups, I hide under a voluminous hoodie. I'm losing weight since there's little at home in our studio with the tiny fridge. I like losing the weight, but not the worry about money, and I hate being actually hungry.

I never find a friend to replace Laurie. I keep my nose in a book to make up for it as I plow through each day with my head down, glasses and overgrown bangs hiding my eyes, hoping for something better to come my way, someday.

CHAPTER THIRTY-TWO

LEAVING ON A JET PLANE

Age: 13, Kauai, 1978

We're on a giant Boeing 747 back to Kauai to visit Pop for the first time, and I've survived extended misery. I'm looking forward to jumping in the water, running on the beach—but not to seeing my dad. Awkward doesn't begin to describe what I imagine that will be like. We've been building up to this visit with a series of cards, letters, and phone calls, but as usual, my gut churns with mixed feelings when I think of him.

Mom sits next to me, with Anita on the other side of her. Bonny's on the other side of me and I'm fiddling with my packet of macadamia nuts, trying to get it open.

"I have something to tell you girls," Mom says. "Gigi and Grandpa Jim are buying us a house on Kauai."

"That's great!" Bonny says.

She's too young to realize what this means—*big changes*. I narrow my eyes. "When is this happening?"

"The house's in escrow now. So—this isn't a visit. We're moving back." Mom crinkles her foil wrapper nervously. "Your dad and I are getting back together."

"What?" My voice is too loud. I hear a roaring in my ears. "What happened to 'I'm stabilizing things now'?"

It's been the worst year of my life, hands down: two half years of junior high at different schools, moving, academic struggle, confusion, harassment by Mexican chicks, compulsive eating, and reading to escape in a series of "forts" near our cramped quarters. In all of that, at least Mom was sober and beginning to really act like a mom, and Pop was three thousand miles away. "And what about Greg?"

I must be shouting, because Bonny puts her hand on my arm and Mom frowns, making that "lower your voice" hand gesture. People are turning their heads to look at us from the aisles.

"We broke up."

I want to puke. I finally really liked Greg. His heart must be so broken. He really loved her. "So, you just decided this—when?"

"Your dad visited a month ago and I—we—fell in love again." She has those red spots in her cheeks. I remember that long weekend with Tina in charge and Greg conspicuously absent—I thought the two of them had gone off together! But really, Pop was here in California, and we never even saw him while they plotted behind our backs.

"Gigi and Grandpa Jim said they'd buy us a house if we got back together. I miss Kauai and our life there. Don't you?" Mom fiddles nervously with the foil of the packet. "Doing this *is* stabilizing things."

"That's so fucked up," I yell, with no volume control whatsoever. "So, Gigi and Grandpa promise you a house and off we go back to that asshole? You're a whore!"

Mom slaps me in the face so hard my head bounces off the seat back. "You don't know anything about it!"

"I know you're not acting like an adult or you wouldn't treat us like this. You'd tell us what was going on. You'd ask what we wanted." My face is stinging, my eyes burning. "Things were better back when you guys were drinking!" It's the worst thing I can think of saying.

I force my way past Bonny and into the aisle, hurrying to the bathroom. I go in and slam the door, locking it.

I'm panting at my reflection: eyes small brown pebbles behind my latest pair of thick ugly Welfare glasses, ginger hair unruly, chubby freckled cheek reddened from Mom's slap.

I hate myself and my life with a profound despair.

I wish I could teleport to another world, like on Star Trek. "Beam me up, Scotty." I shut my eyes and pray to whoever visited me on that moonbeam at the Estate and told me everything would be okay. "Please just kill me now."

Nothing happens. I stare down at the little blue-water metal toilet bowl.

I wish I could transform into another person. I'd walk out of the door of the bathroom and into First Class, grown up and dressed classy, with long shiny black hair and luscious brown skin, confident, sexy, smart, and on my way to somewhere amazing.

I wish my parents cared about what I needed, instead of just themselves—and Kauai. Always Kauai, and its magnetic, addicting pull. I'd started to think we were getting free of it.

I shut the toilet lid and turn to sit on it, putting my face in my hands. My eyes feel dry and hot as beach stones.

I do like Kauai better than the Mainland. I'm sick of all the failed efforts to fit in and make friends, of feeling overwhelmed as I try to blend with hundreds of junior high kids in my aunts' hand-me-down clothes while standing in the free lunch line.

But one good thing has happened. *Now I know I'm good at school.* I get A's wherever I go, even in math now that I'm caught up.

Knowing that I'm good in school gives me a sense of possibilities. Of control. Of hope for my future. Things can't be that bad because I'm at the top of my class. My family may be messed up, but at least *I'm* functional. Someday, somehow, school is what will take me to another place and I'll make my life what I want it to be.

I picture that for a moment: some interesting job involving reading and writing, maybe as a business owner, wearing a suit and heels. Or being a researcher, magazine journalist or a reporter, or even writing novels like the Andre Norton and JRR Tolkien books I love so much.

I'll have a house of my own surrounded by beautiful rosebushes that I never have to leave unless I want to. I'll own a horse, and a goat, and a decent car, maybe a Honda Civic that starts up every morning without fail like my Aunty Jan's. There will be lots of good food in the fridge, somewhere between health food and *badforyou*, and I'll have someone smart and kind who loves me to share it with.

More drama with Mom on the plane isn't a good idea. She probably told me here so I wouldn't make a scene in public. *Like that worked.*

I splash water on my face and go back to my seat.

"If you have anything more to say, wait until we're off the plane," Mom snaps. She looks like she wants to slap me again. "Drama queen."

"I'm done talking." I make Bonny move over to sit next to her, and I won't look at her.

I've been betrayed.

I thought we were building a new life. Stabilizing things. Without *him*. And I was doing my part, working hard to adjust and be a help with everything. I will never trust Mom the same way again.

CHAPTER THIRTY-THREE

THE TIP TOP MOTEL

Age: 13, Kauai, 1978

Pop meets us at the airport. I forgot how big and tall he is; it makes me uncomfortable when I got used to someone Greg's size being the man in our lives. The younger girls hug him, but I don't. He's bald now, and thinner, with a few sad strands of comb-over, and he has a habit of twisting his hands together that I've never seen before. The wrinkles I noticed when Mom left for Guatemala have hardened into grooves. He's a stranger.

"I'm totally clean and sober," he tells us. "It's been a long hard road."

"For us, too." I let him give me an A-frame hug at last. He doesn't ask anything about my life and has no idea what I've been through, and quite frankly, I doubt he cares. He never had much capacity for anyone's suffering but his own.

Kauai's humidity feels like a hot wet blanket. Looking around, I sigh with relief. The multi-ethnic faces around me are people groups I can identify and understand. The two-lane road we call a "highway," with its one stoplight on the whole island, is blessedly familiar. California was so big, busy, and congested that I never really got my feet under me.

Pop's driving a secondhand van with one of his homemade beds in it, and he takes us to the sleaziest motel on Kauai, a cash-only low-rise made out of cement block with a weed-choked parking lot. We reunite as a family in a room with lumpy beds, cigarette burns on the sheets, and a wheezing air conditioner dripping into a plastic bowl. I wrinkle my nose at the geckos all over the window. I remembered their soft, camouflage-colored bodies and little chirps fondly on the Mainland, but I'd never noticed how much they pooped before—the motel room's windowsills are thick with little black turds.

We sit down on the beds for a family "confab."

Pop says the house bought by Gigi and Grandpa Jim is in escrow, and it's only going to be a couple of weeks until we are in our own place where we will each have a bedroom. "You are going to love it," he promises.

He has a job, he tells us, working in a dive shop—but Mom's eyes widen when he says that it pays six dollars an hour and its part-time, so "things will be tight for a while."

Looking at her expression, I'm pretty sure that wasn't what he told her to get her over here with all of us girls on a one-way ticket.

In painful, embarrassing detail, Pop works through a list of "amends" with Bonny and I for hurts from the past, including the Cup Incident. He has the things he remembers written down on a piece of paper and holds it in the trembling hand that isn't clutching Mom's.

There's nothing I can do but nod and say, "I forgive you," because he's so humble and broken, so clearly glad to see us again. Mom gets over the surprise of his lousy part-time job and looks at him all soft and lovey-dovey.

I feel sad and sick for Greg, who I never even said goodbye to. It shouldn't matter so much, but I feel really bad about it, thinking of how he must feel—like we *all* dumped him. Some of us didn't have a choice.

Crowded into a lumpy double bed next to Bonny that night, with Mom and Pop on the queen next to us and Anita on the floor, I contemplate the water stain on the ceiling and think about the "amends" process. People doing the twelve steps do a "searching and fearless moral inventory" in Step Four. And then in Step Eight, they make a list of people they've harmed and become willing to "make amends" to them. In a later step, which was what our dad was attempting to do, they "make direct amends to such people wherever possible."

Apologies for the years of choices that led us to this place and time are a nice gesture, but they don't make things better.

Don't apologize. Just get a fucking job and a house and make our lives better. Be a real parent.

Mom never got much steady work the whole time we were in California with Anita to care for, and Pop hates working so much, he couldn't provide for us without Gigi and Grandpa Jim giving him money all the time. Apologies aside, this motel is not a good sign. Hopefully, the new house will make everything better, as our parents clearly hope it will.

I feel disgusting and guilty because I'm hanging onto anger and I know it. An apology is not a bad place to start, and Pop's sincere. I should give him a chance. But the truth is, I don't want to hope things are going to get better because then it will hurt worse when things don't. Anger feels like armor, like it will protect me.

The next day, we find out that Pop, who's assured Mom we'll have rental to go to until the house is fully purchased, has actually been living in the van he's currently driving. He's running out of money for the motel, so we're going to have to "camp" in the van.

More lies and another setback, but Mom smiles bravely and tells us, "It's only for a couple of weeks until we get the house, and it's not the rainy season yet. We've done this before and it'll be fun, right, kids?"

We're at the county park in the van, a wind-whipped beach in Kapa`a next to the library, when Pop comes back from the pay phone after a call with the real estate agent. "Gigi and Grandpa Jim have decided not to buy the house. They've pulled out of the escrow." Mom's sitting in the passenger seat, and he tells her this through the rolled-down window in a flat voice, his eyes averted.

Holy crap! "Buying a house" was a ploy to get my parents back together—and it worked!

Mom bursts into tears of rage, jumping out of the van to stalk up and down the parking lot, yelling. "Sick, malicious fucks! Those assholes, goddamn it! How could they do this to me, to their grand-children!"

Why isn't she mad at Pop for lying to us? Doesn't she see they were probably all in on it together? But that can't be right. Pop knows he couldn't take care of us by himself, without their house and their help . . .

I scoop Anita up and press her against my chest, a hand over her ear to keep her from hearing Mom's screaming bad words as Pop tries to hug her. She throws him off, sobbing, and stomps away with him in pursuit.

"Come on, Bonny. Let's go to the library." I get out of the van, holding crying Anita. My toddler sister is a soft, sweet bundle of vulnerable, and she's too young to understand all this craziness. She shouldn't have to be frightened by what's going on. Bonny has to skip to keep up with me as I head toward the library, a sanctuary in good times and bad.

As usual, the small concrete block building is almost empty. I carry Anita to the children's section, and we sit on the carpet in front of the rows of picture books. Bonny lies down on her back next to me, inserts her finger into her mouth, and twines her hair around her finger with sniffling Anita cuddled against her side as I read both sisters a story.

I read four Bill Peet books in a row, showing their funny illustrations and using my special character voices and everything. Eventually Anita is calm enough to stay with Bonny and her own book, and I can go get something from the Adult section.

"Haven't seen you in a while." Mrs. Rapozo smiles over her half-glasses. "Missed my best customer. Welcome back."

It's the first time I feel like somebody notices or cares that I'm here, and it matters more than it should—because now we're broke and trapped on Kauai, a place where rentals are scarce and jobs are scarcer—and the winter rains are coming.

CHAPTER THIRTY-FOUR

VAN CAMPING IN WINTER

Van living on Kauai again

Age: 14, Moloa`a, Kauai, 1979

"At least we're sober," Mom says as we set up a tent for Bon and me
to sleep in remote, barely habited Moloa`a, a turn in the road outside

of Kilauea. The family that bought Keiki is letting us squat in their empty field.

"Yay, awesome." I try to fit one long aluminum tube into another for the rigging of the big old canvas tent we've had since Haena, moldy from being stored in a friend's garage. The Moloa`a campsite's rugged, with no usable running water or toilet, a ton of mosquitoes, and right next to a muddy stream. Mom, Pop, and Anita sleep in the van on the bed in back, and Bonny and I are in the canvas tent we set up.

Bonny and I are used to California comforts by now, and I'm painfully conscious of everything about our situation and terrified the kids at my new school will find out how we're living; we're homeless, though Mom and Pop continue to call it "camping," as if we've opted to live this way as a fun vacation.

Gigi and Grandpa Jim, apparently feeling bad about pulling out of the home purchase, and worried about how Bonny and I will do in "those native schools," pay for tuition at a little alternative private school just outside Kapa`a called Island School.

Each morning, Mom and Pop drive Bonny and me to school in the van, and drop us off in front of the dilapidated building. I hop out of the van nonchalantly, as if I wasn't just brushing my teeth in a parking lot and rinsing out of a canteen, hoping I won't need a shower for a day or so when we can go to the public park and use the cold outdoor facilities. I don't let Mom fill up the family water jugs at the hose on the school's grounds, worried that someone will figure out why they're doing that.

And at school, I pretend all is well—and for those hours, it is.

Oddball, smart *haole* kids are the norm at Island School, and for the first time at a school on Kauai, I feel like I really belong.

I love Morning Circle, where we all lie on our backs and do a guided visualization, then start the day with yoga exercises. With ten kids per grade, it's a tight-knit group, and I make some new friends —Megan, Mike, Karen, Jonathan, Kate, Emma, Brian, Greg, Adam, and Bryan. We call our teachers by their first names: Peggy, Tom, Nancy, and Lindsay. We do group learning projects, like a whole class, multi-week game of being settlers taking Velcro-backed "wagons" across the West to Oregon, calculating our journey using math and navigation. For science, we sample pond water in a nearby ditch, uncovering a whole world of tiny wriggling things, and count ghost crab populations on the nearby beach.

School is where I feel good, and I continue to do well. I find mentors in my teachers, and sometimes I even go home and have meals with them and their families—but I don't tell them we're camping, and I like to think no one knows.

We go to a lot of twelve step meetings, too, during which Bon and I read in the van and babysit Anita. Pop's hours at the dive shop are not enough to live on, even with food stamps, so Mom starts cleaning houses and mowing lawns with Anita in tow.

The change of season progresses with the usual big surf and heavy rains. One day shortly after my fourteenth birthday in January, Mom swings by in the van to pick us up after school. She's frowning, worried, her brown hair coiling into curls from the damp of the rain pouring outside. "We have to keep an eye on the stream next to the tent. The ground's kind of low there. We might have to move if it gets any higher."

The rain increases to a roar during the night. Bonny and I lie awake, trying to keep anything from touching the canvas sides of the tent where it will immediately get soaked. It's too loud and scary to sleep, and suddenly Pop unzips the flap and sticks his sopping head inside. He hands us a couple of big black trash bags. "Put your swimsuits on and cover up with these. The stream's flooding, and we have to get out of here!"

CHAPTER THIRTY-FIVE

A FLOOD AND A BIG SURPRISE

Age: 14, Wainiha, Kauai, 1979

The danger of flash flooding carrying all of us away in the middle of the night is very real. We've seen it before in Wainiha, and hear of it annually elsewhere. Bonny and I throw on our suits and push our heads and arms through the garbage bags as makeshift raingear. We begin to tear down the tent and throw all our soaked worldly belongings into the van as the stream, brown and menacing, overflows its banks mere feet away.

Mom turns on the van's engine and aims the headlights at the tent. Three-year-old Anita sits in the open sliding doorway and holds a flashlight on us as well, as the four of us frantically pack up and tear down. Rolling up my sleeping bag inside the wet tent even as it begins to collapse around me, the situation strikes me as funny.

"The Wacky Wilson family, winning at life again!" I giggle, shivering in my swimsuit and garbage bag raincoat.

"Wild Weird Wilsons whining," Bonny giggles in helpless hysteria, and soon Mom and Pop are laughing as we call out variations on our last name. "Wet Wilsons. Wino Wilsons. Wily Wilsons. Wonderful Waffle-loving Wilsons!"

Somehow the combination of mirth and adrenaline carry us until we've piled the soaked, muddy tent, bedding, clothes, and our battered suitcases back into the van. Dripping, panting, the five of us get into the van where it's parked on a higher elevation beside the road.

Laughter dies down to snorting as we wrap up to get warm in our designated towels. The van smells like mud and body odor, and it's steamy with our closeness. The headlights shine through the pouring rain and black, dripping jungle to illuminate the stream, a brown flood spreading to cover our former campsite. The sight makes me shiver and I tighten my towel.

"What next?" Mom says. "It's two in the morning, and we need showers and somewhere to sleep."

"Let's go to Serenity House," Pop says.

This dormitory-like building above Kapa`a is where Pop went to get sober when he eventually decided to—it's a "halfway house" that provides lodging to people in recovery. I've already attended numerous meetings there with Mom and Pop. They've firmly grasped onto "the program" as a place to get support rather than their drinking and using friends.

Pop drives us to the Serenity House parking lot. The program's building is shut up tight, so we dry off, change out of our bathing suits into semi-dry clothes, and with involved maneuvering, figure out how a family of five can lie down together in a van to sleep.

Laughter bonded us, and no one is grumpy even though we're uncomfortable.

I fall asleep like tumbling down a lava tube, and wake up when dawn is gray in the windows, fogged over with condensation from our wet clothing and shared breath. I sneak out of the van, looking for a bathroom.

From the parking lot of the halfway house, there's a view over the bluff to the ocean. As often happens on Kauai, the sun breaks over the ocean and through the clouds like a lighthouse blasting apart fog, reflecting the sky off the ocean in a glorious panorama that gives life to the conditions of the night before. I wander down the damp grass and stare at the sunrise, breathing in the morning, peeing behind a bush, and wishing for a shower.

We squat in the van in the parking lot outside of Serenity House for a couple of weeks, sneaking in for showers after the residents are all in their meetings, and filling our water jugs at the hose on the side of the building. Getting to school is an escape that ends too quickly; in the evenings, we all attend meetings.

I sit near the window of the cigarette-smoke-filled room, trying to be invisible, as I listen to "Hi, I'm an alcoholic" stories of domestic abuse, crime and the lengths alcoholics will go to to get a drink. These awful tales of "experience, strength, and hope" actually make me feel better about our situation. At least we're together, and Mom and Pop really are trying.

One Sunday, Mom and Pop drive us in to church. We've dropped out of "organized religion" and the program is the new religion—but this particular day, we go to Catholic church in Kapa`a.

"Why are we here?" I whisper to Mom as we sidle into a wooden pew, sitting down in front of a mildewy hymnal and unfamiliar padded kneeler.

"Pop wants us to go," Mom whispers back. "Try to hear from God." She has a funny tightness around her eyes. Gigi is Catholic, so maybe Pop's wanting a taste of that spirituality from his past—but I can tell something's up. I may not be doing pupil checks anymore, but I've made it a practice to monitor all of Mom and Pop's moves in order to be prepared.

We muddle through the service: standing, reciting, kneeling, praying. I'm curious about this religion, looking around at the stained-glass windows telling unfamiliar stories. Wind-whipped coconut palms outside cast shadows on them in a strange juxtaposition. The bloodied, agonized sculpture of Jesus on the cross, his eyes rolled heavenward, isn't appealing—but I enjoy the calm, rehearsed feeling of the service. The recitations, the singing, the whole process printed out in a booklet—all of it gives me a timeless feeling of peaceful predictability. The stories told in the stained-glass window scenes seem like they've been there forever, and they will last forever.

I like things that don't change or disappear. Maybe I'll be Catholic when I grow up.

We get back into the van outside the church; Pop and Mom get in the front seats, as usual, me on the storage bench, and Anita and Bonny are on the bed in back.

"We need to have a family confab," Pop says.

I brace myself. Supposedly we all get to express ourselves in "family confabs" but really, this is just how Mom and Pop roll out bad news.

"We have something exciting to tell you." Pop's eyes are suspiciously shiny, like he's going to cry. "Your mom's pregnant!"

Collective shock. Bonny and I turn to each other, our mouths falling open. Mom looks down, pleating the fabric of her muumuu with her fingers.

The wrongness of the situation roars up through me and bursts out of my mouth. "Are you fucking kidding me? You guys can't even take care of the kids you have!"

"That isn't for you to pass judgment on," Pop says. "We're the parents." He glances around the emptying church parking lot, decides we better get on the road, and turns on the van. So much for the family confab.

"If you were acting like parents, you guys would have jobs and we'd have a house. On welfare, five of us living in a car, and you're pregnant? How did you even do that? Gross!" I address my comments to Mom. She's the one who betrayed me by getting back together with Pop.

She still won't meet my eyes. She wraps her arms protectively over her waist, like whoever's in there can hear me. We're driving down the hill from the church toward the main highway.

"Did you mean to get pregnant?" I continue, firing my words like bullets. "Seriously, you thought this was a good time to have a baby? Or did you think about anybody but yourselves?"

"Shut up!" Mom finally yells at me. "You're fourteen years old, you don't know anything about it."

"I know that you can keep from having a baby using something called birth control, and you can get rid of a pregnancy with something called abortion. So why don't you do all of us a favor and get one?" My cheeks feel hot but icy. I'm going to vomit. I can't believe I just said what I did. I think abortion's wrong, but another baby right now? *This is crazy.*

"You crossed the line, you little bitch!" Pop yanks the wheel to the side and slams on the brakes, pulling the vehicle off the road. His face is red and veiny, and if he could reach me he'd be hitting me. "Get out of the fucking car!"

Mom puts her hands over her face, and the younger girls put the bed's pillows over their heads. Everyone hates me for calling bullshit on this, but I can't believe they think the situation is remotely okay. I already feel sorry for what I said, but also believe the truth of it: *Mom and Pop can't take care of the kids they have, let alone a new baby!*

I yank down on the handle of the side door and jump out. "You guys are crazy! I hate you!"

Pop guns the engine. The rusty van spits gravel as it pulls away, the door still ajar.

"Oh my God! I can't believe this!" I watch them pull away.

I burst into tears and stumble off the side of the road into shoulder-deep buffalo grass. I thrash straight into it, heedless, desperate to hide. I fall abruptly into an empty, dry old sugarcane irrigation ditch hidden by the vegetation. I burrow down into the trench, crying hard and hating myself for being so mean and angry, hating what my life is like, hating Mom and Pop.

All of my efforts to make something better for myself seem doomed. I'm going to have to take care of this baby like I had to take care of Anita, and my responsibilities will cripple my ability to escape to college. I'll end up a homeless dropout, cleaning condos and living with some druggie surfer like so many other kids from Kauai . . . "I'll never marry a surfer," I say aloud. "I'm getting off of this island."

Snuffling into my shirt, I try to think logically about the situation.

I'm fourteen and in ninth grade.

I only have three more years with the family. Nothing is going to stop me leaving and making a better life for myself if I stay focused on my goals. Even though I already feel guilty about leaving my sisters behind, I can't help anyone—especially this latest one—if I haven't made my own life work.

Furthermore, Francis is never far from my memories. Something might happen with Mom's pregnancy and she could lose this baby, too. And if things progress, we still have eight months or so for Mom and Pop to get their shit together. Maybe with the crisis of a new infant on the horizon, they will figure out that all five of us living in a van going into winter on Kauai isn't sustainable.

I just have to put my head down, button my lip, and bide my time no matter what insanity comes my way. Fighting my parents only gets me punished—and what if they pull me out of Island School, deciding it's a bad influence? No, I have to resign myself to the situation and make the best of it, as I've always done.

Sleep, a blessed oblivion, claims me.

A tiny tickly feeling wakes me up. It's a four-inch cane spider crawling on my arm, its long hairy brown legs cartoonish. I give a little shriek and shake it off, sitting up. They don't usually bite, but there's always a first time.

Long, fuzzy stalks of six-foot-high grass surround me. All I can see above is a circle of bright blue sky. Fluffy white clouds mock my misery. Fucking Kauai, always so ridiculously beautiful. My eyes feel swollen and gummy, and I've got the mother of all emotional hangovers.

I sneeze convulsively. That gets me moving, belatedly remembering I'm allergic to buffalo grass. I stumble out of the ditch and dust myself off as best I can, my skin prickling and itchy, hives rising on my arms and legs as I continue sneezing.

I need to get somewhere private and rinse off. Cars whiz past me along the two-lane road leading into Kapa`a. I look both ways, trying to decide which way to go down the road.

I really have no idea what to do next. I'm dressed for church in a skirt and a scoop neck tee with sandals. I left my purse in the car, and don't even have a quarter to use a pay phone, even if I knew an adult's number to call. I could hitchhike, but where?

The gravity of my situation sinks in.

I'm hungry, thirsty, penniless, and have nowhere I can think of going for help.

I'm somewhat close to my school. I'll walk to the school. I can spend the night in the playground equipment, since tomorrow's Monday. The plastic tube thing that leads to the slide will keep the elements off, and I can rinse off the buffalo grass allergies with the hose and have water to drink. A night without food will be good for me, and when Monday rolls around, I'll come out of the bushes and pretend I was dropped off as usual.

I walk and walk—hot, itchy, and miserable. The school building is finally visible in the distance when a familiar van pulls over to the side of the road just in front of me.

Bonny opens the van door with a slide and a bang, and I've never been so happy to see her in my life. Our eyes meet and communicate without words how screwed up everything is: *but we have each other.*

"Get in," Pop yells from the front seat. "And not another word out of you about this."

I get in. I don't say another word about it.

CHAPTER THIRTY-SIX

GHOSTS AND BAD MEN

Waiting for school bus pickup at Wainiha store

Age: 14, Wainiha, Kauai, 1979

We eventually get a rental house way out in the Wainiha Valley. An A-frame on stilts at the far end of the valley, the house is buried in a dank mosquito-infested tunnel of *hau* bush next to a large stream that feeds into the Wainiha River.

It's cheap enough for us to afford, and there's a reason. The house doesn't have electricity, so lights at night end up being a racket from the generator, and the mosquitoes are the worst of anywhere we've lived—and from the first day we move in, strange things happen. Stuff is moved. Doors open and shut. Items appear and disappear. I have a constant feeling of being spied upon, especially while showering. One evening, eating vegetable stir-fry over brown rice, Mom says, "I think this place is haunted."

We all agree and tell each other the weird things that make us think so: the sense of cold in some parts of the house. The feeling of being watched. Weird dreams. Cupboards open when they were closed, or closed when they were open. Missing items that turn up in strange places. The front door left open wide, letting in gouts of vicious mosquitoes, when we're all so careful about that.

Bonny and I begin to do everything together, including going to the bathroom. We also keep Anita close—we can't let her out of sight because of the unfenced, powerful stream that runs past the house. She's only three, and it could carry her away.

Living in the van was almost better.

Each day, Bonny and I walk the long muddy track all the way to the main road to wait by the rusty old red gas pumps by the Wainiha Store for pickup by our carpool—and every afternoon we walk all the way back. It's weird to be at our old stomping grounds—in a way, I don't feel like I belong anymore. My time on the Mainland changed me, showed me how small Kauai is, how hard it is to make it here, and that while other places may not be as pretty, they're more hospitable.

One day, Bonny's not feeling well and stays home from school, so I make the trek to get picked up alone. I'm dropped off again in the evening, and head up the dirt road toward the house, kicking a green guava down the same potholed, sandy dirt road where I jumped into puddles with Knight so long ago.

I'm looking better since the Mainland. I've lost the weight from Santa Barbara and, according to the doctor, I've reached my full height at five foot five. Rather than the tall, long-legged build Mom and Bonny inherited from Maga, I'm curvy: my breasts have filled in to a generous 32C, and I inherited Gigi's small waist and delicate ankles. Wearing my first pair of contact lenses and a new pair of Ditto jeans that make the most of my athletic butt, I put a little sway in my hips as I walk down the dirt road into the jungle, bookbag dangling as I daydream.

If Island School had a prom, I'd wear a flowing strapless dress with a tight waist and blow the guys at school's minds. I'm such a tomboy. Good ol' redheaded surfer girl Toby. Maybe they'd see me in a different light in a dress. But there's no prom . . .

The rumble of an approaching truck interrupts my fantasy, and I move to the side of the road. A mud-spattered pickup truck pulls alongside me, filled with sturdy young local guys and a welded rebar cage full of baying, drooling hunting dogs. Everyone is filthy from a pig hunt that appears to have been fruitless.

The truck slows to a crawl, bumping along the dirt road abreast of me. "Eh, *haole* girl," the guy in the passenger seat says. "You like one ride?" He grins, a scary effect.

"No thanks." I swing my bookbag up and put it on over my shoulder. I wish I hadn't brushed my hair and swayed my hips. I thought I was all alone.

"You look hot. We think you need a ride to cool off," says one of the guys says from the back of the pickup. I glance over—there are four of them altogether. "Come on up here and sit with us. We'll take you wherever you want to go."

I walk faster. My heart's thundering. "No thanks. I like walking."

"So, what, we're not good enough for you? Stuck-up bitch," the guy in the back says. He puts his hand on the side of the truck bed, getting up. Tattooed muscles in a thin wife-beater tank bunch as he prepares to jump out and grab me.

I drop my bookbag and leap into the jungle, a leafy mass of Java plum, thick grass and tangled *hau* bush. I'm fast, and panic makes me faster. I hear them yelling behind me, the dogs barking. I have a terrible image of them letting the dogs out, unhooking their guns off the back of the truck cab, and hunting me down.

I run faster, weaving through the trees until I encounter a stand of *hau* bush so dense that there's no way to get through it without climbing, so I climb and crawl until eventually I don't hear anything from behind me. I scramble up a leaning *hau* bush trunk the size of my thigh, holding on with my hands and walking with my feet. I get high enough to pop my head through the canopy.

The sky's dressed in dazzling clouds surrounded by the rugged green-clothed slopes of the valley. Off in the distance, cobalt ocean glitters. It's the same view I had from Knight's tree fort all those years ago, only further back in the valley. The view couldn't be a bigger contrast to the submerged green gloom of the tangled *hau* bush grove I've battled through.

They won't find me up here, and the dogs can't reach me. Unless they shoot me, I can't see them getting me down.

I'm safe for the moment.

I do some meditation as I sit on my high limb, closing my eyes and breathing, trying to decide what to do and when to do it. Thinking about how long it would take for the men to get bored looking for me, waiting for me. I eventually climb down, and, after checking that the coast is clear, retrieve my bag, and run all the way to the house at the very end.

Mom and Pop begin driving us to the bus stop each day after that. Finally, they pull us together for another family confab. Lamplight softens our faces because the generator is too expensive to run.

"Part of our recovery is that we're not taking any help from your grandparents, and we're just not making it financially here," Pop tells Bonny and me. "This house isn't working out, either. We have to move back to California, where I can at least get a job that pays the bills and there will be good medical care for your mom and the new baby."

I don't need a calculator to figure out that we aren't making it, but I'm sad to leave Island School and have to adjust to another school in California again. I've never understood the weird push-and-pull Mom and Pop have going on with my grandparents, and with Kauai, but I definitely won't miss living in Wainiha.

CHAPTER THIRTY-SEVEN
HMONG TV

Me holding baby Wendy when she arrives, Isla Vista, California

Age: 14-15, Isla Vista, California, 1979-80

At the Los Angeles airport, Maga eyes my dad without affection and doesn't hug him. "Hello. The children are welcome," Maga says, and the distinction is not missed by my parents. She was not, apparently, in favor of my parents getting back together.

"Thanks for giving us a place to land," Pop says. "We'll pitch our tent in the yard and get out of your hair as soon as possible."

"Uh-huh. Let's get on the road." There are none of the usual exclamations on our cuteness or how we've grown. After all, it's been less than a year since we wore out our welcome on her living room floor the last time.

The drive to Santa Barbara from L.A. is beautiful, and I lean my face on the window of the Vista Cruiser and watch the coastline roll by. The ocean's color is translucent green jade, and it smells different in California, kelpy and strong. The hills are velvety golden swells dappled with deep green live oaks, and I enjoy the graceful, lazy circles of the buzzards surfing with updrafts of the valleys.

Pop says we're going to "stand on our own two feet" and he'll do "whatever it takes" to provide for us, but the Estate was the last time he actually tried, and even working part-time was more than he could handle. Sober Pop is still moody and irritable, a huge worrier who doesn't like other people, and now there's no alcohol or *pakalolo* to take the edge off.

I don't understand him. We're so different. I'm not afraid of challenges, and I've already decided that getting an education and working are how I'm going to have a different life than this one. A *normal* life. Maybe I'll never be as rich as Gigi and Grandpa Jim, but I'm going to make sure I never have to worry about being homeless, getting washed away in a flood, or where the next meal's coming from.

And Mom? She's a hard worker but never pursued anything enough to have marketable skills. Having kids every four or five years is a real handicap for a woman. I won't fall into that trap. I'm going to stay focused on my goals.

"We're ba-ack!" I sing out as I throw myself into Nancy's arms in her room. Now that she's in high school, it's stuffed with clothes and the walls are carpeted in football game and dance souvenirs. It smells like bubblegum and popularity, and I stifle a twinge of envy.

"Where's my Anita?" Nancy exclaims, and my littlest sister, face aglow and green eyes sparkling, launches into Nancy's arms. They formed a strong bond when we lived here the last time, and are delighted to be reunited.

Bonny comes in for more hugs with Nancy. We turn Nancy's radio up super loud to the same Bee Gees song that Patricia's listening to in her room. Patricia's grown into looking like Cindy Crawford, with just as much style, and she comes out of her inner sanctum to join the party. All of us girls dance around in the living room, singing *"Stayin' alive, stayin' alive, ah, ahhh, ahhh!"* while doing John Travolta dance moves.

Maybe coming back to the mainland is exactly what we all need. Maybe we're finally done with Kauai. Maybe we've broken the island's strange and compelling hold, a hold that has begun to seem as negative to my parents as Gigi and Grandpa Jim's filthy lucre.

Mercifully, Pop gets a job right away at a hardware store and lumberyard in Santa Barbara, where he works a full forty hours a week cutting wood and helping old ladies find nuts and bolts. We get the cheapest place we can find after a couple of weeks at Maga's house, an apartment in Isla Vista, the same college town where we lived in a converted garage before.

Our unit is half of a duplex in a small quadrangle completely inhabited by Hmong refugees. The families are packed twelve to a two-bedroom unit, so our family of five in the same amount of space seems luxurious by comparison.

Mom explains how the Hmong are a hill tribe from Vietnam and Laos who helped the United States in the Vietnam War, and this is their reward: coming to America and not being slaughtered by the North Vietnamese.

Bon and I share a trash picked waterbed in one bedroom, Anita sleeps on the couch in the living room, and the new baby will stay in the other bedroom with Mom and Pop. We've sold the van coming over to get money for the tickets, and now Pop drives our "new" car, an elderly pistachio-colored Pinto, to work each day.

The hardware store is a nasty adjustment for Pop. He gets home and goes straight to bed, hardly taking a shower, on his first day. The familiar black cloud of depression is thick around him. I hope he'll get used to it and not fall off the wagon and drink, unable to deal with the stress of full-time work on the Mainland with no surfing.

Mom enrolls Bonny at Isla Vista Elementary where she's in fifth grade, within walking distance of our apartment, but I'm in ninth grade now and need to go to high school. The closest one is called Dos Pueblos High, and it's across town in the foothills.

"Take the bus to school and get yourself registered," Mom says to me. "I'm looking for a job, and I have to take Anita with me." The pregnancy's making her tired, and Pop has the car, so we all have to fend, getting ourselves around.

I look up bus routes on a kiosk and wait for one that takes me by the high school's address. I get on the bus and sit self-consciously, avoiding eye contact with anyone, as the vehicle sways and clacks along. There are a lot of University of California Santa Barbara students on the bus, elderly people, and people riding to work at jobs that require logoed pockets.

I stare out the window at raw new developments peeling back the skin of the earth. Beyond our route, dun hills dotted with olive-green oaks roll into a heat-shimmering distance marked by buzzards and telephone poles. It's hard to believe that just a few weeks ago I was in lush Wainiha, swatting mosquitoes and worrying about rapists and ghosts.

The worlds I've occupied feel so different that it's almost like the plane ride is a transporter device. I spot the sign for the high school, and tug on the cable for a stop.

Hunching my shoulders in a stiff new backpack Gigi bought me, along with stiff new jeans and stiff new Reeboks, I get off the bus and walk up into a big, new, sprawling concrete school decorated with a flagpole on roped-off grass. I'm carrying my birth certificate,

immunization record, and my last report card from Island School—
all As, of course.

At the office, a clerk looks at me over half-glasses. "You're registering? Where's a parent or guardian?"

"They had to work." I give her confident eye contact, like it's
totally normal for a fourteen-year-old to take a city bus to a high
school and register herself. Mom and Pop had their rebellion,
running away from their families and going hippie-surfer-druggie in
the jungle, but going normal is my rebellion. From now on, I'm going
to pretend I'm normal until it's true.

"Well, I guess you can do that. Okay. Here's some paperwork
they need to sign. Let me look up some classes that aren't too full."

She gets me enrolled and prints out a schedule, turning to bawl
over her shoulder, "Dawn! New student tour!"

Dawn looks up from a computer at the back of the room. I
recognize her face between wings of curling-ironed hair, and she
remembers me—I can see it in the way acne-pitted cheeks lift up her
glasses in a smile. She takes my schedule from the office lady and
glances at it, coming through the flapping half door into the office
area. "Toby. I think I knew you at Goleta Valley Junior High."

"Good to see you again, Dawn."

Dawn shows me around, and I end up eating lunch with kids I'd
known briefly before. My adjustment to "D.P." as it's affectionately
called, gets off to a good start.

Back at home that evening, we sit down for dinner around a
garage-sale Formica table set in the kitchen window. Mom's made
soup and corn bread, and I'm so hungry I go for seconds as we all
compare notes from the day. Heading back to my chair, I glance out
the plate glass window and freeze where I'm standing.

Our Hmong neighbors are watching us, clustered three deep,
upturned faces illuminated by light spilling out of the window. Their
faces are as rapt as if we were a live sitcom. They have shorter
stature, wider faces, and narrower tilted eyes than the races I'm
familiar with. Most of them are wearing American clothes, but a few
of the women are wearing traditional garb: brightly colored fabrics

sewn in intricate geometric patterns, worn in padded layers with a high, twisted headdress like a turban on their heads.

"Mom. Pop. Look out the window."

My parents turn to gaze outside. The Hmong stare back, unabashed. Some of them smile and wave.

There are at least twenty people watching us.

"Why are they staring?" Bonny asks. "It's rude."

"Maybe it's not rude in their culture. Maybe they've never seen white people eating before," Mom says.

"Maybe they're hungry." I immediately wish I hadn't said that because the bowl of soup I've just served myself is mostly broth, and it was the last of the pot. We're the kind of poor right now that's not truly hungry; it's just monotonous and consists of staples like rice, cabbage, expired baked goods and no options. Looking out at the overhead light reflecting off of dark eyes fixed on the corn bread, I suspect these people have been a lot hungrier than that.

"Ignore them," Pop says, with an imperious note in his voice that reminds me of Gigi. He uses the spatula to pry loose another square of corn bread. "Even if they're hungry, we can't do anything about it."

This is true.

We eat all of the soup, and the leftover corn bread gets fried and becomes breakfast the next morning. There are no leftovers to share even if we wanted to—and where to begin? There are so many of them.

Eventually, we get used to being the Hmongs' evening entertainment. Even after we've been living there for months, they gather around the window outside to watch us, and wave and smile every time we look up.

Things seem to settle during the next few months. With the Hmong surrounding us, our poverty feels like wealth as we hear them scream, fight, fart, and have sex on the other side of our wall and across the narrow driveway. During the day, the women wash laundry in their bathtubs inside, then hang it on lines crisscrossing the concrete driveway. They tote their babies, and cook up pots of strange-smelling stew. The men sit around on their haunches on the stoops, smoking and gossiping in a tongue that reminds me of mynah birds "talking story."

Mom makes friends with one of the Hmong women, Myxie, who speaks some English. Myxie begins sewing a baby carrier for our coming brother or sister in the Hmong tradition, a lengthy project: two square panels, elaborately embroidered and quilted, with long red sashes that go over the shoulders and around the waist to anchor the baby against front or back. It's so elaborate that I wonder if it will be ready in time as Mom's pregnancy progresses, but she seems to enjoy working on it and coming over to show it to Mom.

I buy a bike at a garage sale and begin riding to school. In spite of arriving hot and sweaty, as it's mostly uphill, biking keeps me in shape and helps me relax. I notice and record in my journal that I need to exercise every day, or I get edgy and emotional. I'm trying hard to be positive these days and keep my stress under control—all part of passing for normal.

I qualify for free lunch but make my lunch at home so I don't have to get in the free line. My home-packed lunches are cold corn bread and an apple, or a cottage cheese sandwich, which Mom says is "perfectly nutritious" but has the disadvantage of being strange and soggy.

"What kind of sandwich is that?" Dawn asks one day at lunch, pointing to the wheat bread from the day-old bakery oozing cottage cheese and Mom's homegrown alfalfa sprouts.

"Low calorie." I take a big bite, eyeing her down.

"Okay," Dawn says doubtfully. I forgot to eat the squishy mess in secret in the bathroom stall. People will accept any kind of food oddity if counting calories is a part of it—and I'm becoming increasingly worried about my weight as I mature into a body that doesn't feel like mine anymore.

I want to be slim and hard-bodied with small boobs. Instead, I've got an hourglass shape. I begin to get attention from guys, whistles as I zoom by on my bike—and I'm nervous at the unwanted notice, remembering the pig hunters and their truck.

Act normal 'til it is normal is my new motto. Staying away from overcrowded, not-normal home as much as possible, I join the soccer team and run around every day after school for practice, or study after school at the library—but I eventually have to get on my bike and ride back to my claustrophobic home. There's no privacy to be had anywhere, and I need somewhere to retreat to.

I take the screen out of our bedroom window, which looks into a six-foot gap between our building and the next. The Hmong are using this hidden strip of ground for growing giant red opium poppies, florid as a Georgia O'Keefe painting. I climb out the window, looking at the poppies to see if the tiny cuts they make in the poppy pods are bleeding more of the black sap they'll make into hash. I've read about opium harvesting and I want to see them do it —but I never catch anyone back there.

Standing on the windowsill, I turn around and pull myself up onto the flat, tar paper-covered roof. I look across the houses from above and watch the sunsets alone. On non-school days, I go up and lie on a towel with my book and pillow, listening to a tiny portable radio and reading, or writing in my journal in the evenings until the stars come out. It's almost as good as my old tree fort at the Estate in Hanalei, another lifetime ago.

Bonny and I still get along well. She's reconnected with her best friend, Kim, from when we lived in the area before and is enjoying fifth grade. On weekends, Bonny and I ride our bikes all around the town, exploring. We spot crayfish in the tiny park pond in the middle of town and, using bacon on a string, catch hundreds of them to boil at home and crack out of their shells.

The Hmong are also foraging—the ocean all around us is a marine sanctuary, but they clearly don't know that as I see them passing by with bags loaded with clams, fish, sea urchins, even starfish, all destined for the soup pot. One day when I come up to my rooftop retreat, I'm confronted by the maggot-filled heads of deer they've shot and put up there to dry. They smell so bad and draw so many flies, I can't go up on the roof for months.

Everything mortifies me these days, not the least of which is the embarrassing vastness of my pregnant mother. A pregnant woman wears a sign around her midsection proclaiming, *I HAD SEX.* And when the sign points to your dad, and you know about the gross activity that goes on to get pregnant, mortification is the only possible response.

Mom's belly is a vast mountain that heaves and ripples with the powerful movements of the baby. Her hair is long, curling, and lustrous. Her flat breasts have filled, her nails are shiny. She exudes contentment as she waddles back and forth across the highway toting a red STOP sign for her crossing guard job at Bonny's school, or squats to weed the garden she's carved out of our postage stamp lawn.

I'm equal parts fascinated and repulsed by what's happening to her. Mom shows us a photo-illustrated book on childbirth from the library, and the baby's head "crowning" gives me nightmares. Getting a ten-pound baby out through that hole seems to defy all the laws of physics.

"You just forgot how big I was with Anita," Mom pants as we take an evening walk as a family along the bluffs above a sunset-streaked Pacific Ocean, an evening ritual she and Pop usually do with four-year-old Anita. "I was huge with Anita. All of you were ten-pound babies, except you, Toby. You were only eight pounds."

I lift my nose in the air, eyeballing Bonny with mock snootiness. "I'm the petite one."

"More like a redheaded Oompa Loompa," Bonny says, with a shove that makes me stagger. She has a quick wit that keeps everyone around her laughing. Her future beauty shines in the flash of her eyes and whirl of her creamy-thick blonde hair, though she's still got the uneven teeth and chubbiness of almost-adolescence. Her legs are longer than mine, making her my height at only ten.

Anita, at four, is an elfin sprite. She's shy and gorgeous, with pink cheeks, a beauty mark on the stem of her neck, and the same green eyes Bonny and Pop have. A little silver tabby cat, she ghosts quietly through our tiny apartment until she ends up in my lap and I'm brushing her dandelion-gilt hair yet again.

The trail of droplets dotting the dusty path behind Mom that evening turns out to be amniotic fluid, and her labor begins before we get back to the house. Mom and Pop grab her bag, and off they go to the hospital in the Pinto.

Bonny, Anita, and I play Parcheesi and read stories and go to bed together in the waterbed. I drag the phone out of the living room into our room so that when Pop calls I won't miss it.

He doesn't call until the next morning. "You have a sister— Wendy Ellen." His voice sounds like change rattling in a rusty can. I'm so relieved that Mom and the baby are okay that I make pancakes for Bonny and Anita for breakfast.

I just knew there would never be another brother after Francis.

Mom and Wendy come home a few days later. Wendy's adorable: blue-eyed, dark-haired, with a strong pair of lungs. We do a "photo shoot" with each of us holding her, posing with Mom's hospital flowers.

Holding her, I fall in love again. There's just nothing like a baby: that milky smell, the helpless sweetness of her weight in my arms. That I ever said what I did about her seems obscene now that she's here.

Myxie, our Hmong neighbor, has finally finished the beautifully stitched baby sling, and Wendy spends her first months wrapped close to Mom, wailing her unhappiness into Mom's breasts. Wendy's colicky, not good news in our tiny apartment. Even the neighbors on the other side, all twelve of them or so, are worried and stop by to ask after the baby as Wendy's crying keeps everyone awake into the night.

Pop becomes withdrawn, and his black mood intensifies as Wendy wails on, inconsolable. Anita comes to sleep with Bonny and me, displaced as the baby of the family, but in typical Anita fashion, there's no fuss or drama—she simply appears down by our feet or wedged between us.

Mom takes Wendy to the doctor. The baby comes home with both of her feet in casts. "Her feet are turned too far inward. The casts are going to help straighten them out," Mom says. The casts do not improve Wendy's outlook on the world.

Mom's bubble of contentment has burst. Her thick hair falls out in handfuls. Her eyes are red-rimmed, and she stares into the distance, nursing or joggling Wendy. She's barely keeping the crazy at bay.

I do what I can, helping fix meals, cleaning, and taking care of Anita after school. Bonny and I take her with us on her little bike with training wheels on long rides along the baked-dirt bluffs, or into town to shop or fish for crawdads. We harvest freakishly large vegetables from Mom's garden that we trade at the health food store for tofu, free-range eggs, and Dr. Bronner's that we can't get at the discount stores where we often shop.

"Never seen tomatoes this big." The health food store manager goggles over the cardboard boxes Bonny and I carry in balanced on our bike handlebars loaded with glossy eggplant, brain-sized broccoli, and tomatoes like small pumpkins. He holds one up, marveling, and weighs it. "Pound and a half. What's the secret to these giant vegetables?"

"Horse manure." Mom's love of gardening with all things manure has not abated. The first thing she did after having us shake the dirt out of the dug-up grass of the former lawn of our minuscule yard was locate a stable. She then asked if we could haul away their manure, which they were happy about, and she volunteered us to shovel it into bags to keep the garden supplied.

We're in Isla Vista for a year, and Wendy eventually grows out of her fussiness. I start tenth grade, and I've got a crush on a fellow soccer player, Philip, who lives in Isla Vista too. I go to his house after school and watch TV with him, sitting on his couch holding hands while his parents are at work. I'm hyperaware of his long muscular body beside me, his fresh pink cheeks, the dark curls beside his ears.

I'm even considering bringing him over to meet my family. I never bring anyone over because our funky, crowded, tiny apartment in the middle of the makeshift Hmong village is *Not Normal*. But I know Philip well enough by now to know that he'd like my secret fort on top of the roof now that the Hmong took down the deer heads. Maybe he'd even kiss me up there. I get all tingly imagining his mouth touching mine.

One morning, Pop has an unfamiliar spark of animation in his eyes, and he tells me, "Be home for a family confab."

My gut knots. Not another confab!

That evening, Mom and Pop gather us in the tiny living room, sitting on Anita's couch-bed. Pop leans forward, and the light falls on his big, square hands, battered and scraped from handling lumber. The deep creases in his face have lifted upward—the black fog of his angry depression is gone, and his eyes gleam with excitement. Even Mom, who's been quiet and preoccupied since Wendy's birth, is smiling, bouncing Wendy on her knees.

"Good news, girls," Pop says. "I've been looking for a job back on Kauai for months now, and I finally got one. We're going to be caretakers for a nice estate back in Hanalei Valley."

I let down my guard.

I quit monitoring Mom and Pop, got caught up in my own life as a teenager, and forgot my parents' other addiction: the lush paradise island of Kauai, with its drip-castle mountains, lush waterfalls, and pristine, uncrowded surf.

Of course, I don't agree to go back to Kauai meekly.

I rage, slam doors, and accuse them of selfishness. "Just when I was starting to like my life!" I cry, thinking of Philip and the soccer team and my little, hard-won group of friends. Mom and Pop are unmoved, fixed on returning to their drug of choice.

"You might like your life here, but I hate mine," Pop says. "The grind of the nine to five. Cold, crowded surf. All these people packed in one space. Kauai will be different this time. We have a job and a place to live, from day one."

The reservations are made, the tickets purchased. The only bright spot is that Gigi and Grandpa Jim, alarmed by my hysteria about attending Kapa'a High where I'm just sure that Kira Yoshimura is the reigning queen, agree to pay for the tuition for Bonny and me to attend Island School again.

Dawn and my other lunchtime buddies make me a mock yearbook and sign it with good wishes. "You're so lucky, going to live in Hawaii!"

Ha. If they only knew how we lived. I nurse the flame of resentment with angry poetry and angst-ridden journal entries. Philip finally kisses me, but it's a sweet and devastating kiss goodbye.

CHAPTER THIRTY-EIGHT

TARO FIELDS AND SWANS

Me with my sisters and cousin Jennifer

Age: 15, Kuntz Estate, Hanalei, Kauai, 1981

We get a ride from the airport to the new estate where we'll be living and working with our old friends Tom and Cheri Hamilton. Piled in the back of Tom's pickup, their surfboards temporarily gone, we make a left turn onto a potholed, sandy-dirt road in the middle of town next to the Wai`oli Hui`ia Church, the scene of my attack after hula lessons so long ago. Seeing the spot still gives me an internal shiver.

The taro fields on either side of the narrow road, square plots filled with water and fed by a system of canals, reflect a deep blue, layered sky filled with rosy-edged cumulus clouds. The *kalo* plants themselves have large, heart-shaped leaves of dark green on slender, upright stems like anthuriums. White egrets and herons stand still as statues in their midst, hunting small fish. The stunning backdrop of the three mountains that frame the main house, Mamalahoa, Hihimanu, and Namolokama, are gushing waterfalls and seem to have their rugged valley arms extended open in welcome.

The owner's house is a modern multi-story masterpiece in silvery cedar set off by a big, deep green pond with two swans circling in it within an acre or so of lawn. The whole estate is set like a jewel in the framework of the fields.

Our new boss and his family are out of town when we arrive, which is a good thing because the "caretaker cottage" we're supposed to live in turns out to be a one-room shack with no electricity or bathroom. The five of us females stare at two unfinished rooms in semi-horror: the shack's only plumbing is the kitchen sink.

Mom swivels to glare at me, daring me to speak. "I'm sure we can make this work." She shifts Wendy to her other hip. "We can rig up an outdoor shower and build a composting toilet."

"Yep, no problem. I'll fix it up!" Pop is undaunted by this setback and galvanized by his escape from the lumber mill. I roll my eyes and stomp off to keep from saying all the things I'm thinking. Mom and Pop are still really good at getting work and babysitting out of me as punishment for sassy comments.

Pop continues to be cheerful and energetic as he takes the owner's truck to town and buys lumber, nails, and screens to expand the guesthouse. He drops us off at Lihue Library, where we stock up on books, and he borrows one on composting toilets.

He builds the toilet outside the kitchen window of our cottage, following plans in the library book. The finished product is a five-foot-high box accessed via a ladder. There's a hole in the top of the box to squat over. A big handful of leaves and grass clippings is kept in a bucket and dropped in when we finish. The broken-down waste can be raked out the front through a small door and used on the garden.

We even get to use real toilet paper, not just leaves like at the Forest House. It doesn't smell, and he sands the hole so splinters don't go into our butts if we sit on the hole. But, it's positioned right in front of the kitchen window where our bare asses are hanging out for all to see, and there's no surround. The shower he rigs up is also exposed; a hose tied to a Java plum tree with an old wooden pallet to stand on so the ever-present mud doesn't get on our feet while showering.

I WILL NEVER BE ABLE TO BRING A FRIEND OVER TO THE HOUSE IN case they have to go to the bathroom because there is no privacy whatsoever. Apparently, it's too much work for Pop to build a privacy surround for either area. I get assigned yard work when I point out the limitations. "If you've got energy to complain, you've got plenty of energy for work," Mom says.

The location out in the middle of agricultural land is out of range of any of the usual town comforts and normal zoning, so the utilities at the estate are "off the grid" and consist of a solar water heater, a generator, and a well and cesspool for the main house only.

With no electricity but a generator that sounds like a sledge-hammer running at top speed, and a budget that doesn't include batteries, I don't even have my little transistor radio anymore—even if it could have picked any music up in remote Hanalei.

Pop gives me ten hours a week of his job hours now that I'm a strong and sturdy fifteen, just like the old days at the Estate. Bonny gets hours as well. In addition, we put in Mom's food garden in a raised concrete bed designed for that purpose but overflowing with weeds.

So far, my experience of Kauai sucks. We're cut off from

everyone and do nothing but work. Once again, my only escape is reading.

Pop's "renovation" of the shack finally ends. Bonny and I share a section of screened-in porch at the front. We bicker so much in the tiny six-foot by ten-foot space that Pop loses his temper one day as we're screaming at each other.

"You want to be by yourself, Toby, you got it," he growls. "Anything to get you out of the house."

I help him build me my own room out of screen and plywood, tacked onto the back of the house. It's a six-by-ten box with no access to the main house, and screen on three sides as a cost-saving measure. As an angry almost sixteen-year-old with no phone, TV, or transportation, this suits me just fine. I retreat to a homemade bed with a foam mattress on it, enjoying a view of the taro fields in private splendor through screened walls.

We buy another van, and carpool to Island School with a couple of other North Shore families. I reconnect with my Island School friends from our last stint on Kauai without any trouble, but our house is so isolated that a car is necessary for getting anywhere close to my friends. My buddy, Megan, lives in Anahola, thirty minutes away, as do Kate and Emma, British twins who also attend our funky private school. I can't find my old friend Tita, and I hear she moved into Kapa`a and is attending the high school there.

With the racial barriers from the past just as impervious as ever, there's no one to hang out with nearby. Out of boredom and necessity, I get back into surfing and buy my first surfboard at a garage sale. It's a seven-foot, single-fin, light blue Channin "gun" designed for big surf, but I take it out almost daily in any condition.

With nothing to do but chores at home, I find new motivation to get out in the surf and improve on my own. After school and chores, I ride my bike down the potholed dirt road through the taro fields, the Channin precariously balanced under one arm.

The salty gym of the ocean is the place to take all of my angst out on. I attack the waves with all of my frustration, and they can take it and spank me right back. I'm reminded again that nature is a place that can absorb and transform my frazzled emotions. In my sleek black Speedo tank suit or my new green bikini, on any given day I'm out in the ocean, hooked on the challenge and adrenaline rush of surfing.

Surfing. We joke that it's the only thing to do on Kauai, but what a thing it is. I start out at the beginner spots, sand bars along Hanalei Bay where I don't have to be embarrassed by how bad I am at first— but I've absorbed a lot from being around surfing all my life, and I've already got "wave knowledge" from swimming and bodyboarding and my early start when we lived at the Kauikeolani Estate. I can read the lineup, choose a spot to take off where the wave will peak, and be able to tell when I need to straighten off because it's going to close out in front of me.

All of this helps me progress rapidly. Within a few months, I've graduated to paddling out at my parents' favorite spot, Hanalei Bay. Sometimes I even surf with Mom and Pop while Bonny babysits the younger girls. The first time I get a tube ride, where the lip of the wave curls over me, I'm filled with an exhilaration that makes me yell in triumph after I kick out the back successfully—and the other surfers grin, hoot, and give me "shaka." It's a friendly place that day, even though I'm one of just a couple of women out in the water.

I'm beginning to understand Kauai's addictive quality, and it has everything to do with the exuberant beauty of the place itself, and its great surf.

Reconnecting with old friends at Island School is great, but the "off the grid" world at home still feels desperately small, a shoe that never stops pinching. When I want to make a phone call, I have to ride my bike up to the pay phone in town—and change is coming to the old Ching Young Store building. It's being cleaned up and remodeled, and Aunty Clorinda reigns over a new, freestanding post office building a block or so away.

1981 rolls around, and Pop gets into the new sport of windsurfing, teaching me and Bonny to sail first. Like most sports, I pick it up quickly and graduate to shorter boards as they are developed, and work on mastering moves like jibing and waterstarts. We all enjoy this new sport, which feels like the perfect marriage of sailing and surfing.

Pop and I get along better now that I'm surfing and boardsailing —we have an interest to share, and Pop and I always get along best when he's teaching me something. He opens a new business giving windsurfing lessons while Bonny, Mom, and I do a lot of his caretaker job hours. He gets a business loan and buys rental windsurf equipment, and pretty soon Bonny and I are helping load and unload the student windsurfers at nearby Anini Beach Park, even teaching lessons ourselves when he needs help.

I start dating, mostly other surfers, and I go out with a smart, hardworking kid named Greg. We surf together, and he gives me a driving lesson in his little Honda that ends when I run off the road and almost crash into a fence. We take a hike up to Sleeping Giant, a remote mountain near Kapa`a, and with the heat of our exertions, a glorious view, and a cool breeze drawing us together, we kiss and make out.

It's pleasant, but I thought it would be more exciting—earth-shattering! Captivating! A sonic boom of physical sensation!

I sense my capacity for these feelings, but they remain elusive. I want sex to be meaningful: deep, intense, total rapture, and fulfillment. Maybe reading so many romance novels has given me unrealistic expectations, but I'm still not going to settle for anything less than the full experience of falling in love and passion.

Mom drags me to our family doctor in Kilauea for birth control, over my protests. "I'm hardly even dating," I grumble in embarrassment.

"But you're going to. And you want to be in control of what happens with your body," she says.

I have to admit, having several months' worth of birth control pills does give me peace of mind. I'm grateful to Mom for making me look the issue in the eye. Getting pregnant would be a disaster for my aspirations, and she loves me enough to know this.

CHAPTER THIRTY-NINE

EXPERIMENTATION ALLERGIES

Pop teaching me to windsurf

Age: 16, Hanalei, Kauai, 1982

The first time I ever get drunk is at an adult party at night on a sailboat anchored in Hanalei Bay. There are some young people there, but I'm definitely the youngest. I'm handed shots of tequila, which go straight to my head. Dizzy and giggling, I strip off my clothes with the rest of the partiers, and soon we're all jumping off the side of the boat, skinny-dipping, shrieking and laughing as rock music echoes across the Bay.

One of the guys dares me to take one of the windsurfers tied up to the boat out for a naked sail, and some part of me can't help but rise to the challenge—the same part that climbed a forty-foot tree to play on a raft of vines, and will surf and jump off waterfalls when none of the other girls will.

I pull up the sail from the water by the stretchy uphaul. Keeping my balance with difficulty, naked breasts swinging, I reef the boom in, angling downwind. Overhead, a vault of stars is rendered fuzzy by my lack of glasses, and, sliding by under the windsurfer, the water is a glassy black abyss that, when I inevitably fall off, feels cold and filled with unfamiliar monsters.

I end having to paddle the windsurfer back, and am stone cold embarrassingly sober by the time the boat's lights fall on my naked-ness. "Nice form!" comes a drunken holler. I seriously consider sailing away to shore, but the wind's died. I end up climbing the ladder onto the boat and enduring razzing until I can find a towel.

Out in my screen box bedroom, I write about the experience in my journal. I don't like the way drinking makes me feel—out of control, silly. I'm four times more likely than other people to become an alcoholic since I'm the offspring of alcoholics, and I worry about that.

The worst episode of this experimentation phase happens at a party when I drink too much and end up in a sleeping bag on the beach, making out with Greg's older brother home from college, a guy I barely know. Waking up in his arms, both of us crusty with dried salt from night swimming, I have no idea how I got there. I crawl out of the sleeping bag and check my panties, deciding I'm still a virgin because they're the only thing I have on and look clean.

My best possibility in getting off Kauai lies in going to college, and to do that I need to stay focused. I'm in very real danger of getting accidentally pregnant or derailed from school through some stupid alcohol or pot-related blunder, and I'm meant for bigger things than struggling to make ends meet at some menial job in this beautiful backwater just so I can surf.

An anti-drink and anti-drug decision hardens into resolve.

"That's it," I tell my friends after the Sleeping Bag Incident, taking my decision public for accountability purposes. "No more drinking or pot, or I'll get stuck on this rock."

My PSAT scores make the *Garden Island* paper as they're in the top ten percent in the nation. My grandparents, allowed back in our lives because of their help with the Island School tuition, encourage my college dreams.

"We'll take you to look at schools," they say, which means colleges in California near them. I give lip service to being interested in that—but I've got my sights set on faraway new places like Boston and New York. I want to see everything, try everything, and have a much bigger, better *normal* life: one with a fulfilling, interesting job and fat paychecks.

ALL WE HAVE IS A GIANT COLUMN-SHIFTER VAN FOR ME TO LEARN to drive on. I'm well past sixteen and still don't have my license, purely due to neither parent wanting to teach me. After much begging and trading work for the lesson, once I have my permit Pop agrees to instruct me. Between clutching, gassing, and braking the huge vehicle, I bump the van into the gravel pile we use for filling the potholed road. On impact, I giggle hysterically—we haven't even made it out of the parking area.

Pop is not amused. "That's it. I'm not teaching you. This is too stressful."

"Everything is too stressful for you. I don't know why you even had kids."

"I never wanted kids. Your mom wanted you." I've never heard

Pop say his truth quite so clearly before. I do know the story—it's been told often enough. Mom got pregnant with me when they were in college, and their parents made them get married—and from then on Pop was an unwilling sperm donor. Pop yanks the keys out of the ignition and gets out of the van. "You can figure out getting your license yourself, Never Enough Girl."

Never Enough Girl. The nickname hurts, as if my ambition and dreams are something bad, something shameful. I rest my head on the steering wheel and cry as he slams the door.

I TRADE BABYSITTING THE NEIGHBOR'S TODDLER SON FOR USING her phone and getting driving lessons in her stick shift VW Bug. Now I only have to walk down the long-ass muddy road to the house at the end of the taro fields to use the phone extension she puts out for me in her garage. Calls to my friends Megan, Kate, and Emma usually go like this: "Can I spend the night at your house and never come home?"

Twins Kate and Emma are originally from Europe, and have sophisticated style from traveling all over the world with their hippie mom. Kate's funny and hyper, always full of fun and creative ideas; Emma is more mellow. Pretty much anything goes at their house. I can tell that they're sometimes as unhappy as I am, and finances aren't easy.

Megan has it the best of the four of us. Diana, her mom, is a lovely woman who teaches music at our school. Things are clean and fun at her house, and there's always plenty of food. Some of my happiest times take place lying on her bed with the other girls, listening to music and talking about boys.

Kate dates a local guy, the only one of us to do so. Kimo's adorable, gentle, and fun with a great sense of humor. He makes me wish I'd had a chance to get to know Hawaiian boys better, but bad memories have put me off. Attending Island School with other *haoles*, I don't even see the kids I used to go to school with in Hanalei.

In spite of teasing from my friends, who've already cast off their outmoded virginity, I'm waiting to fall in love before having sex. I'm a romantic surfer girl "Anne of Green Gables," complete with red hair and a reading fetish.

One day, a boy I've known since I first went to Island School shows me a scribbled poem on his geometry paper. "I'm making lyrics out of this math poem," he says. "'The square root of the hypotenuse' could be a catchy title. Next stop, top forty!" He laughs.

Math poetry becoming song lyrics? *Yes, please.* Brian has a keen intelligence, and for years, as I've shuttled back and forth between schools, whenever we're together we compete to get the best scores. Smart guys are sexy.

This particular day, the sun hits his auburn hair and lights a fire in the depths of it. I've always admired how Brian could pick up any instrument and play it, but now I notice him physically too. His longish red hair is curlier than my strawberry blonde, but otherwise, down to our eyes, we're as matched as twin ginger bookends.

A constraint falls over our usual banter. I catch him looking at me when I'm sneaking looks at him, and it feels hot and scary and different from the relationships I've had so far. Nothing happens, but I notice every small uniqueness about him: full lips that would be too soft if not opposed by a square jaw. A compact surfer's body sprinkled with delicious freckles like nutmeg. Dexterous musician's hands, sensitive and confident.

After play practice one day, the room clears out as he plays an improvised, original song on the school's old upright. I lie on the stage next to the piano, floating with my eyes closed on the sound as if it were a rich and colorful magic carpet. His music is like my art and writing—something that arises from within, unstoppable and necessary.

The song ends. "Let's take a walk," he says.

We leave the building and cross the road to the beach across from school. Brian's hand feels like the only real thing in the world at that moment; his warm, firm grip is keeping me from flying away like a balloon on the breeze.

This. This is what I've been holding out for.

The wind hums in the branches of a beach heliotrope tree we take shelter under. Brian's wearing board shorts for surfing, his default outfit, and he takes his shirt off with a quick and graceful movement, dropping it to the sand. I love looking at him, and the tiny dimple beside his mouth tells me he knows it.

He takes off my glasses. I take off his. We set them on his shirt near our feet. His eyes, level with mine, are a fascinating umber flecked with mossy green, rust, and gold. I see my outline reflected in their shiny surface. My eyes look like his, so I know what he's seeing, too. Our similarity feels amazing, like finding a missing part of myself I never knew was gone.

His skin, buttermilk with cinnamon sprinkled on it, covers a lean muscled body. I touch him tentatively, drawing a hand down his arm, over his shoulder. Each touch trails fire through my fingertips and raises chicken skin on him, making his stomach clench. His nipples, the size and color of pennies, tighten into currants. He strokes me in similar fashion, then slides his hands up my arms to cup my face, drawing me closer.

We're just inches apart, hazel eyes gazing into hazel eyes, and we slowly lean in for the kiss we can't wait for any longer. I step into a red room of sensation, a spell cast from just the connection of our mouths. The waves crash on the beach behind us, the ever-present wind shushes through the branches of the tree, and our arms circle around each other in a perfect fit that makes each of us sigh with recognition and relief—"Oh, it's *you*."

Over the next weeks, we sneak to the beach often to meet under the heliotrope tree and kiss until our lips are raw and our bodies quiver.

I don't even tell my close friends about our relationship. It's a small school, and neither of us feels ready for the usual teasing, as if in telling others we'll dilute what we have—at least, that's the way I feel about it. And as our relationship intensifies, I want him to be my first.

I tell Brian so, one afternoon under our favorite tree. "I'm a virgin. I've been waiting to be in love." I can't get enough of looking at his firm, lush mouth, tracing it with my fingers, kissing and tasting it. His is a beauty that's crept up on me, a subtle delight I almost missed. "I have champagne. And a tent."

I've broken into my stash and started the birth control pills. I want to be with him in every way I can, and it's keeping me up nights. He doesn't say he loves me too—but that's okay. What he doesn't say is in his eyes, hands, and kisses.

We tell our parents we're spending the night at our friends' houses. We're going to hike the Na Pali Coast and set up the tent and . . . do it. My imagination boggles at that point, educated as I am by Barbara Cartland and Joan Collins. I can't wait to be transported into the bliss of sensual oneness.

I get into Brian's car on Friday afternoon for Mission Deflowering. My backpack bulges with a bottle of champagne, bedding, and tent. I've even swiped a rubber from one of my sexually prepared friend's wallets, just in case Brian doesn't have one.

We pull away from the school and take a left, headed for the North Shore. Brian's clenching and unclenching his hands on the steering wheel. "I have to tell you something."

He stares straight ahead. I see an unfamiliar muscle in the square line of his jaw.

"What?" I restrain myself from my old habit of bouncing on the seat with excitement.

"I know what this means to you. And I need to tell you that . . . I don't feel the same."

I turn fully toward him. "What?"

"You said you wanted to be in love, you know, for this. And I'm sorry, but I just don't feel the same. I don't want to take advantage of you. So . . . I don't think we should go through with it." He still won't look at me.

Somehow, we're still driving, moving through space. I'm pinned through the heart like a butterfly to a corkboard, breathless and dizzy with pain. All I can think of is getting away. "Stop the car."

"We should talk about this. I do care about you." Brian begins to pull over, but it isn't fast enough for me. I open the door. The asphalt and red Kauai dirt speeds by. "Wait!" He sounds panicked.

He gets the car mostly stopped and I jump out, stumbling and almost falling. I reach back and grab the pack filled with supplies for our special night.

My eyes feel as hot as the volcano goddess Pele's intense fire. I incinerate him with my gaze as pain turns to rage. "You're gonna be sorry." *Anger is armor.* "I'm the best you'll never have." I slam the door.

It's a pretty good exit line. That's a tiny comfort, but not nearly enough for having loved someone and offered everything, only to be turned down.

I turn away and break into a jog, headed back to school to phone for a ride. He calls after me, but I speed up, running full tilt down the road. Tears choke me. My first broken heart feels very much like an actual stab wound to the chest.

CHAPTER FORTY

AN ENEMA FOR THE PAIN

Age: 17, Hanalei, Kauai, 1982

Everything about home has begun to chafe.

Our morning breakfast, made from boiled chicken feed: "Why pay more for the packaging when it's all the same ingredients?" says Mom, buying a fifty-pound bag of mixed cracked corn, rolled oats, flax, and barley scratch from the farm supply store.

The Meher Baba quotes taped on the refrigerator:

"Don't worry, be happy."

"Mastery in servitude."

"No amount of prayer or meditation can do what helping others can do."

Yogananda's quotes were deeper. Why did we have to change gurus? That happened somewhere along the way, and I was too caught up in my teenage life to pay attention.

The refrigerator itself annoys me. Small and rusty, it's run by turning on the cacophony of the generator once a day for an hour, the only electricity we have.

The composting toilet outside the kitchen window rankles. It's functional, but doing my morning poop in public stresses me out. Pop can't be bothered to build a screen for the composter, nor anything around the "shower," that hose tied to a tree. Now that I'm a well-rounded seventeen, showering in plain view irks me even more than the stone-cold water. "Why are you so fussy?" Pop says. "Nobody cares."

"I care," I say, but that's never mattered.

Daily rain blows into my little screen room, covering my few possessions in mold. When it really rains, I have plastic blinds I can go outside and roll down, but I have to get soaked doing it. When it really, really rains, which it does often in winter, the roof slant of my tacked-on room is too flat and water backs up and rolls down the inner wall, soaking everything it touches.

The alternative is to go inside the crowded family shack and sleep on the floor of the living room—too claustrophobic even to contemplate.

The endless yard work of Pop's caretaker job takes the annoyance to a whole new level because I get the tasks that require a strong back. Standing in mud in the pond with a sickle to chop back the thick, choking buffalo grass is one of my chores. Cane spiders, their environment disturbed, run up my body, and I almost hack off a limb more times than I can count trying to get them off me. Shoveling gravel into a wheelbarrow to fill the potholes and puddles in the road to the estate is my chore, along with chopping encroaching *hau* bush with a machete or chainsaw and digging out the multi-bulbed stumps of banana trees.

I wear my bikini for all these tasks, telling myself I'm getting a tan and getting in shape. Wearing my bathing suit also saves having to wash filthy work clothes at the Laundromat since we don't have a washer.

No phone. No car. No music. No TV. Nowhere to go, or shop, or hang out with friends. I miss Brian and our secret meetings; I miss our easy friendship just as much. I'm frustrated, isolated, and claustrophobic all the time I'm not in school or out surfing.

Surfing becomes an escape, a way to discharge energy, a place to socialize. I can "talk story" with the other surfers in the parking lot or out in the break. I'm improving, though being a girl counts against me.

There's no respect from other surfers. If you fail to make a takeoff even once, no one will let you in to the takeoff spot to try again. But I know a lot of people from growing up here, and eventually I find a lineup where I can usually get waves; out at the big Hanalei break, I hang way inside and pick off the smaller waves no one wants.

Taking off, left foot forward because I'm a "goofy foot," angling down the wave and pumping the board to pick up speed on the liquid, moving surface, drawing up tight to tuck under the lip, making it out the other side—that's when I stop thinking or feeling anything but totally connected with the energy moving through the water. There's a shared power in riding waves, just like riding horses —a merging that's greater than the sum of its parts.

I struggle because of weak arms and not being confident, and I don't like being one of just a couple of women surfers. I work on strengthening my arms at home by lifting gallon milk jugs filled with water and doing squats and lunges as I go about my yard work.

Surfing puts me back into the "tomboy" role I've always had in spite of my body's betrayal into curviness. After my home chores, I become "one of the guys" and pile into vehicles with boys from school and the neighborhood to go out wherever there are waves.

Evenings in Hanalei are when there's some of the best surfing, as the wind is often offshore, helping hold the waves' shape. The sandbar next to the Hanalei river mouth is crowded with parked trucks filled with guys and their families and girlfriends, passing joints and sipping beer, watching the sunset and telling stories of the waves they caught that day. Sometimes I spot Knight with his posse of friends, but we never speak. He's becoming a model and a surf star, and is too exalted to say hi to me.

The canoe club team comes into the river mouth from their ocean practice, pushing upriver. Their shoulders swing in sync, keeping the beat with, *"Hup! Ho!"* from the steersman as the beautiful wooden canoe trimmed in yellow slices through the water. Parked on my baby blue Channin, I sit in classic surfer pose on the beach: ass on my board on the sand, arms looped around my knees, one hand clasping a wrist. I'm a part of that scene, and it feels good. I'm a surfer chick; not a beach babe like Bonny, who's become frighteningly beautiful.

Going anywhere with Bonny has become hard on my ego. "Back off, she's only thirteen!" I tell my surfer friends, who hardly glance at good ol' buddy me but are agog at Bonny. She's grown to five foot ten and strolls down the beach on long tan legs with about an acre of white-blonde hair bouncing in the sun.

I'm mouthier, angrier, and more frustrated than ever. Mom and Pop have no idea how hard it is to be seventeen and living our weird, smothering lifestyle—which is how I've begun to see it. One day, in a rare moment alone at the beach with Mom, I tell her how I'm struggling. "I'll die if I don't get off this island. I think about killing myself sometimes. I can't end up trapped here."

"Always such a drama queen," Mom says. "Never Enough Girl."

I walk away so she won't see the tears spill over, adding to my "drama queen" reputation—and I stop trying to communicate. She's never understood my drive to excel, my hunger for normalcy, my need for a broader world.

I WAKE UP WITH A PAIN IN MY ABDOMEN ONE MORNING, A stabbing sensation that makes me curl around myself in my little foam bed, moaning. I'm hot all over, my mouth is dry, my lips chapped, and skin burning. I try to get up and walk to the house to tell Mom I'm sick, but when I stretch my legs out, the agony in my stomach makes me curl up again.

"Help!" I pound on the wall behind me, a wall that connects with Mom and Pop's room. "Help!" My voice is raspy and small.

How did I get so sick, so fast?

I have to vomit, suddenly and overwhelmingly, and barely make it to heave up my empty stomach outside the little door of my room.

Bonny comes in answer to my pounding and her eyes widen as she sees me lying on the floor of my room, smells the vomit outside my door.

She fetches Mom. By then I have diarrhea, which doesn't really work with the composting toilet, and my cries of agony at having to walk and climb the ladder. The owners are gone from the main house, and Mom and Pop half-carry me upstairs to the only real bathroom on the whole property. I'm shaking and burning with fever and weeping from the pain.

Mom consults her home remedies book and decides I have a blocked bowel. "We need to give you an enema."

I'm too weak and delirious to protest.

Mom plies me with water, which I throw up, and inserts the enema. She barely gets me onto the toilet in time. When there's blood in the toilet, and I become incoherent and am still vomiting, my fever around a hundred and four, she and Pop confab and decide I have to go to the hospital.

The hospital.

None of us have gone to the big white square cube of Wilcox Hospital in Lihue since Anita was born. Mom and Pop hate hospitals and Western medicine and we have no health insurance, but they finally load me in the van, leaving Bonny in charge of the younger girls.

I clutch a barf bucket, lying on the bed in the back of the van, flickering in and out of consciousness as we speed down the road. At the hospital, I shriek like a banshee when the doctor palpates my abdomen.

"Appendicitis," he says. "You got here just in time. We have to operate."

I'm too far gone to notice much but the colored lights overhead as they wheel me down the hall toward the operating room—but just before they take me in for the surgery, a gunshot victim arrives.

Getting shot on Kauai is a front-page news event—it *never* happens. I lie on my gurney, writhing in agony, puking up the fluids they're pumping into me via IV, as they rush the bloody gunshot guy past me into the hospital's one operating room. The doctor, already prepped in a blue gown and gloves to do my surgery, does him first.

They can't medicate me because they're going to put me under, so it's another two hours before I'm finally wheeled in after they finish with the gunshot guy.

"Frontier medical conditions," the surgeon, on rotation from Oahu, grouses as he changes into clean scrubs with a nurse's help. "I can't believe this place. It's like the fucking outback."

I'm wheeled into the operating room and the man looks down at me, examining the smooth, flat, caramel-colored expanse of my belly, sliding his gloved fingertips across it like it's a fresh canvas and he, the painter. He looks up at me and his brown eyes, all I can see above the paper mask, are kind. "So pretty. I don't want to mess you up with a big ugly scar. Nurse, shave her so I can do a bikini line incision."

"Right away."

This means more delay, and I'm pretty sure I'm dying. "I don't care," I croak. "Just do it. Just get this over with, please."

He shakes his head. "You'll thank me later."

The nurse shaves my pubic area and tapes everything off, and finally the anesthesiologist puts a mask over my face and ends my suffering.

The surgeon gets my appendix out just before it ruptures. I recover rapidly from the first operation any Wilson has ever had at Wilcox Hospital, and do indeed write a card to thank the doctor for taking the time to cut me just above my pubic bone, leaving a seam of scar that can be hidden under my bathing suit.

THAT SUMMER, ISLAND SCHOOL DECIDES TO CLOSE THEIR HIGH school program and only operate a middle school. This decision is terrible for me personally as an eleventh grader. Now my choice for senior year is Kapa`a High School, with every post-traumatic terror that invokes, or homeschooling myself.

I'm determined to make my high school record as good as it can be for college. Homeschooling, in addition to being too isolating, won't help my grade point average.

The news about Island School throws me so far into desperation that I get an idea: I could go back to Santa Barbara by myself. Perhaps I could live with Maga and finish high school at Santa Barbara High. I bet I could even make my patchy high school resume look good with extracurricular activities, maybe Student Government or a sports team. I could go to a prom and have a real high school experience my senior year!

I trek down to the neighbor's house and tell her I have to make a long-distance call. I give her five dollars of babysitting money and, standing in the dirt-floored garage with the phone pinched through the door that leads into her kitchen, I make my call.

"Toby?" Maga's deep, intimidating voice summons up a memory-picture of her bold blue eyes, the tall long-legged frame Mom and Bonny have, and the long ripple of strawberry-blonde hair I inherited. "What are you calling for?"

We've had a good relationship since the days of crashing at her house, but I've never called her by myself before. I've never had the sense that she thinks of me as a granddaughter—more like a niece or a cousin to Nancy and Patricia, her daughters so close to my age.

"I'm calling to ask a big favor." I take a deep breath, hold it. Squeeze my eyes shut. "Can I come live with you for my senior year of high school? I promise I'll help out. Do yard work. Clean your house."

"Sure. Of course." Maga hardly takes a moment to think about it, something I love about her. "Nancy's gone at college and you can have her room. Patricia's still in the house, going to City College. And you know that I work, so there won't be any handholding." She's brisk, no-nonsense, with all the nurturing of a platypus. I've often thought my mom had it hard as her oldest, but as a grandma she's great.

"Of course, Maga, I don't expect that." I'm hopping with excitement, raising little puffs of dirt on the floor of the neighbor's primitive garage. "I'll do anything you want."

"Put your mom on," she says. "I want to talk this over."

"I have to go home and get her." I bite the side of my finger. Mom and Pop might decide to be difficult about this. I can't get my hopes up.

Surprisingly, they're thrilled. "This is a great solution," Mom says. "I was so worried about what to do."

I didn't know they felt that way. The broadcasting of my misery wasn't totally missed after all. I thought they'd be happy to get their mouthy firstborn with all of her complaining off their hands, but even Pop seems downcast as I start packing.

I'm even more taken aback by outpourings of grief from my sisters as I give away my mildewy possessions and pack my few clothes. Bonny sits on my bed, helping me sort my jewelry, her eyes the blue-and-yellow they go when she's upset.

"You'll write me?" Bon's hair is cut like Farrah Fawcett. She looks like her too, her tall body decoratively draped over the beat-up sleeping bag in my tiny room. We've been the two passengers in a lifeboat through all of our family storms. I still can't quite believe I'm climbing out and swimming for the horizon without her. I wish I could take her with me, but Mom and Pop would never go for that— she's in line to pick up my chore load.

"Of course I'll write. Maybe even send you a care package full of Kraft Mac' & Cheese." I get a smile out of her as we remember our binges on Maga's *badforyou* food.

Anita sits on a scrap of rug in the corner of the tiny space, watching. She's been crying on and off all day, tears seeping out of her big green eyes. I feel the sickest about leaving when I see her precious face. This morning I took her for a walk alone, up the long dirt road to the gardens behind the church, and French-braided her hair in a crown around her head, studded with plumerias, to say goodbye. I have a pure, unalloyed affection for her—probably because of all the babysitting I did when Mom and Pop were too deep in their drinking and using to take care of her like they have Wendy.

Outside, Wendy is having one of her tantrums. The most emotive of us besides me, she's loudly objecting to my departure as Mom tries to explain.

"NO!" She shrieks. "No, no, no!" Her wails make my tummy tighten up. They always have.

"I better go help Mom with Wendy. Bon, why don't you put my jewelry in a Ziploc bag?" I say. "I'll just keep the real gold stuff. You guys can share the silver and whatever else." I don't want anything to weigh me down. Giving them my stuff makes me feel a tiny bit better.

Outside my room, Wendy is howling into Mom's blue denim work muumuu. Mom looks pinched and sad, and she pats Wendy's back helplessly.

"Let me take her for a walk." I say. "We'll go feed the swans." Wendy loves feeding the swans.

I take her chubby, sticky hand and we walk across the lawn to the pond. I glance down at her wispy head. She's only wearing a diaper and a pair of tiny red plastic rain boots, and she slowly hiccups into silence. My heart squeezes me breathless.

I can't believe I'm leaving my family.

But I have to.

I'm fighting for my life. If I stay, I have to go to Kapa`a High and face the bullies I've been hiding from since fifth grade. For all my bravado, it's too scary. I'd rather strike out on my own to the mainland.

The swans, necks regally bent into arches, white feathers gleaming against the green glass of the pond, swim eerily toward us without raising a ripple on the water.

Wendy knows where the food is stored in a big Rubbermaid container. She pops the top and leans over, reaching in with the scooper. I follow her as she toddles back to the edge, sprinkling the feed into a trough above the water.

Immediately, the water erupts with tilapia, an introduced fish of the cichlid variety, whose population has exploded in the contained setting of the pond with access to the swans' food. I grab a nearby scoop net and scoop ten or twelve big flapping ones out and toss them on the bank in the grass. We don't eat them because they taste bad. Instead, we put them around the papaya and banana trees as fertilizer.

Wendy squats to watch the swans, her hands tucked between her tummy and thighs. The swans reach in among the boil of fish to eat, dabbling their black beaks and lifting their long snowy throats so the food can go down. I sit beside Wendy and put an arm over her. I can't imagine my life without my sisters in it, but I'm going to have to. "I love you."

Wendy throws her arms around me in the tightest hug, burrowing into my side.

Mom and Pop take me, alone, for a goodbye beach picnic at the End of the Road, Ke`e Beach, site of so many sunsets when we lived at the Forest House and a thousand family outings since. It's bittersweet to eat my favorite treats like Brie and French bread and have my parents' full attention on my last night with them. Pop takes pictures of Mom and me: walking along the sand looking for *puka* shells, clowning together in front of the camera.

They love me as much as they're able, enough to let me go.

CHAPTER FORTY-ONE

THAT FINAL PUSH

Age: 17-18, Santa Barbara, California, 1982-3

I lug a single suitcase, stuffed with all my worldly possessions, into

Nancy's old room in Santa Barbara. Her clothes and mementoes still fill every inch of the room, so I set the suitcase on the floor next to the bed to make it mine. I put my pillow on the bed and claim that too. School starts right away the next morning.

Maga and Egidio indulge in a carafe of red wine at dinner and a loud and good-natured argument on whether or not the Mafia is still running Naples (Maga says yes, Egidio claims no.) Patricia is gone, working at her job or class. I wolf down penne pasta with marinara and an iceberg lettuce salad, and consider how lucky I am to have a hot shower, flushing toilet, and TV after dinner.

I feel guilty to be here and have these comforts when my sisters are at home, eating brown rice, beans, and garden vegetables, and reading by the light of kerosene lamps. When I picture that scene, I miss them. Thinking about the family is a mistake. I turn up the radio in Nancy's room.

No way out but forward. I need to keep my eyes straight ahead to accomplish all the goals I have for my senior year. I can't look back; this is the chance I've been working toward for years.

Maga and Egidio's modest 1960s ranch house is located on a keyhole-shaped loop of road in the foothills of Montecito. Built on a gulch of fire-prone eucalyptus trees, this place has been a solid family home for Nancy and Patricia their whole lives, and a some-time landing pad for us. Being here feels familiar but challenging on my own.

"No handholding," Maga warned me. She's made it clear she hasn't signed up to be my substitute mom, and frankly that's a relief. That also means that she drops me off the next morning on the road down below Santa Barbara High with a map and a bus schedule, on her way to her job at the unemployment office.

For the third time, I walk toward a school holding my birth certificate and immunization record to register myself. On my way, I pass the beautifully groomed expanse of the football field. Near one end is a cluster of girls, several in cheerleader uniforms, painting a large cloth sign for an upcoming game.

This is my chance to meet some kids at the top end of the social ladder on my very first day.

"Fake it 'til you make it," I mutter to myself, a saying from the twelve-step program. I trot down the steps of the bleachers onto the football field. I'm wearing jeans, Reeboks, and a scoop neck T-shirt that makes the most of my curves. I hope to look cute enough to blend, and approach the girls with a confidence I don't feel.

"Hi. Can I help with that?"

One of them turns to give me a once-over. She's blonde and pretty, wearing one of those pleated cheerleader skirts. "Sure. Grab a paintbrush."

I unsling my backpack and drop it on the ground, pick up the paintbrush, and kneel beside her, filling in the outlined letters with the color she's using, yellow.

"Olive and gold," I say. "Nice." I remember the school colors from when I went to junior high, briefly and long ago.

"I haven't met you before." Pretty Blonde is checking me out and I seem to pass muster. "My name's Allison."

I imagine this kind of moment at Kapa`a High, and am willing to bet my reception would have been a lot different. I feel a glimmer of hope that I've made the right choice. "I'm Toby. From Hawaii. I'm headed in to register for this year."

"Hawaii! Oh my God! What grade are you in?"

"Senior." This is the tricky part. Everyone has their friend groups by senior year. If I'm going to break in at all, I'm going to have to work hard at it, and I'm braced for that. "I wanted to get off my little rock of an island and go to a real high school."

"Well, you've come to the right place," Allison says proudly, sitting up on her knees. "This is the varsity cheerleader team. Everybody, this is Toby." She makes a gesture, and all the girls look up and smile, waving their paintbrushes. "Let's show her how we do it in Santa Barbara!"

And just like that, I'm in. It feels like a miracle, and maybe it is.

Allison and a cluster of cheerleaders walk me to the office, exclaiming at my bravery in registering by myself. I sit with them at lunch, and get invited to a house-to-house scavenger hunt party that week.

The scavenger hunt is a blast. We zoom around town, hopping in and out of Allison's car in a "team," asking for bizarre items from strangers ("Do you have a spork?") and posing for Polaroid photos in front of Santa Barbara landmarks we have to check off a list, such as the famous plastic cow outside the ice cream parlor. It's the most fun I ever remember having as a teenager.

"Fake it 'til you make it" carries me on, and I become a Student Government member, the backup editor for the school paper, a runner on the track and cross-country team, and a lab helper in Physics class to earn extra credit because math remains my academic Achilles heel.

I buy a secondhand bike and ride down narrow, winding Sycamore Canyon Road every day to school, staying after to run with the cross country and track team or do student government activities. In the evenings, I ride the bike through the powdered gold light and red tile roofs of Santa Barbara to catch the bike bus, with its carrier on the back, up into the foothills.

I study *How to Win at the SAT* workbooks at the library, and take the test twice, hoping to improve my scores. Both times I get a perfect 800 on the verbal/written portion, but I can only inch the math score up another twenty points into "above average" by doing the workbook.

Things are not going as well at Maga's. Patricia is friendly but seldom around. Nancy's room, where I'm camping out, is where I'm assaulted by homesickness for my quirky family, for the lushness of Kauai, for surfing. Maga and Egidio's dinnertime argue-fests, a norm for them, abrade my sensibilities and I withdraw into my room, listening to the radio, doing homework, and studying college brochures.

The other place I hang out when at the house is in the canyon. I take my drawing tablet or journal and sit in my old hideout under the deck, the secret spot where I made a fort when I was thirteen and played Barbies.

When I feel sad or lonely for the family, running soothes me. Going up the road, along the dirt track to Westmont College and jogging around the grounds lifts my mood. Sometimes I run for hours after school, until my thoughts and worries are finally quiet and my body is tired enough to sleep.

I keep going to the Christian Young Life Club that organized the scavenger hunt. While I'm wary of being proselytized to, I'm also semi-interested—hell, I've eaten off banana leaves with my fingers, had my third eye anointed, chanted the Hare Krishna, and been expected to kiss a pair of shoes. Jesus can't be any weirder than that.

The thing that draws me most is that the nicest kids in school, like Allison, go to Club.

On a Young Life campout, they tell us that Jesus died to give us a new life and that all we have to do is accept that gift. After the campfire message, the leaders send us out into the dark to think about it.

Sitting in my surfer pose under unfamiliar pine trees, I look up at stars that are the same in California as they are in Hawaii, reducing me to a dot in the scheme of things—and consider the message that God cares about me.

I know that already, in a deep place. I've known it since the angel told me that things would be okay when we thought I was going blind. I matter, and I have something I'm meant to do in the world. I don't know what it is, but if I have Jesus, I won't be alone trying to figure it out. And I don't want to be alone anymore, struggling to make my dreams happen on my own.

I bow my head and pray.

I like how much more "normal" it is to be Christian than a Krishna, Bahai, or Yogananda follower, and choosing my own religion feels like the first really adult decision I've made. It's great to have Someone to rely on and pray to and to be able to name as my Higher Power.

The Young Life leaders are a wonderful little family. They live only a block up the street from Maga's house, and they have a toddler who reminds me of my own little Wendy. I meet with them weekly to learn about the Bible, and I babysit Taylor for them.

They invite me to move into their house as a part-time au pair, exchanging free food and lodging for babysitting Taylor. "It seems like you aren't that happy at your grandmother's, and we could use the help," Bob says. Bob's a thoughtful, hard-working dad who helps out at least fifty percent when he's home. Wendy, his wife, has a big smile and always looks like she's wearing tennis whites. Their house is small and perfect, the bathroom clean, the lawn neatly mowed.

"I'd love it! Thank you."

With little fanfare and a big hug of thanks to Maga, I haul my suitcase up the street from my grandmother's house to the Ludwicks' tidy bungalow, and they install me in their pretty guest room.

Bob and Wendy are loving and generous with each other, and steady and structured as parents. They have a dog that they care for like a family member. Being in their home inspires me, clarifying amorphous dreams I've had of my own future.

"This. This is the kind of life and family I want someday," I whisper to myself as I settle into my pretty bed.

Middle-class, not poor.

Owning a home instead of renting.

Driving a decent car, not a live-in van.

Going to church on Sundays and eating steak once a week, instead of meditating and eating tofu.

Jogging and the gym instead of surfing as a compulsion.

Owning a dog that you love enough to take to the vet—not drop off at the dump or give away to a stranger.

Hiring a lawn service, instead of being the lawn service.

Preschool, piano lessons, orthodontia, Scouts, and even college for the kids.

I'm still on a mission to be *normal*. It's my rebellion.

I get serious with my college applications by November, and apply for Stanford and Harvard as well as a raft of second-tier colleges.

I know Ivy League is a stretch—but on the plus side, I have good test scores and a 4.0 GPA; on the negative, I lack extracurricular activities, I've been to three different high schools, I'm white and poor. My chances are slim for getting a good college offer, but I stay positive as I fill out earnestly worded essays and carefully completed applications well before deadline, without any adult help.

This is what I left Kauai for. This is my shot, and I'm taking it.

CHAPTER FORTY-TWO

AND SHE'S OFF

Bonny and me, teen years

Age: 18, Santa Barbara, California and Kauai, 1983

I go to Disneyland, and to football games, and to the prom with the older brother of one of my friends. I write articles that are printed in the school newspaper. I get excited about majoring in journalism so I can write as a career. I cover school events with my disposable camera for the newspaper and yearbook, earning social cachet.

My college acceptance letters come in spring, and Bob and Wendy rejoice with me when I get a full scholarship offer from both Boston University and nearby Westmont College in Santa Barbara. It's *happening!* I'm really going to college, and all on my own.

I graduate in the top sixty in my class of six hundred, walking around SBHS's vast football field in Nancy's too-long, borrowed graduation gown from last year. My parents don't come to my graduation, claiming they can't afford it—but I try not to let it get me down. This is my road to walk, one they never understood, anyway. I'm the only kid in the stadium wearing a lei, a big carnation one sent from my family on Kauai.

I did it. I'm going to college at Boston University, on a full ride scholarship—because that will be the most exciting, glamorous, different...and the furthest from Hawaii.

A ticket home to Kauai to visit is my graduation present from Mom and Pop; it's been a year since I've seen everyone. Planning for my trip, Mom tells me that the whole family got "saved" at a church that started up in the fellowship hall where I used to have hula lessons.

"The hymns and choruses would echo across the taro fields. It was so wonderful, we just had to go sing with them," Mom says, and I picture her, in rubber slippers and her denim work muumuu, standing in the red dirt of the neighbor's garage to use the phone just like I used to do. "We all went up and prayed at the altar. We're Christians now!" I'm astounded at this, but hopeful it will give us something in common.

I spend the summer after graduation going to an educational program in Europe, paid for by Gigi and Grandpa Jim, who are thrilled I'm actually going to college. I see Paris from the Eiffel Tower, windsurf on a lake in Bavaria, eat sublime chocolate in Germany, and watch the gondolas from the Bridge of Sighs in

Venice. I fall in love with glassblowing in Murano, am swept away by the club scene in London, swim for hours in Greece, eat ice cream in Rome, and hike the Alps to pick actual edelweiss in Austria.

Seven countries later, my eyes are filled with the sights, sounds, and scents of a great wide world that's so much bigger than I've ever known. And finally, I go home for two weeks before I start at Boston University.

Coming down the steps off the Aloha Airlines flight onto the familiar tarmac, my hair lifts off my head in the warm, moist, plumeria-scented breeze of Kauai. Tears sting my eyes, and I know, running to embrace my three sisters in the shade of the funky open airport, that however far I go, this addicting island will always feel like home.

Adorable Wendy embraces my knees, sweet Anita my waist, and Bonny, now grown into an almost six-foot goddess, gets my arms. Mom and Pop, tan and grinning, both hug me at the end. They all pile me to the eyeballs in homemade plumeria lei as people do in Hawaii when someone graduates. A moment I wish would never end passes too quickly.

A lot has changed for the family in the year I was gone. Gigi and Grandpa Jim built them a house in Princeville, the former cow pasture on the mesa above Hanalei Bay. Pulling into the new place's clean cement driveway, I raise my brows—they're driving a Toyota station wagon and a shiny truck, and the huge house has beige wall-to-wall.

"Watch out or you'll be getting respectable or something," I tease Mom, looking around the brand-new home.

"Gigi and Jim might have bought us the house and cars, but I'm still growing my own sprouts," Mom says, pointing at a variety of mung bean, sunflower, and alfalfa decorating the sink in familiar glass jars covered with rubber-banded cheesecloth. She's planted a papaya and banana patch and, in spite of neighborhood covenants, has a henhouse started and is deep in compost development.

Pop, meanwhile, has expanded his guitar playing to worship music, picking out classics like *Jesus loves me, this I know*. His business teaching windsurfing lessons is booming. He finally seems to have found work that he likes, and a venue for his music where it can be appreciated.

"Got a friend coming over for dinner tonight," Mom tells me after I get my suitcase stowed in one of the downstairs rooms. "A nice guy who's been helping your dad and me learn the Bible. We're all volunteering at a youth camp in Koke`e this coming week; I hope you don't mind because we're all going."

"Sure." I'm determined to be pleasant and cooperative, though the last thing I want is to spend my first night home having family dinner with some fuddy-duddy old Bible thumper, and the rest of a precious week before college volunteering at a religious camp.

The fuddy-duddy old Bible thumper turns out to be late twenties, six foot four, with the lithe muscles of a surfer. Mike has to bend to give me a welcoming hug, and his shoulders block out the light. Dark hair contrasts with eyes the color of crushed glass, and they seem to see all the way into my soul. "So, you're the wayward daughter I've been hearing so much about."

"I guess. Not very wayward, actually. Normal is my rebellion." I laugh self-consciously.

"I've been praying for you with your parents. It's great how things worked out for your family. Congrats on your graduation—I hear you did really well."

"Thanks." It feels way too intimate that he's spent time *praying* for me! Heat flashes over my cheeks, and I look away.

My sisters are helping Mom with dinner in the kitchen, but I catch Bonny's eye. She's grinning at my discomfiture.

"Toby's on her way to college at Boston University." Mom's voice is indulgent as she brings a pot of her Swiss chard and brown rice soup to the table. "She's going as far away from Kauai as she can, getting all high *maka maka*." The pidgin phrase means someone's getting above themselves.

"Mom! I just want to—you know. Reach my potential. Do something important. I have to leave Kauai to do that." I trip over my awkwardly self-important words. "I'm majoring in journalism," I tell Mike.

"As long as you don't write about Kauai and how great it is," Mike says, and we all laugh. The Cone of Silence about Kauai is still firmly in place as far as media goes.

Pop is playing his guitar in the background, his default mode for social situations. He puts his instrument away, and we all sit down. Mike is next to me, and I have to hold his big warm hand as Pop says a simple grace.

Around the dinner table we end up having a lively discussion about the reasons people move to Hawaii and why they leave.

"The islands either accept you, or spit you out. We've had both," Pop says. They reminisce about some of our moves back and forth from Kauai, joking about our various living situations. It feels good to be far enough away from those desperate times that here, in the comfort of this big new house, we can laugh about them.

Mike crumbles bran-laced corn bread into the vegetarian soup with every appearance of enjoyment, and I like him for it. My mom's cooking is known for unusual ingredients. "I've had both, too. I came to Hawaii for the surf in 1975, when I was nineteen." He tells us about chasing his passion for big waves from Maui to Kauai, dealing weed and falling on hard times in his early years, but determined to stay for the surf. He ended up living in a tool shed in Wainiha feeding the Ham Youngs' pigs before a dramatic conversion to Christianity. "Just like the prodigal son."

I know exactly where those pigs are and what they look like. Watching the Ham Youngs slaughter a hog with Knight will always be burned into my memory. This man might be the most striking and charismatic individual I've ever been instantly smitten with, but he's all wrong for me. Hard-core surfers like him have an all-consuming addiction to waves, and I'm never going to fall for someone like that. I'm on my way to Boston University and a whole different kind of future—a *normal* life.

As the evening progresses, I flirt with Mike a little, tossing my hair and letting my dimple show. There's no harm in it. I'm totally committed to my course of action, headed for the Mainland, and no *surfer* is going to derail me.

Over the course of the week at the youth camp where we're both volunteering, we're on the same tug-o-war team, our bodies crashing into each other, giving a hundred percent to pull our team to victory. We hug exuberantly afterward.

Somehow, that simple hug is imprinted everywhere all over me.

Mike's totally competent and can fix anything, including one of the broken-down cars and a stove that won't light; everyone turns to him for help and leadership.

One day he invites me on a hike outside the camp. We move fast, almost running, weaving through Kauai's stunning high elevation forest. I have to work hard to keep up with his long legs and endurance. He gives no quarter—he expects me to match him, and it's invigorating to try.

Mike has brought me a rigged-up fishing pole, and we leave the established trail and bushwhack through jungle he's already explored, fishing for trout in a hidden Koke`e stream. I love every minute of the adventure, and delight in catching my first Kauai rainbow trout; showing it to Mike feels as good as getting an A in physics. He's brought a camera to capture the beauty around us, and he tells me about his love of nature and the many interesting jobs he's had, from carpentry to fine dining waiter. I tell him stories about growing up here on Kauai, and we discover that we were in Hanalei at the same time: I was twelve and he was twenty-three. We laugh in amazement that we existed in this same tiny place and time, together—and yet so far apart.

I can't stop watching his graceful height and swallowing a flight of butterflies when he's near, even while telling myself repeatedly that he's too *old* for me and all wrong; he doesn't fit with a *normal* life. I'm only eighteen. He's twenty-eight—and a *surfer*!

Mom and Pop organize a bonfire and goodbye picnic for me at Ke`e Beach on my last night before I leave for Boston. Their new friends from church come, and some of our old friends too, like Tom and Cheri Hamilton who looked in on us so long ago at the Kauike-olani Estate. There's potluck and sparklers, singing with guitars, a sunset that flames glory over the ocean, and the layered magic of the Na Pali cliffs.

I'm sandwiched by my sisters, sitting in the cool evening sand with the flickering bonfire lighting the dark ocean. Affectionate Wendy cuddles me on one side, gentle Anita on the other, while Bonny, all wit and attitude, keeps us laughing.

I wish I could slow down time, turn every moment to honey and watch it drip by. I'm already feeling the wrench of having to leave my sisters after such a short, sweet visit. Tears are close to the surface when I get up to take a break and get my emotions under control.

Mike catches hold of my arm and gives a gentle tug, pulling me aside into semi-darkness under the *kamani* trees.

His hand is large and beautifully shaped, rough from the construction job he's working. I wish I could look at it a lot longer. Maybe turn it over, explore those calluses with my fingertips. I'm fascinated by everything about him, even these little details, and I can't figure out why. *Why him? Why now?*

Mike clears his throat. I gaze up into crystal-blue eyes filled with shadows and reflections from the bonfire. Dark hair in salty tufts halos his head. "If you ever need help in the big, bad city . . . write me." He slips a bit of paper into my hand and folds my fingers over it. "I'd like to keep in touch. You know, if you need advice or anything."

Every simple, innocent contact burns my skin and scares me. He's all wrong, too old, not the right type. Not normal.

He's extraordinary.

"You know writing is my thing," I tell him.

He laughs. "Well, it's not my thing, but I'll make an exception. We can be pen pals."

"Pen pals." I back up a step and press my fist, clutching the paper, against my chest. "Okay. Sounds nice."

We gaze at each other a long moment. My heart pounds like a sledgehammer. I wish he'd kiss me, and I think he might wish he could too—but instead he gives a brisk nod. "Okay then." He turns and walks away, disappearing into purple shadows.

I open my hand and stare at a torn-off bit of lined paper, scrawled with his name and address in bold, slanting block letters.

"Not bad for an old guy." Bonny's sneaked up next to me to deliver one of her pithy observations. "He's hot."

"It's not like that." I close my hand so she won't see the address in it and fan my warm face.

"But it could be. I saw how he looked at you."

"He's a surfer. I'll never be with a surfer." I elbow her, and she pushes me, and a minute later the years have rolled back and we're roughhousing and giggling with the love and closeness we've always had.

Sunset gilds the iconic, rugged silhouette of the Na Pali Coast in a wash of gold. My last day as a kid on Kauai ends with the dying light.

EPILOGUE

Mom and I visit the Forest House and make fern crowns

Maui, Hawaii, age 50+, 2015

I'm sitting with a couple I've been working with in family therapy—
I've been a full-time counselor for close to twenty years now, holding
degrees in psychology, human services, and social work.

The dad, Ikaika, is a buzz-cut, mixed-heritage man with the
Hawaiian Islands tattooed around his muscular forearm. Lisa, the

359

mom, is a petite Japanese woman with a black plume of lustrous hair she has to move aside to avoid sitting on. I'm helping them with some parenting techniques for their middle grade children. The older child, a boy, is depressed and has been mouthy and failing classes, and the younger has social problems. I'm still assessing their situation after one initial session and figuring out a treatment plan.

"So how's this week been?"

"He still so sassy," Ikaika says, with a tone that implies one session of therapy isn't working. He and his son butt heads a lot, which I suspect has to do with his unrealistic expectations and an "old school" strict communication style.

"What about the reward and consequence plan we set up for when he mouths off?"

"We haven't followed through," Lisa sighs. "It's hard keep up with it all. We both have jobs, the kids have activities, and then there's my mom in the house. . ."

I let a beat go by, letting us all think on this a moment. Ideas are only as good as their implementation, and if the plan was too involved, it wasn't a good plan. I don't want the parents to give up because something isn't working. It's my job to help them find something that is.

The mom is the one who dragged them all into therapy, so I know I can count on her. Now I need to engage the dad, using language and a metaphor that will motivate him to try new things. He's wearing a Raiders tee, so I decide to try a football analogy.

I turn to a big whiteboard propped against the wall. "Let's make a list of what's getting in the way of making changes so everyone in the family can win. As your family coach, it's my job to help you guys find a plan that leads to success—which means everyone in the family is getting what they need."

We make good progress problem solving as I draw on the board in an abbreviated version of a football play. An animated sparkle brightens Ikaika's eyes; he's engaged with this, seeing it as a team challenge now and not criticism on his parenting. He even jokes about joining his son in a pushup contest when he talks back. Lisa easily transitions to the new analogy.

Near the end of the session, Lisa gives me a meaningful glance and goes out to check on the kids. She's trying to get me to "talk sense" to her husband, who she sees as the main parenting problem.

"Toby. I know dat name," Ikaika says, with a lilt of pidgin. I glance at him, wondering why he's bringing this up. We've been through the initial "where you from, who's your people" of a first session that's part of the culture here in Hawaii. Credibility with this family was increased when I told them I grew up in Hawaii and have worked in the public schools on Maui for the last twelve years. I'm *kama`aina*, or "child of the land," a long-time resident, not a *haole* fresh off the airplane.

"At least you're not telling me you had a dog named Toby. That's what I usually hear when people comment on my name," I tell him.

Ikaika laughs. "I knew a *haole* girl named Toby on Kauai, back in grade school."

"You did? Because I grew up there!" Kauai's population remains small, and people who are "grown here not flown here" are fewer than sunrise shells on the beach. "Did you go to Hanalei School?"

"Yeah. We were in class together. Dat girl, she had hair like you— and freckles." His voice sounds warm, not critical, and his whole face smiles. "I knew when I heard your name that you had to be her."

He wanted to take my measure first, before he said anything. I'm not surprised by this at all. Hawaiians are usually outwardly friendly, but slow to open up to real relationships outside of their immediate circles. Many people try to settle in the Islands, enamored of palm trees and good weather, but those who last are few. Complicating race relations further, the native Hawaiians' trust was betrayed and their lands stolen. They invented *aloha*, but they also were fierce warriors with very long memories.

I never forget I'm the wrong color to do anything but earn my place here and prove I'm worthy of their trust.

"What are the chances?" I tug a wayward lock of my hair. "This always made me stand out back then."

"Remember Mr. Nitta? That's the last time I saw you."

"Of course. Remember the tidal wave kits? My parents nevah have the right stuffs fo' go inside." I do a little pidgin, too.

"Ho, so crazy. You think my family was going fo' do dat kine?" He laughs, crinkles beside his bright brown eyes, and I recognize him suddenly, that kid I knew—one of several brothers, a wiry, funny middle child, always in motion, from a big hardworking family who lived at the back of Hanalei Valley. We grin at each other, members of a tiny and exclusive club.

"You were so good at drawing and writing stories," he says. I'm embarrassed that he remembers so much about me, and I don't remember much about him but his laugh. "Where'd you go after fifth grade? You just disappeared."

"It was hard being *haole* there," I say evasively.

Ikaika drops his eyes. "I know it was bad. I remember those days. I'm Kira Yoshimura's cousin. For all we did back then, I'm sorry."

Kira Yoshimura. The bane of my elementary school existence is summoned before us by her name. Petite, with lovely hula hands, shiny mynah-bird hair, a mouth like a cherry lollipop, and hard brown eyes.

He's Kira's cousin. Was he one of those in the group that beat me with sticks and lily bulbs after hula practice? Those faces have mercifully blurred in my memory, but forty plus years after those events, I feel tears well up. I cover my mouth with my hand as we gaze at each other, suddenly two kids on the playground again—two kids who might have been friends if they'd been allowed to be.

I saw Kira Yoshimura once, thirty years ago, when I was twenty-one. Surrounded by my wedding party, I was headed in to a rehearsal brunch at the ritzy Princeville Hotel. Kira was still tiny and beautiful, wearing the fitted hostess muumuu of the resort, a plumeria pinned behind her ear. She walked toward us, and I recognized her instantly. My heart stuttered with old terror, and I froze.

Kira's face beamed into a genuine smile. "Toby!" She exclaimed. "Oh, girl, you so pretty! And you're getting married, congratulations!" There was not a shadow of antipathy in her demeanor as she set the menus aside to hug my rigid body. Somehow, I introduced her to my fiancé and the rest of the wedding party as "my classmate from Hanalei School." She led us into the banquet area, seated us, and gave me a friendly wave goodbye.

I wondered, for years, how Kira could appear to have so completely forgotten her bitter hatred and cruelty toward me. To this day I don't understand it.

And now, seated beside her cousin Ikaika, I remind myself that I have nothing to fear. In fact, I'm the one in charge here, the "coach," the one with the answers. I've worked damn hard to come all this way and sit in the "expert" chair, and I do it to help.

"I'm sorry," Kira's cousin says again. "We don't act like that anymore. I don't let my kids hate *haole* like that."

"Mahalo. This means more than I can say."

How could he know how surreal this moment feels, how filled with grace? My hands tremble as I set down the clipboard. I'm broadsided by this collision with my past as my hands come up to cup my cheeks, and my eyes overflow. His apology washes over me, a priceless gift.

"Thank *you*," he says. "Now you helping us. So funny, eh?"

"I can't believe I've met you again, and here of all places," I tell him. "We've both come a long way."

"All the way to Maui," he says. We both laugh, because moving from one island to another is a very big deal when you're *from here*.

We stand up and hug, because Hawaii people are huggers, and we go out to the waiting room. He announces to his wife and kids that we're classmates, two of the few that went to a little school amid the taro fields of Hanalei in the 1970's. More hugs ensue.

This family is going to do great in therapy, and my chest is tight with happiness that I get to be a part of their lives.

Me and Mike, engaged 1986

I pick up my travel bag and lock the beautiful home I own halfway up Haleakala on Maui. I get into my highly reliable Honda Civic with my husband Mike, who is driving me to the airport. After I stow my bag, we hold hands as we drive down the volcano. We've been married more than thirty years now, and it's been a constant adventure. Our kids are grown and gone, and we've been finding the "empty nest" a satisfying place to be.

How an eighteen-year-old college-bound kid and a twenty-eight-year-old surfer fell in love and stayed that way for so long is a tale for another day.

"I'm nervous about this trip to Kauai," I tell him. "It's a big deal to go back there."

Mike glances at me with those blue eyes I never get tired of. He squeezes my hand with his big warm one. "It'll be good for you and your mom."

Mom and I are continuing to heal the wounds of the past, and as part of that, she's invited me to return to some of the places that have haunted us—we're visiting the Forest House together one last time, while it's still standing. Our tiny abode in the jungle is slated to be torn down to make way for a state park.

"I hope going there will give us both some closure."

"It'll be interesting, that's for sure. The island's changed so much," Mike says.

"I'm glad the Forest House is still there, and I love it that Mom wants us to go see it again, together." Mom's joie de vivre is still the same after all these years, and I'm looking forward to having time alone with her to reminisce about those wild days.

THE JUNGLE ARCHES OVER US, LUSH AND THICK, AS MOM AND I pick our way down a muddy track I last saw forty-plus years ago. Damp, embedded rocks are slippery obstacles. The little Chihuahua that Mom's pet-sitting tugs on her leash, an additional hazard for a fifty- and seventy-year-old making a journey back in time.

"Maybe rubber slippers weren't the best choice," I observe as familiar red Kauai mud sucks at our shoes.

"What else would we wear?" Mom says. It's true. "Rubbah slip-pahs" are the footwear of choice in Hawaii.

Mom and I have had a bumpy journey, both in our relationship and in life after we left this island. We're trespassing down memory lane, and the gash of bulldozed track we're on was once a boulder-strewn path where I learned to ride a bike.

The lullaby of the stream alongside us casts a spell that ignites memory. I look up to catch the way the light filters through giant tropical vines dangling from Java plum, guava, rose apple, and bread-fruit trees. Bamboo grass and ferns carpet the forest floor. A shama thrush trills a liquid song from somewhere nearby, and I'm trans-ported back to when I lived here, in the shadow of drip-castle moun-tains wrapped in empty beaches and aqua surf.

Mom and I both gasp in shock as we reach the little cottage that we called the Forest House.

The building's listing to one side, and the roof is caved in. A limb must have fallen from the giant monkeypod tree that looms over the house, a tree that didn't exist when we were last here. The paint is peeling, and the front door hangs open like a missing tooth.

The three *lokelani* rose bushes, marking the abandoned graves of Hawaiians, still survive in the front yard—the only thing that's the same.

We go to the back door since the front porch is crushed. The back steps, too, have disintegrated into the leaf mold of the yard, but I grasp the jamb and pull myself up into my childhood home. I turn and give Mom a hand. "Thank God we came now. This won't be here at all much longer," she exclaims.

The sea's primitive termite treatment so long ago gave the wooden walls inside the cottage a silver hue that hasn't changed. But in the kitchen, once painted yellow, mold has grown over the walls in lichen-like patterns. Memories flood me as I stand in front of the rotten counter and broken shelves where Mom kept gallon jars of mung beans, brown rice, and whole wheat flour flecked with bran.

We are rendered silent by the ravages time has wrought here.

Veils of rotting screen drift over the handmade wooden bedframe I remember lying on to read in the window, my little sister sleeping beneath me. The room looks harshly abandoned, a giant hole in the roof admitting leaves and branches that fill the corners.

I take some pictures with my phone. Feelings are jumbled and clogged within me, and I see them jostling in Mom's eyes too. Mom and I share hazel eyes, the greens and browns of the stream that sings beside us, but this is one of the first times we're totally in tune with each other and no words are necessary.

There was a time when I wanted to get as far away from these walls as I possibly could—and I did. I transformed myself from bare-foot hippie in Hawaii to middle-class mental health therapist living in the Midwest, married with two kids, two careers, and two cars. Since then, I've come full circle: now, at my home on Maui, I recycle, organic garden, practice yoga, surf, and spend all the time I can outside.

"This place was all I ever wanted, but I couldn't stay here," Mom's voice is thick with grief. "The *mana* was too strong." The *mana*, spiritual power, of this elemental location, combined with hallucinogenic drugs, drinking yeast, and studying the occult, brought on the psychotic break that took us all to California while she recovered.

"I know, Mom. I loved it here too." I support Mom with a hand back down out of the cottage and we walk around to what used to be the front yard. I can't help glancing under the porch as if my beloved puppy, Argos, will miraculously reappear—but it's filthy and dark, with a smell of mildew that makes my nostrils tighten.

I look over in the direction of Taylor Camp, the hippie encampment next to our house—and gasp again.

The forest has been bulldozed into vast mounds of rotting logs. Sunlight blasts an open wound where jungle once sheltered many homes made of plastic and bamboo. This particular stretch of Haena jungle was purchased by the state of Hawaii for park development long ago, but plans are obviously progressing to make the area a fully usable property.

Mom picks up a windfall orange from the familiar tree we used to feast from, now struggling to live in the shade of the invading monkeypod. She peels the orange and hands a section to me.

As I bite into the sweet-tart, juicy fruit, I see this yard again as it was: the clothesline, with our towels drying crunchy-hot. The plywood privy nestled in banana trees. Jungle surrounding the open glade, the trees' susurrating voices enhancing the sound of the stream. Makana Mountain behind the cottage, a jutting, green-clothed spire. Antique roses sheltering humble graves near a lush vegetable garden. Hand-sickled grass where we'd lie naked in the sun to dry after baths in the stream.

I'm glad that this will be a park and not just another opulent vacation rental for out-of-towners. *Everyone* will be able to enjoy this place, not just the privileged few.

We make our way down to our former bathing spot on Limahuli Stream. Mom reminds me how we used Dr. Bronner's Biodegradable Soap and tried to leave no footprint before that concept became a buzzword.

We truly left no footprint here. Instead, this place left a mark on *us*, all the rest of our lives: a deep-buried longing to live in the shadow of the mountain and hear the song of water. Mom and I listen to the stream, watching the clear water flow over the mossy rocks where we used to jump in and shriek at the cold. Our eyes wander over the beauty, and the destruction, and we take it in to think on later.

Pinky the Chihuahua provides a welcome distraction as she picks her self-important way, plump bottom and curly tail wagging, to the path leading down from the house toward the ocean.

"Guess we should go down to the beach." Mom follows Pinky, her steps slow and careful, a twist in her back hunching her. She looks small on the path ahead, a bent older lady with a funny little dog.

My heart squeezes with a new kind of sorrow because when we lived in this enchanted place, Mom was tall and long-legged, her rippling brown hair catching glints of sun, a surfer Ali McGraw with a big smile. I ran after her, barefoot, freckled, and golden. Pop followed, carrying Bonny on his shoulders and his surfboard under an arm, his blond head as high as the sky.

I spit the seeds from the orange into my palm and slide them into my pocket. We pick our way around devastation wrought by chainsaws, finding a path long buried in vines and grasses, and as we go I feel a deep gratitude that Mom and I could come here and see this place again before guardrails, pavement, and *Keep on Trail* signs corral this wilderness.

Seeds from the tree that sheltered our little house lie slippery in my pocket. I've got a knack for growing trees, a glimmer of Mom's famous green thumb. Maybe in another forty years, we'll still be eating juicy Hawaiian oranges from this unforgettable spot.

ACKNOWLEDGMENTS

Me with a toad, age 4

Dear Readers:

Kauai, for all its magic, can be a brutal place, and many who appear in this memoir are gone now. Here's what I know so far:

Dead:
Minka: Died in the 1980s, leaving two young children.
Kenny Bryan: Disappeared in 1992. Presumed murdered.
Melanie Adams: Killed in high school, hit by a cane truck.
Chris (Knight's friend): Drowned surfing.
Ginger (Kala's mom): Killed in the Anahola flood of 1992.
Aunty Jan: Died in her fifties of ALS (Lou Gehrig's disease).

Onward and upward:
Toby: Author and therapist, married over thirty years to blue-eyed surfer Mike who she met in 1983. They have two grown children.
Bonny: Magazine publisher, lives in Hawaii with her family.
Anita: Married, living in California.
Wendy: Living in California with her family.
Mom and Pop: Divorced, still sober and active in twelve-step programs, doing good works and living "green" in Hawaii.
Tita: Married to a helicopter pilot with two sons, she now rides an Arabian stallion across the deserts of Saudi Arabia.
Kira Yoshimura: last I saw her, working in the hospitality industry.
Kala Alexander: Big wave surfer, waterman, actor, father, and activist. He lives on Oahu and appears regularly in movies and on television.
The Wilcoxes at the Big House: They and extended family were fictionalized in *The Descendants*. (All homes on the original property, including the Big House, are now available to stay in as vacation rentals.)
Tom and Cheri Hamilton: Parents of two awesome sons and Bethany Hamilton, pro surfer, shark attack survivor, and worldwide inspiration.
Island School: Now Kauai's premier private preparatory academy.
Knight Richardson: international surf legend.

Memoir caveat:

This narrative is based on a true story. ***Freckled*** is how I remember things. Where possible I fact-checked, but as with all firsthand eyewitness accounts, impressions will differ.

For instance, for the longest time I remembered Mom looking on and not helping Bonny and me during the "cup incident." When I fact-checked, she said she and Anita were gone on a walk with the stroller when those events occurred. Finding that out actually made me feel better, but the trauma of the time had distorted my memory of it. If I got something wrong, I apologize—I have done the best I could, to be as truthful as I could.

I have also changed some people's names and basic descriptions. Kauai is a small island and Hawaii is a small place. Anne Lamott has famously said, "Own everything that happened to you. Tell your stories. If people wanted you to write warmly about them, they should have behaved better."

That is true. And it's also true that we writers are the ones holding a pen and chiseling someone's actions into history without their knowledge or permission. I tried not to be unkind in my telling of events and descriptions of people and places as I remember them.

This book would not be possible without the midwifery of my incredible friend Holly Robinson. Her first published book is her memoir, ***The Gerbil Farmer's Daughter*** (2009), and from the time she came into my life, we've been talking about my memoir project. She's a ghostwriter, celebrity biographer, and women's fiction novelist, and thus uniquely qualified to help people tell their life stories. Even with all that experience, she had her hands full coaching me!

Writing a memoir can be therapeutic, but it's not therapy. A good memoir is primarily a story for the consumption of others, and ripping open your soft parts, spilling your guts, and then assembling something entertaining out of that mess—well, it's not for the faint of heart.

Holly kept telling me this book would be good, maybe the best I'd written (and I've written more than thirty fiction novels.) She said the book was important, even as publishers turned it down as "too small" and "too niche." She said *Freckled* was more than just my story: it was a glimpse into a unique era and lifestyle in a sublime place. Reading this memoir would enrich others' lives, and help them make sense of their own.

I began to succeed more and more with my fiction, and for years at a time I set *Freckled* aside for writing that was easier, more fun, and paid the bills.

Ongoing, Holly fed me memoirs others had written and novels that she thought would stimulate my mind: *Wild* by Cheryl Strayed, *The Glass Castle* by Jeannette Walls, *The Liars' Club* by Mary Karr, *The Unheard* by Josh Swiller, and more.

I became hooked on memoir, on trying to figure out how other writers had made a cohesive narrative arc out of the mishmash of vignettes that are real life. It wasn't until Holly gave me *Don't Let's Go to the Dogs Tonight* by Alexandra Fuller, that something clicked in my brain.

Dogs is so spare, so unsentimental, so "just the facts" in the most horrific of times and inhospitable of African places. The book is hauntingly beautiful in its understatement. The love in Alexandra Fuller's bizarre family comes through, clear and powerful.

I finally found the tone I wanted, the feeling I hoped to leave the reader with: *in spite of everything, there was a lot of love in my family too.*

Writing this book was so intense that it was like giving birth and being the baby struggling to be born at the same time. I did the first draft in a mere six weeks, hoping to find mental and emotional relief when it was finally over. I laughed out loud and cried rivers. The memoir took over my life, derailed my publication schedule, strained my marriage and all my family relationships. It's been terrifying, wonderful, painful and joyful . . . and something I just had to do—my personal Everest. Thank you, Holly. I couldn't have done it without you.

Kim Rogers, a wonderful photographer and writer, provided an early edit and the cover photograph. Thanks for being a witness and cheerleader, Kim! Shannon Wianecki, another journalist friend, ran an eye over an early version of manuscript and gave feedback. And Christine Pride, an independent editor specializing in memoir, also did two passes through the manuscript. Then, my wonderful friend Angie Nakamura Lail, a local girl from Hawaii who's read ALL of my books, stepped up to copyedit, and Shirley and Jamie typo hunted. This book needed a lot of help, and I was happy to have all of the input I could get.

Mom and Pop, I love you guys.

I hope you can feel that in every page. I'm so proud of *us,* of all the healing work we've done to get where we are. It was a bumpy journey, and not pretty many times, but I've come to appreciate so many things about both of you through this life review process: your strength to rebel against conventional forces and make your own way in the Kauai of those days, your determination to live life on your own terms, and most of all, your courage in getting clean and sober and staying that way for over thirty years.

I hope sharing our story helps even one person get free of substance abuse and press on with their family into healing, no matter how challenging the process is.

I also want to thank Mike Neal, my dynamic, talented, and amazing husband, exactly the right man for me—who is just as relieved as I am that I ended the book where I did. Thank you for being my one big true love!

To my sisters:

Bonny, you're my best friend, confidante, courageous fellow survivor and overcomer, outrageously beautiful to this day. I love you even more for having gone down this road into the past, realizing that you walked almost every step of the way with me as we grew up together. I thank you for your unswerving support and incredible resilience. You are simply awesome.

Anita, you came into my life at the perfect time to be the recipient of all my blooming maternal instincts. You were always so easy to love. I adore you, and one of my life's great sorrows is that somehow you didn't know it. We have never had enough time together.

Wendy, you're a kindred spirit. Always stirring the pot, speaking your truth, feeling your feelings and expressing them beautifully—I see myself in you, and I love you for it and so much more. I'm excited to see how parenting, writing, and creativity manifest in your life, and I celebrate that we get to share these things.

To my children:

I'm sorry that I've always been an over-sharer. Thanks for being there for me, inspiring me, fulfilling my fondest dreams, and making me proud every day. Thank you for being, along with Mike, the family I longed for. You have made my dreams come true.

To Kira, Knight, and all the schoolyard bullies out there: someone's probably bullying you, at home or at school. Ask for help rather than acting your pain out on others because the pain you inflict will haunt you, and can't be undone.

Seeing how I reenacted bullying on my sister Bonny was one of the most painful realizations I had writing this book. Though it's textbook stuff I see as a clinician, it made me sad all over again.

To victims of bullying: the best revenge is a well-lived life. To kids bullied in school for any reason: red-haired, poor, black, white, Asian, Mexican, Guatemalan, Micronesian, zitty, chubby, four-eyed, dorky, dweeby, ditzy, and a million others: you might need to retreat, but never give up. Persevere, and someday you'll look back and see how your wounds made you stronger. Your life is what you make it in the long run—don't let a bully win by stealing your future.

One of the many things I realized in writing this memoir was our isolation from the local people on Kauai. I didn't see the totality of that until I was writing this, finding that not one close friend in my early life was Hawaiian or mixed heritage due to the race issues of the time. It saddens me that this is the truth of my experience, even as a third generation *kama`aina*. I love the Hawaiian culture, and as an adult, I've healed that a lot through working for the Hawaii public schools for twelve years as a counselor, making friends with local folks, doing therapy with them, studying the culture, and writing about it all in my fiction mysteries, the *Lei Crime Series*, *Paradise Crime Series*, and more.

Kauai is the most beautiful and enigmatic island of a Hawaii that's much more of a tapestry made up of distinct threads than a "melting pot."

My story is just one more thread.

With much aloha,

Toby Wilson Neal

REFERENCES

Hawaiian Style 12 Days of Christmas: Music and lyrics published by Hawaiian Recording and Publishing Company, Inc., and copyrighted in 1959.

ABOUT THE AUTHOR

Award-winning, USA Today bestselling social worker turned author Toby Neal grew up on the island of Kauai in Hawaii. Neal is a mental health therapist, a career that has informed the depth and complexity of the characters in her stories. Neal's police procedurals, starring multicultural detective Lei Texeira, explore the crimes and issues of Hawaii from the bottom of the ocean to the top of volcanoes. Fans call her stories, "Immersive, addicting, and the next best thing to being there."

Join the TW Neal newsletter to learn about new nonfiction titles as they are available.

MORE TITLES FROM TOBY NEAL!

Interested in reading Toby Neal's fiction series?

Lei Crime Series
Paradise Crime Series
Romances
Romance Thrillers
Young Adult

Visit TobyNeal.Net today to learn more!

CONNECT WITH TOBY

Facebook: https://tobyneal.net/TNfb
Twitter: https://tobyneal.net/TNtw
Pinterest: https://tobyneal.net/TNpin
Instagram: https://tobyneal.net/TNin
BookBub: http://tobyneal.net/TNbb
Google +: https://tobyneal.net/TNggp
Goodreads: https://tobyneal.net/TNgdrd

Join the TW Neal newsletter to learn about new nonfiction titles as they are available:: https://tobyneal.net/TWNnf

Join my Facebook Fan Group,
Friends Who Like Toby Neal Books, for special giveaways and perks!
http://tobyneal.net/TNFriends